A CULTURAL
HISTORY OF ANIMALS

VOLUME 2

A CULTURAL HISTORY OF ANIMALS

GENERAL EDITORS: LINDA KALOF AND BRIGITTE RESL

Volume 1
A CULTURAL HISTORY OF ANIMALS IN ANTIQUITY
Edited by LINDA KALOF

Volume 2
A CULTURAL HISTORY OF ANIMALS IN THE MEDIEVAL AGE
Edited by BRIGITTE RESL

Volume 3
A CULTURAL HISTORY OF ANIMALS IN THE RENAISSANCE
Edited by BRUCE BOEHRER

Volume 4
A CULTURAL HISTORY OF ANIMALS IN THE AGE OF ENLIGHTENMENT
Edited by MATTHEW SENIOR

Volume 5
A CULTURAL HISTORY OF ANIMALS IN THE AGE OF EMPIRE
Edited by KATHLEEN KETE

Volume 6
A CULTURAL HISTORY OF ANIMALS IN THE MODERN AGE
Edited by RANDY MALAMUD

A CULTURAL HISTORY OF ANIMALS

IN THE MEDIEVAL AGE

Edited by Brigitte Resl

Oxford • New York

English edition
First published in 2007 by
Berg

Editorial offices:
First Floor, Angel Court, 81 St Clements Street, Oxford OX4 1AW, UK
175 Fifth Avenue, New York, NY 10010, USA

Paperback edition published in 2011
© Brigitte Resl 2007, 2011

Berg is the imprint of Oxford International Publishers Ltd.

Library of Congress Cataloging-in-Publication Data

A cultural history of animals / edited by Linda Kalof and Brigitte Resl.
  p. cm.
 Includes bibliographical references and index.
 ISBN-13: 978-1-84520-496-9 (cloth)
 ISBN-10: 1-84520-496-4 (cloth)
 1. Animals and civilization. 2. Human-animal relationships—History. I. Kalof,
Linda. II. Pohl-Resl, Brigitte.

 QL85C85   2007
 590—dc22   2007031782

British Library Cataloguing-in-Publication Data

A catalogue record for this book is available from the British Library.

ISBN 978 1 84520 369 6 (volume 2, cloth)
    978 1 84788 818 1 (volume 2, paper)
    978 1 84520 496 9 (set, cloth)
    978 1 84788 823 5 (set, paper)

Typeset by Apex Publishing, LLC, Madison, WI

Printed in the United Kingdom by the MPG Books Group

www.bergpublishers.com

CONTENTS

ILLUSTRATIONS

INTRODUCTION

CHAPTER 1

CHAPTER 2

CHAPTER 3

CHAPTER 4

CHAPTER 5

CHAPTER 6

CHAPTER 7

SERIES PREFACE

A Cultural History of Animals is a six-volume series reviewing the changing roles of animals in society and culture throughout history. Each volume follows the same basic structure, and begins with an outline account of the main characteristics of the roles of animals in the period under consideration. Following from that, specialists closely examine major aspects of the subject under seven key headings: symbolism, hunting, domestication, entertainment, science, philosophy, and art. The reader, therefore, has the choice between synchronic and diachronic approaches: A single volume can be read to obtain a thorough knowledge of the subject in a given period from a variety of perspectives, or one of the seven main aspects can be followed through time by reading the relevant chapters of all six volumes, thus providing a thematic understanding of changes and developments over the long term.

The six volumes divide the topic as follows:

Volume 1: A Cultural History of Animals in Antiquity (2500 BCE–1000 CE)

Volume 2: A Cultural History of Animals in the Medieval Age (1000–1400)

Volume 3: A Cultural History of Animals in the Renaissance (1400–1600)

Volume 4: A Cultural History of Animals in the Age of Enlightenment (1600–1800)

Volume 5: A Cultural History of Animals in the Age of Empire (1800–1920)

Volume 6: A Cultural History of Animals in the Modern Age (1920–2000)

General Editors, Linda Kalof and Brigitte Resl

Animals in Culture, ca. 1000–ca. 1400

BRIGITTE RESL

Bears and wolves were hunted to near extinction, sheep and cattle shrank in size, pheasants and rabbits were introduced as new quarries for hunting, dogs and horses were subjected to selective breeding, lions and elephants were imported as luxury goods to be displayed in royal menageries: between 1000 and 1400, social and cultural developments and the associated increase in human intervention with the natural environment had serious unforeseen effects for the animal populations of Europe. Drastic changes occurred in all spheres in which humans and animals interacted, whether in the roles of animals in such aspects of everyday life as farming, hunting, and entertainment, or in the more abstract fields of religion, science, and philosophy; all these were variously manifested in literature, art, and symbolism. The centrality of animals within medieval culture is abundantly reflected in the surviving source material; animal fables and zoological encyclopedias in the broadest sense are among the most widely distributed texts of the period, and hardly any building or illuminated manuscript survives that does not feature animals in its decoration. This rich variety of source material provides ample basis for the reexamination of some common modern assumptions about the human–animal relationship in medieval Christian Europe and offers many unexplored avenues for future research.

Studying the cultural history of animals is difficult at all times, not least because it is impossible to write a history of animals that is not tangled up with

human history. This was famously pointed out by Robert Delort in a book
with the programmatic title *Les animaux ont une histoire* (Animals have a history) that in many ways started off historical research into animals as subjects
in their own right.[1] The questions about medieval animals upon which most
historians concentrate concern the boundaries between humans and animals
and the ways in which these changed over this period, or on the extent to
which the rediscovery of ancient zoology transformed the human perception of
animals. Such problematics are ultimately designed to further our understanding of human nature rather than of animals themselves. In this sense, historians
who study animals today are not so different from medieval philosophers, who
themselves thought about animals primarily in order to obtain a better understanding of human nature.[2]

Alongside this central conceptual problem, the study of the cultural history
of animals between the eleventh and the fourteenth centuries shares difficulties
common to all medieval research in respect of the imbalance in the social origins of the source material available. The vast bulk of the extant textual, visual,
and material data was produced by or at the command of a small minority of
the population, namely the secular and ecclesiastical elites. Consequently, our
perception of the cultural history of medieval animals is restricted and derives
primarily from the concerns of the upper classes. The survival of a wealth of
works of literature that feature animal protagonists, for example, ensures that
the majority of studies of medieval animals are concerned with their textual
manifestations. Reynard the Fox is therefore a much more frequent subject of
scholarly inquiry than are medieval foxes, and research by literary historians
is necessarily one of the key pathways that the cultural historian in pursuit of
medieval animals must follow. But alongside the abundantly evidenced popularity of animals in elite cultural contexts, the investigation of the role of animals in everyday and popular culture in a broader sense has proved harder to
sustain, not least because of the difficulties in finding source material. Certain
textual genres, such as legal and administrative documents, can occasionally
allow a deeper insight into contemporary attitudes than sources produced exclusively by and for the elites.[3] Ultimately, however, as is so often the case with
cultural history, reading the sources against the grain is usually the only way
of broadening the scope of the inquiry. This method can provide fascinating
insights into attitudes that otherwise seem to be difficult to access, such as the
uses of animals in popular games and feasts.[4] Equally, new approaches can be
developed by supplementing the restricted textual sources not only with visual
material, but also with data provided by disciplines outside the conventional
reach of cultural history, such as archaeology and archaeozoology.[5] But while
a deeper and wider understanding of the cultural meanings of animals can only
be achieved by studying all the evidence available, whatever its form or genre,
such an analysis carries its own dangers; the excessively simplistic comparison

of sources that are completely different in nature and emanate from separate discourses has lain at the root of many stereotypical perceptions of animals in the Middle Ages.

In this regard, it should be emphasized at the outset that one of the biggest obstacles to the study of cultural meanings of animals between 1000 and 1400 lies in language and terminology. Throughout this volume, the term *animal* is used in its modern sense to mean *nonhuman animal*. In many medieval texts, however, *animal* was used in its strictest Latin sense to refer to all breathing, moving, living beings, that is, to humans and nonhuman animals alike. In this language system no single word was available that corresponded to our modern animal in referring to all nonhuman animals. As we shall see, modern scholars who neglect this difference can all too easily jump to anachronistic conclusions. But before discussing evolving medieval conceptions of animals in more detail, let us focus first on the changing roles of animals in everyday life.

Humans depended on animals in the medieval period in numerous ways; they required their motive power for agricultural and transport purposes, they consumed their flesh and their by-products, and they derived from them the raw material for clothes and medicines. Between 1000 and 1400 the human population of Europe grew steadily; at the same time, the economy was being thoroughly transformed. Around the first millennium, wealth was grounded in land ownership and rural networks of exchange. The main source of food was cereal grown on aristocratic and monastic domains concentrating on subsistence farming. By 1400, however, wildernesses had been pushed back in most regions of a Europe that was now densely covered with towns and crisscrossed by interconnecting roads. Regional and long-distance trade were an increasingly important source of income in an economy largely based on money. Not surprisingly, the considerable social and economic changes of this period had serious consequences for animals as well as humans. They occurred, moreover, in conjunction with a consistent amelioration of the global climate between 1000 and 1300. Both rising temperatures and increasing populations encouraged an expansion in agricultural production and an intensification in the exploitation of marginal or previously unused land. The extensive clearing of woodland and the draining of wetland reduced the natural habitats of many species and deprived them of their usual sources of food. Deforestation, for example, pushed bears and wolves further and further toward the margins of civilized Europe. On the other hand, the drive to enhance agricultural productivity, accompanied by the invention of new technologies in plowing and traction, intensified the exploitation of animals such as oxen and horses and had far-reaching consequences for the breeding of the latter in particular.

Around the turn of the fourteenth century, however, this lengthy phase of sustained growth came to a halt. The deterioration of the climate that marked the first signs of the little ice age brought an abrupt end to agricultural expansion, and there began a sorry series of famines and plagues that severely depleted the human and animal populations of Europe. The natural catastrophes that occurred during the fourteenth century were certainly particularly devastating, but medieval chroniclers were assiduous in their reporting of floods, famine, and pestilence throughout the medieval period. When they did so, it is noteworthy that they remarked upon the horrific consequences for humans and animals alike. The *Annals of Klosterneuburg* in Austria, for example, record that the Danube flooded in 1194, causing destruction to humans and cattle (*homines et iumenta*). In the following year, a famine killed humans and cattle (*homines et iumenta*).[6] During an outbreak of pestilence in Austria and Hungary in 1271, dead people and livestock (*pecora*) were buried in ditches.[7] Such reports increase significantly in number during the fourteenth century, but also in detail, and animals become the causes as well as the victims of disaster. Crops might be ruined by severe weather conditions such as droughts and floods, but also by swarms of locusts; according to the *Annals of Neuberg an der Mürz,* parts of Austria suffered from the insects in three consecutive years from 1338 to 1340.[8]

Accounts of famines in medieval chronicles that feature animals can contain some rather disturbing details. *The Annals of Heiligenkreuz* in Austria, for example, report that a famine of exceptional severity hit Hungary in 1243, just after the Tartars and Cumans had devastated the area; more people died of hunger than had done in the atrocities of wartime. The famine was so extreme that people were driven to eat dogs, cats, and even their fellow humans. As a consequence, wolves roamed the land and people fearfully hid inside their houses.[9] Assessing the factual value of such information is not an easy task; wolves ranging freely and threatening humans is a topos often deployed to express the collapse of civilization and the concomitant return of wilderness and chaos. Indeed, the whole entry for the year 1243 in the Heiligenkreuz annals is full of the apocalyptic imagery commonly used by contemporary chroniclers, who read the advances of the Tartars as signs of the impending end of the world. What does become apparent, however, when reading through a succession of such chronicle entries, is the extent to which their human authors emphasized animals in their accounts, whether by describing domesticated animals as their fellow victims of catastrophe, or, in contrast, by deploying the intrusion of wild beasts into the space proper to humans and domesticated animals as one more marker of civilization in crisis. Whether or not these are topoi, they show not only the importance of animals to the perception of events, but also where contemporaries liked to draw the boundaries between species.

The image of humans eating cats and dogs is another stereotype frequently deployed to emphasize the severity of a famine. True or not, the grim message this conveyed was that humanity was under such a threat that conventional taboos had to be broken; cats and dogs were certainly not part of the regular diet of medieval Europeans. In principle, medieval dietary rules were established by religion. The Old Testament books Leviticus and Deuteronomy provided a general framework, but one that could be variously adapted. Pigs, for example, were eaten by medieval Christians regardless of biblical restrictions on their consumption. The Christian religion also imposed strict guidelines for days and periods of fasting. The consumption of meat was forbidden on many occasions such as during Lent or during the vigils preceding religious feasts. Fish, however, could be eaten on such occasions. This encouraged some curious and imaginative classifications, whereby all animals swimming in the water, including ducks, geese, and even beavers could be regarded as fish. This loophole was soon closed by more specific legislation that deemed all birds, including water birds, to be forbidden food, together with beavers; the latter's tails, nevertheless, could still be eaten on fast days.[10] Apart from inspiring such taxonomical anomalies, these rules also had economic consequences; in coastal towns, for example, the demand for fish opened up opportunities for employment, while monasteries developed elaborate fish farms.

Food was also class specific in the Middle Ages. The ability to access and afford foodstuffs and clothing materials of different types was generally regulated by economic constraints. The diet of peasants continued largely to be based on cereals and tended to feature meat only if they could hunt it down, whereas the aristocracy consumed meat on a regular basis, with special treats reserved for feast days. White bread too was a luxury food reserved for the rich—and their hunting dogs. Nothing illustrates this divide more clearly than the kitchen account books of noble households, monasteries, and urban hospitals; these catalog foodstuffs by type and cost and specify the groups within the household for which they were bought. In late medieval hospitals, for example, the masses of the resident poor were fed on a diet of pottage and rye bread and might look forward to meat only on a few feast days. But the better class of inmates, the corrodians, had contracts detailing the provision of meat to which they were entitled, sometimes as often as three times per day.[11]

Meat for human consumption was obtained not only from the rearing of cattle and poultry but also through the hunting of wild animals. However, in the central medieval period, hunting for food was essentially an activity of the lower classes. For the rich, the primary attractions of hunting lay elsewhere, whether in training for military activities, exercise, entertainment, or, not least, the display of their wealth, status, and power. Hunting was a masculine pursuit *par excellence*; women could participate, but only in carefully restricted ways. And just as hunting dogs were a male domain, so women had pet dogs instead. Literature provides a famous example of the distinction; compare Tristan's powerful hunting dog Husdent with Petitcreiu, the tiny lapdog with a bell

FIGURE 0.1: *Lapdog*. Johannes von Valkenberg, *Graduale*, Universitätsbibliothek Bonn, MS S 384. © Institut für Realienkunden—ÖAW.

attached to its collar presented to his lover Isolde to amuse her during his absences.[12] (See Figure 0.1.)

While the hunting of animals for food had no significant impact on animal populations in medieval Europe, hunting as a vehicle for the display of symbolic capital did. In this regard, certain animals, such as bears and wolves, carried a particular cachet as trophies, as they were seen as natural competitors of the huntsmen. Both species, but particularly bears, were already suffering from the persistent reduction of their natural habitats. Those that survived this were instead hunted to extinction in many areas. In Portugal, for example, bears were considered so special yet so rare that the privilege of hunting them was reserved for the king.[13] Similarly, the hunting of wolves, sometimes interpreted as a consequence of the threat they posed to humans and domestic animals, was instead driven mainly by the fear that they might steal the hunters' prey.[14] Other species too, such as foxes and lynxes, were hunted primarily because they represented a threat to game. Yet even as some species were being extinguished through hunting, others were introduced into many parts of medieval Europe for that very purpose, whether birds of prey and hunting dogs, or new forms of quarry such as rabbits and various types of fowl.

Hunting is one of the best-documented areas in the cultural history of medieval animals, not least because of the wealth of surviving manuals.[15] These inevitably record the cruelty of many hunting practices, but they are also among our best sources for the more positive side of the human treatment of animals. Those that were kept to assist in hunting—horses, dogs, and birds—were looked after with great care. Apart from demonstrating the value set on these animals, the manuals demonstrate that the inhabitants of medieval Europe were well aware of the particular preferences of different species. Many of them report, for example, that birds required a calm environment and good food, including tasty snacks of mice or eels; they should be protected from cold and drafts as well as from natural predators such as weasels and polecats.[16] Further evidence for the huge interest in hunting as well as the associated expense comes from sources as varied as aristocratic household accounts or the Statutes of the Fourth Lateran Council, canon 15 of which proclaimed: "We forbid hunting and fowling to all clerics; wherefore, let them not presume to keep dogs and birds for these purposes."[17] All the evidence available, including the consistent reiteration of prohibitions such as this, only serves to confirm that for many clerics the pleasures and social cachet to be derived from hunting prevailed over the requirements of ecclesiastical discipline.

Animals also furnished the raw materials essential for the production of clothes in the medieval period. As in the case of food, these uses were class specific and subject to variations determined by the broader social and economic developments of the period. This is particularly obvious with regard to sheep; the growing demand for wool led to a huge increase in their numbers across much of Europe.[18] Animal skins were also used to produce leather, another raw material used in the manufacture of items of clothing; this too influenced the character and scale of livestock husbandry. Furs were no less important. The prices and availability of different furs varied widely by region and species, for example, between those of commonly available animals such as cats or foxes and more prized ones imported from specific regions, such as martens and particular species of squirrel from northern Europe.[19] As the material wealth of many inhabitants of medieval Europe continued to increase, the growing demand for good-quality clothing eroded established social boundaries of consumption, as reflected in the rising demand for budge—fine lambskin. Many European governments were sufficiently concerned about the potential dangers of such developments to introduce sumptuary legislation intended to reinforce the social hierarchy by limiting access to such luxury. Particular materials were reserved for the elites to ensure that class distinctions were visibly displayed and perpetuated. Details such as the type and quantity of fur trimmings permitted on dresses and coats were subject to legal regulation, providing the cultural historian with a wealth of information about the species and breeds bred or hunted for these purposes. In fourteenth-century England, for example, the wives and daughters of craftsmen and yeomen were not allowed to wear "fur or budge," but only the furs of lamb, rabbit, cat, or fox.[20] Similarly, the commune of Bologna in 1398 forbade women to "wear any garment lined in any fur, namely ermine, … or marten, entirely or partly sewn to the garment …, save that they are allowed to wear furs (except ermine) for the edges of sleeves. … However, this clause does not apply to women, of whatever condition, aged 40 or over (of whose age their own statement should suffice), nor to the wives and unmarried daughters of knights and doctors of law and medicine."[21]

Holy men and women were no less constrained by convention in their diet and dress. Since they avowedly followed the ideal of poverty expressed in the life of Christ and obeyed by the early Christian communities, fasting and the rejection of any form of luxury were standard motifs of holiness. Hagiographical works in particular can provide us with numerous insights into the usage of animals for food and clothing, often in the form of the saintly repudiation of familiar social practices that persisted throughout the medieval period. Religious figures who did not adhere to the accepted norms of a life of austerity could expect criticism. Saint Wulfstan of Worcester (d. 1095), for example, usually wore humble varieties of clothing, but to keep warm in winter, he preferred sheepskin to the cheaper alternatives. According to his biographer, William of Malmesbury, he was often asked why, if he must insist on wearing animal skin, he did not choose that of cats instead; the saint was accustomed to reply that he had heard "people singing the *Agnus Dei,* 'Oh Lamb of God,' but never the *Cattus Dei,* 'O Cat of God'; so I would rather be warmed by the lamb than by the cat."[22]

Animal skins were, of course, a treasured raw material for purposes other than the production of leather. In our period, they formed the basis for the production of parchment, still the main material to be written upon before to the gradual introduction of paper. Parchment was routinely produced from sheep skins, but in late medieval Italy goat skins were also popular, and the finest results were achieved by using calfskin, especially that of newborn and stillborn calves.[23] The production of such material could assume industrial proportions in those institutions that had routine need of it, such as the major monasteries. In medieval medicine, too, animal parts were a key ingredient in many remedies, the recipes for which had often been inherited from classical antiquity, through the works of Dioscurides and Pliny the Elder. A scholarly interest in such matters became established within the universities from the twelfth century onward, existing alongside popular practices that made frequent reference to the pharmacological and magical properties of materials deriving from animals in the accounts of tried and tested popular medical practices.[24]

The varied and considerable consequences for animals of the cultural and economic developments taking place in Europe between 1000 and 1400—from the impact on their habitats to the balance of species within the ecosystem—are obvious. But did these changes also affect attitudes toward animals? Human claims to superiority over the rest of creation are often seen as taking decisive shape during the central Middle Ages, but scholars have disagreed as to whether the attitudes to animals established during the early centuries of Christianity began gradually to disappear in this period, or whether the intellectuals of the time were in fact reinforcing an existing human–animal divide.[25] In order to assess this crucial issue it is essential to begin by considering the arguments inherited by medieval theologians from early Christian thinkers who had elaborated them on the basis of scriptural exegesis, but within the context of classical learning.

Part of the problem lies in language and taxonomy. Initially, medieval Christians used the Latin word *animal* in its original sense to refer to all living, moving, breathing beings, human and nonhuman alike. This was the long-established view, as expounded, for example, in Pliny's *Natural History*, dating from the second half of the first century AD. In the seventh book of that work humans are discussed in part by means of a comparison between them and animals, or rather, "the other animals": *cetera animantia*. Pliny's principal taxonomical category, therefore, is *animantia*, and this encompasses both humans and nonhuman animals. He then progresses in the next book of the *Natural History* to the "rest of the animals": *reliqua animalia*.[26] *Animalia* and *animantia* are synonymous for Pliny. In both categories he included all breathing living beings, including humans, all kinds of animals, and fish, but he excluded plants and minerals. This concept of the term *animal* is perpetuated by another particularly influential work, Isidore of Seville's *Etymologies*, written early in the seventh century. Isidore explains that "they are called animals (*animal*) or 'animate beings' (*animans*), because they are animated (*animare*) by life and moved by spirit."[27] That this definition is intended to include humans is apparent from several other passages of Isidore's work, as for example when he observes that "we call any animal that lacks human language and form 'livestock' (*pecus*),"[28] or when he reproduces a favorite example from classical rhetoric to explain the difference between specific and generic: "The general (*generalis*) nouns, because they denote many things, as 'animal', for a human and a horse and a bird are animals. ... The specific (*specialis*) nouns, because they indicate a sub-class, as 'man', for a human being is a type (*species*) of animal."[29]

The biblical exegetes and early Church fathers of late antiquity were particularly required to elaborate upon the differences between humans and other animals when commenting on the hierarchy of God's creation. Their general statements usually derived from the very specific context of the creation narrative set out in the Old Testament book of Genesis. That humans were animals was not debated, but only their privileged status in relation to other beings. When Latin writers such as Isidore strove to distinguish humans from other animals in this context, they tended to follow in classical and exegetical tradition by employing terms for the latter that were conventionally used in reference to domestic animals, such as *pecus;* this usage also corresponded with that of the Latin version of the Bible current in Isidore's day. In vernacular languages, on the other hand, there existed at that time no word for humans and nonhuman animals as a single life-form group, nor even one that encompassed all non-human animals. Even in those languages that derived from Latin, *animal* was not used in the Middle Ages. In Old French, for example, *beste* was used to refer to nonhuman animals and found its way into English as *beast* in the twelfth century, when it came to substitute for the Old English *deor,* "deer," which has the same root as the Middle High German *tier. Beast* has a Latin origin in *bestia,* a word that usually referred to wild animals, and initially, *deer, tier,* and *beast* were usually reserved for wild animals in the Middle Ages. From the twelfth century onward, however, *beast* came to be commonly applied to all animals, whether wild or not. Finally, from the fourteenth century onward, the word began to be displaced by *animal* in the sense in which it is still in general use today. These linguistic developments obviously need to be considered in the context of the changing understanding of the idea of *animal,* but they also had a direct consequence for the description of the distinction between animals and humans in our sources. Once a word had emerged in common usage that encompassed all nonhuman animals, it was no longer necessary for authors to reiterate or explain the distinction between humans and animals, since an explicit boundary between them could now be established through language alone.[30]

The shifting of these concepts is reflected in the evolution of one of the crucial texts for the transmission of zoological knowledge through the medieval period: the *Physiologus* and its variants, the bestiaries. The *Physiologus* encapsulated the dominant approach to animals in early medieval scholarship and remained one of the key reference works for the understanding of animals thereafter. Its origins again lie in late antiquity, a period when the early Church fathers saw the study of animals, and nature in general, as vital to the interpretation of meaning in the Bible, and as a source of moral exempla, but were little interested in it for other purposes. Augustine, for example, explained how essential it was to understand a snake's habits in order to grasp the full significance of the many passages in scripture in which such reptiles feature prominently: "an ignorance of the numerous animals mentioned ... in [biblical] analogies is a great hindrance to understanding."[31] For a similar reason exegetes were often at pains to explain the animals that appeared in the biblical passages on which they were commenting in the light of knowledge derived from classical natural history. The most popular source of such information about animals was Pliny the Elder's *Natural History,* often mediated through the excerpts provided by Solinus in his *Collectanea rerum memorabilium* (Collection of curiosities). These exegetical commentaries then became repositories of knowledge about animals in their own right. Ambrose's *Hexaemeron*—his commentary on the six days of the Creation—would, for example, have an immense impact on the medieval understanding of animals. It was similarly within the prevailing cultural context of biblical interpretation that the *Physiologus* emerged to become the prime point of reference for early medieval European theologians grappling with the nature and significance of the exotic near-eastern fauna that they routinely encountered in the Bible but that was wholly unfamiliar to them in their everyday experience.

The *Physiologus* in its many variants became one of the most transmitted texts of the medieval period.[32] In the form that had become standard by the ninth century, the compilation contained about thirty-six chapters, each concerned with a specific animal, plant, or mineral; those dedicated to animals are by far the most numerous. Each of the animals was introduced through a description of its characteristics—or rather its supposed characteristics—followed by moralizations about it drawn from biblical passages. Several were interpreted as symbols of virtue and of Christ, such as the lion, stag, panther, and unicorn, while others, among them the wild ass and the ape, represented vice and the devil. All the animals that appear in the *Physiologus* were mentioned in the Bible, so their names should have been recognizable to the faithful. But elephants and lions were every bit as unfamiliar to almost all the inhabitants of early medieval Europe as the phoenix or the unicorn. They might nevertheless have known—courtesy of the *Physiologus*—that elephants give birth in water, or that lions brush away their tracks with their tails in order to make it impossible for hunters to follow them. They would also have had the opportunity to see representations of such beasts in church decoration, intended to remind them that God resurrected his son on the third day after his death, just as lions breathe life back into their dead offspring after three days, or that the phoenix lives for 500 years before committing suicide and being reborn. These animals thus took their place in the favored repertoire of moral exemplars familiar to medieval Europeans. The fact that many of them were either unfamiliar or wholly fantastic can only have helped. Even if anyone had wanted to study the actual behavior of these creatures, they would have had little chance to do so; the lack of any contradictory information helped to sustain unchallenged the orthodox reading of their symbolic meaning. As anthropologists have demonstrated, mythical animals are often preferred metaphors because they occupy positions furthest away from humans in most taxonomical hierarchies; the clear boundary thereby established between them and humans enhances their value as exemplars.[33]

From the twelfth century onward, the familiar corpus of information enshrined in the *Physiologus* began to undergo some remarkable transformations. In Great Britain especially, but elsewhere in Europe too, there emerged out of it a new genre of texts: the so-called bestiaries. M. R. James suggested a system of classification for these bestiary manuscripts that has since been broadly accepted, albeit with further refinements. Those he identified as the "first family" of the emerging tradition essentially consisted of an expansion of the *Physiologus* through the integration into its text of passages from Isidore of Seville's *Etymologies*.[34] But it was the next step in the evolution of this tradition that was to prove crucially important because it involved a complete reworking of the text. In the so-called second-family bestiaries, the marked increase in the number of animals included leaps immediately to the eye. Most of these new additions were familiar, indeed often domestic species; these too could now be understood symbolically. The ways in which the behavior of such animals could be read metaphorically were meanwhile expanding too. Moralistic interpretations, and the didactic guidelines to be derived from them, were still based on the characteristics of the animal in question, but these now incorporated observations from nature, as can be seen, for example, in the entry for the lamb. Lambs were a symbol for Christ throughout the Christian tradition, based on Old and New Testament passages alike. The book of Isaiah (53:7) compared the death

FIGURE 0.2: *Ram. Bestiary* (around 1200), Aberdeen University Library, MS 24, fol. 21r. © University of Aberdeen.

of the promised savior to that of lambs at the sacrifice: "He was oppressed, and he was afflicted, yet he opened not his mouth; like a lamb that is led to the slaughter, and like a sheep that before its shearers is dumb, so he opened not his mouth." According to the gospels of John (1:36): "[John] looked at Jesus as he walked, and said, 'Behold, the Lamb of God!'" There is no shortage of such exemplary sheep in biblical typology. Yet there was no chapter devoted to them in the *Physiologus*, nor in the first-family bestiaries. In the expanded bestiaries of the second generation, however, sheep, rams, and lambs each have a dedicated chapter of their own. (See Figure 0.2.)

The lamb has a particularly extensive entry in MS Bodley 764, dating from the mid-thirteenth century. The chapter begins in the customary manner by explaining the animal's name according to its Greek or Latin roots: "The lamb is called 'agnus' in Latin either from the Greek word for pious, or from 'agnoscere', to recognize." It proceeds by explaining this etymology: "because above all other animals it is able to recognize its mother, so much so that if it is in the middle of a large flock, as soon as its mother bleats, it recognizes its parent's voice and hastens to it, seeking for the familiar source of its mother's milk." Not only do lambs have superior hearing, the ewes that bore them share the same extraordinary talent for voice recognition: "And the mother will pick out her lamb among many thousands of others. Their bleating appears to be the same, and they look alike, but nonetheless the mother can pick out her offspring from the rest and will treat only this one with motherly care."[35] After this detailed description of the behavior of ewes and their offspring, the text proceeds to anagogic and moral allegory, explaining with reference to John 1:36 that "[t]he lamb is a symbol of the person of our mystic Saviour" and outlining how it refers more generally to the Christian flock: "[t]he lamb is also any one among the faithful whose life is blameless, and who obeys his mother the Church, recognising her voice and coming to her side and obeying her commandments." The entry concludes with a final reference to scripture: "Lambs are blessed in the Gospel: 'Feed my lambs' [John 21:15]."[36] (See Figure 0.3.)

At first glance, the overall structure of such an entry is not so different from a typical chapter of the *Physiologus*, but there are two essential differences, first in the selection of a domestic animal for comment, and second in the emphasis of the description on naturalistic features. It should be noted, however, that the discussion of ovine behavior is not based on actual observation by the bestiary author or any of his or her contemporaries, but on the description of lambs in Isidore's *Etymologies*. Yet while the account is derived from a recognized textual authority, the choice of motif is still significant. That the appeal of lambs and sheep now lay as much in their nature as their anagogic function becomes even more apparent if one compares similar chapters in other second-family bestiaries. Although in MS Bodley 764 the chapters for sheep, rams, and lambs all begin with descriptions of the animals' behavior before progressing to their

FIGURE 0.3: *Agnus Dei*. Breviary, Chorherrenstift Seckau, Graz, Universitätsbibliothek, MS 789, fol. 255r. © Institut für Realienkunden—ÖAW.

spiritual meanings, in other texts, such as the *Aberdeen Bestiary,* the authors went much further, retaining only the zoological parts of the text, and omitting all references to scripture or contemplation of their subjects' allegorical significance.[37] Animals could now function as social role models independently of explicit reference to the Bible and the interpretations derived from it. It is essential to point out, however, that the additions to bestiaries in the twelfth century did not consist exclusively of domestic and familiar animals. Some fabulous ones were also incorporated into the tradition, but from the same sources from which zoological information about familiar animals was taken, and in similar fashion. Interestingly, however, the didactic purpose of such creatures was generally to exemplify immoral behavior, as in the cases of the manticora and the griffin, both of which are described as killing humans.

To account for the increase in the number of familiar animals used as exemplars, Willene B. Clark suggested that the developments in the bestiary tradition be located within the broader interpretative context of such changes as advancements in animal husbandry, the revival of classicism, and the emergence of new forms of spirituality.[38] A comparison of second-family bestiaries with compilations of knowledge about animals in other contemporary genres, whether encyclopedias or other types of natural history collections such as Alexander Neckam's *De naturis rerum* (Of the natures of things), tends to prove her point. In Neckham's work, written just before 1200, the range of animal examples is radically expanded from that found in the *Physiologus* and even by comparison with the content of the recently enlarged bestiaries. Domestic animals again feature prominently here, but while the second-family bestiaries remained wedded to new examples taken from textual authorities, such as Isidore or Hugh of Fouilloy's *Aviary*, Neckam was prepared to draw inspiration from a much wider variety of sources. The domestic animals to which he devotes most space are those treasured as companions and pets of the aristocracy, such as hunting dogs and apes.

The expansion in bestiaries occurs at the same time as the shift in the concept of *animal*, and the emergence of the new usage of *beast* that allowed a clear distinction between humans and animals. But such a distinction is by no means expressed with equal clarity across all genres. Evidence from art and literature, for example, has instead been cited as indicative of a gradual blurring of boundaries. An increase in the use as exemplars of those animals most akin to humans, such as apes and dogs, and the growing popularity in Gothic art of the depiction of hybrid creatures, half-human and half-animal, have been mentioned in this context.[39] In all these instances, however, it is essential first of all to review the evidence within its specific milieu. Different contexts called for different types of animals. In texts emanating from the spheres of religion and learning, for example, wild, imaginary, and exotic animals predominate in the earlier medieval period, until domestic ones appear more and more frequently from the twelfth century onward, as we have seen. More or less the opposite appears to be the case in literary genres, where unicorns and other mythical beasts begin to feature only from the twelfth and thirteenth centuries.[40]

It is interesting to note that while animal examples were already immensely popular in literature in the early Middle Ages, the preference then was primarily for native species. Although theologians seem to have preferred legendary beasts as moral exemplars and liked to focus on defining clear boundaries between humans and other animals based on criteria such as reason and the ability to talk, a completely different picture emerges from the study of contemporary works of literature. The animals found therein are not only usually familiar, but they are equipped with powers of reasoning and speech. It is not possible to explain this discrepancy as a consequence of the different social contexts of the authors; instead, the distinction derives from questions of genre and audience. Already at the court of Charlemagne poets made regular and colorful uses of animals in their tales. In Alcuin's "The Cock and Wolf," for example, the cock is caught by the wolf but manages to escape by asking the wolf to sing for it. As soon as the wolf opens his mouth, the cock escapes to a tree and shouts back at him: "Whoever grows proud without reason is deservedly deceived, and whoever is taken by false praise will go without food, so long as he tries to spread about empty words before eating."[41] Although this story bears some resemblance to ancient beast fables in its basic structure, no specific model for it can be identified.[42] The author's originality is even more strikingly displayed in Sedulius Scottus's poem "The Ram." Here, the narrator mourns the death of his ram Tityrus, a gift from his patron, after the animal had been stolen by a thief and then tragically killed by the dogs set upon the latter's trail. Before the ram is torn apart, he and the dogs exchange arguments.[43] Both of these poems were written by members of the clergy and, moreover, are replete with biblical quotes and references. Sedulius's ram, for example, is in many ways modeled upon the biblical example of the death of Christ. Examples such as these invalidate the drawing of any clear distinction in attitudes to animals between the religious and secular spheres. Instead, it has to be accepted that what mattered was the occasion. Christian theologians may have spent their time arguing about the difference between humans and animals when actively engaged in the interpretation of Scripture, but such churchmen had no difficulty in bestowing language and reason on animals in their poetry or in using them to convey moral messages.

Animals as protagonists in literature become more frequent with the rise in courtly romances from the twelfth century onward. This led to the creation of some stock characters who would enjoy a long tradition. Around the middle of the century the story of Ysengrimus first appeared in the Low Countries, introducing not only the eponymous wolf but also Reynard, the fox whose name would become synonymous with beast fables for centuries, and other familiar characters such as Tibert the Cat. Twenty-eight distinct versions of the *Romance of Reynard the Fox* are reported to have been in circulation in France by 1250.[44] These tales represent only one strand of the burgeoning literary interest in animals. To cite only some of the more famous examples, Marie de France adapted classical animal fables for the entertainment of a courtly audience, while not long afterward, in the early thirteenth century, the monk Odo of Cheriton was also writing beast fables, in his case for monastic communities.[45] Despite their differences of style and moral interpretation, both Marie and Odo primarily used native species in reworking classical fables for their respective audiences. The only exceptions in Marie's fables are lions, which are usually employed to represent fair monarchs, and apes; for his part Odo was more prepared to mention exotic beasts, but all of them, in a clear nod to his religious upbringing, can be found in the *Physiologus* or in the bestiaries. The appearance of the imaginary animals that had entered the Christian world of learning in the time of Bible translations and early exegesis in works of courtly literature too is another reflection of the expansion of learning in the twelfth century.

The only monsters found across the genres throughout the medieval period are dragons; in folkloric tales, for example, they frequently appear in their many vernacular forms as *worms* to typify the wilderness they were believed to inhabit. Dragons and serpents had long been deployed in a similar way in the religious genre of saints' lives. Animals in hagiography often serve as a way of demonstrating a saint's affinity to God. Only God can influence nature, but through his intervention, saints can, too. The most common interaction between saints and animals in earlier hagiographical works involves the encounters of the former with the serpents and dragons that commonly symbolized evil in general, or the devil more specifically. But not all struggles between saints and reptiles have to be read as straightforward conflicts between good and evil. In many cases, they simply demonstrate the saint's power over the wilderness, over those areas that ordinary men could not control, including the wild beasts that inhabited them. This can already be seen in the early medieval period, for example, in the case of Hilary of Poitiers, who the sixth-century author Venantius Fortunatus records as demarcating with his crook the zone on the Mediterranean island of Gallinaria, which serpents were not allowed to enter; Saint Patrick famously went further when he expelled snakes from Ireland altogether.[46] Jacques Voisenet has argued that most of the appearances of animals in medieval hagiography ultimately derive from models provided by Gregory the Great in his *Dialogues*. In only one of their ten appearances in the *Dialogues* are dragons or serpents associated with the devil, in a story where he enters a serpent in an attempt to chase Saint Martin out of his refuge.[47] (See Figure 0.4 for a saint, in this case Saint George, and a dragon.)

Voisenet's analysis supports Le Goff's reading of the encounter between Saint Marcellus of Paris and a dragon, a story first recorded by Venantius Fortunatus. Le Goff argued that the actions of the dragon-slaying bishop should not be understood in the context of any intended association between the reptile and the beast of the apocalypse, thereby "making this an explicit episode of evangelization." He interpreted it instead as "an episode in material civilization"

FIGURE 0.4: *Saint George and the dragon: early fourteenth century, Sankt Stephan, Obermontari.* © Institut für Realienkunden—ÖAW.

and an "example of medieval construction" as a result of which, after the land had been drained and cleared—including of wild beasts—the bishop could be seen to act not only as a spiritual but also as a political leader in helping to consolidate the interests of his community.[48] Such stories of bishops as the anchors of urban communities in their struggles against the countervailing forces of wildernesses and wild beasts remain common textual topoi in the eleventh and twelfth centuries, when the story of the bringing of the relics of Saint Donatus of Epirus to Venice shows that dragons were still not necessarily meant by hagiographers to be understood as allegories for the devil. In an earlier version of the saint's life, Isidore of Seville had already described the bishop's fight against a huge beast, "larger than dragons in Indian fable," which had preyed upon sheep, goats, oxen, horses, and men, before the bishop finally dealt with it. In 1125, during a crusading campaign, Venetians came upon the saint's relics and decided to take them back to Italy. The dragon's bones were rescued as well and displayed behind the altar in the church in Murano.[49]

In other respects, however, this example prefigures changing attitudes. From the twelfth century in particular, the expansion of horizons through the military campaigns of the crusades, diplomatic missions, or the rapid growth in long-distance trade gave medieval Europeans the opportunities to meet the exotic animals they had hitherto known only from texts, and in particular, from the Bible. Marvels of the imagination could now be seen in the flesh, and many were eager for the experience. Amongst the luxury items imported to medieval Europe were exotic animals in increasing number and variety. The birds of prey and types of game introduced in connection with hunting have already been mentioned. Other species were imported for different forms of entertainment; monkeys, for example, became favorite companions in aristocratic households, while elephants and lions were displayed in royal menageries.[50] These developments further stimulated a growing interest in the naturalistic observation of animals, as reflected in Matthew Paris's journey to London to draw the elephant that had just arrived in the king's menagerie, and its expression in new textual genres, such as Emperor Frederick II's famous treatise on hunting with birds, written in the early thirteenth century.[51]

Similar outcomes could result from the efforts of those who ventured to see exotic species in their natural habitats rather than in European capitals. Late medieval reports of travels to the Far East provide particularly revealing indications of changing perceptions of foreign fauna. Initially, these texts tended to repeat established stereotypes, taking their cue from such texts as the ancient geographical works of Megasthenes and Ktesias, usually transmitted to the medieval period through their reception by Pliny and Solinus.[52] According to these sources, the Far East in general, and India in particular, were populated by such creatures as unicorns or griffins. At first, medieval travelers were happy to repeat this received wisdom. Marco Polo, however, took a distinctly different line in recording his experiences in Asia during the last third of the century. When he encountered a rhinoceros on Java, for example, he was stunned; he thought he was seeing a unicorn, but the single-horned beast before him did not match up to his preconception:

> They have wild elephants and great numbers of unicorns, hardly smaller than elephants in size. Their hair is like that of a buffalo, and their feet like those of an elephant. In the middle of the forehead they have a very large black horn. You must know that they do not wound with their horns, but only with their tongue and their knees. For on the tongue they have very long, sharp spines, so that when they become furious against someone, they throw him down, and crush him under their knees, wounding him with their tongue. Their head is like that of a wild boar, and is always carried bent to the ground. They delight in living in mire and in the mud. It is a hideous beast to look at, and in no way like what

we think and say in our countries, namely a beast that lets itself be taken in the lap of a virgin. Indeed, I assure you that it is quite the opposite of what we say it is.[53]

The droll confusion of this late thirteenth-century traveler inspired Umberto Eco to speculate about the cognitive processes that occur when humans are confronted with previously unknown phenomena; they attempt to explain what they perceive through the concepts available to them.[54] In a way, however, what is happening here is rather different, because Marco Polo would not have been surprised to meet a single-horned creature in the East. On the contrary, he would have been expecting to do so, just like those travelers before him who wrote sightings of such beasts into their accounts even though from all that we can deduce from the routes that they took they cannot even have come across the rhinoceroses that might have confused them. When Marco Polo saw his rhinoceros, therefore, he was not confronted with the unknown, as Eco suggested, but the known; he assumed he had come across the single-horned creature with which texts and images alike had familiarized him. His problem was rather that the animal before him looked so very different from the stereotypical unicorn of courtly culture.[55]

On other occasions when Marco Polo comments upon Far Eastern fauna, however, he better exemplifies the cognitive process studied by Eco. For he frequently did come across creatures of which he had no preconceived idea, and which he duly struggles to describe. His account of the animals he saw in Malabar, for example, discusses various strange-sounding creatures, such as tarantulas that looked like lizards, in terms that are clearly indicative of some kind of misunderstanding. But in general what Polo insists on is not familiarity, but difference: "Over the whole of India, all beasts and birds are different from ours, with the exception of one bird alone, the quail. Their quails are, without doubt, just the same as ours; but all the others are strangely different from ours."[56] As he continues with his report one recognizes that what lurks behind some of his more perplexing descriptions is a way of categorizing animals that differs substantially from a modern zoological one. Polo claims, for example, that Indian bats are much bigger than European ones and, just in case the reader is not aware of what he means by *bat*, he adds: "bats, namely those birds that fly by night and have neither feathers nor plumage."[57] Within this different classificatory framework, it is easier to imagine how a tarantula might somehow be regarded as a type of lizard.

Does the growing interest in describing animals by careful observation—as represented by authors as diverse as Frederick II, Matthew Paris, and Marco Polo—rather than relying upon stereotypical information mean that animals were taken more seriously in general? The legal prosecution of animals is sometimes cited as evidence that such a change in attitudes was taking place in the later Middle Ages, when there occur many cases from all across Europe of animals being put on trial for crimes they have committed. In several such thirteenth- and fourteenth-century trials, pigs were found guilty of murder of children and hanged. The deputy bailiff of Mantes and Meullant detailed the costs incurred in the imprisonment and execution of a pig that had committed infanticide, including money for the animal's upkeep in jail and the execution-er's wage.[58] The subjection of animal behavior to legal control is not an entirely novel phenomenon, since the issue had already been abundantly addressed in the early medieval law codes. At that stage, however, any legal action against animals essentially entailed the prosecution of their owners. The definition of the space animals were allowed or forbidden to enter is a recurrent theme in medieval legislation. Pigs were considered a particular problem because of their voracious nature. Many towns issued laws against straying pigs: "No one shall keep pigs which go in the streets by day or by night," the Civic Ordinances of York stated in 1301.[59] By the later Middle Ages, however, the animals them-selves are considered, like humans, to have legal responsibility for their ac-tions, and any failure to abide by their obligations to the community renders them similarly liable to penalty. The trials and executions of animals resemble public punishments of humans in fulfilling various functions, from displaying the authorities' power and control to providing spectacles for the people. They also served to remind communities of boundaries and rules, enabling authori-ties to use these occasions to exert control over their human subjects or foster their sense of collective identity. As far as contemporary concepts of *animal* are concerned, the remarkable feature of such cases is not the attribution of reason to the unfortunate beasts, because there is no proof that this ever happened. But what they do show is that animals were regarded as full members of the community. The executioner of Mantes and Meullant was given a new pair of gloves for killing the hapless pig, just as he was for performing his duty on his fellow humans.[60]

We have to acknowledge that the big question that dominates so much of the discussion of animals in the Middle Ages—the distinction between humans and animals—is much more complicated than some modern commentators have made it. It should be apparent by now that it admits of no clear-cut or consistent answer, and that source genre and context have a crucial influence on where the line is drawn. As the aforementioned examples have demonstrated, the notion that animals are the so-called other cannot even be consistently sustained in the ecclesiastical sphere. Humans were, for example, among the creatures added to bestiaries in the period when their content was being signifi-cantly expanded, even in those manuscripts that were undoubtedly produced within a monastic environment for a monastic audience. But probably the most convincing evidence of all in this regard comes from scientific taxonomies. In the twelfth and thirteenth centuries, texts discussing the categorization of

nature were written by clerics, often with the intention of providing compilations of exemplars for preaching. In many of these cases humans were included
within the chain of beings, either at the beginning or at the end, depending on
whether the classification was carried out in ascending or in descending order.
One such natural history collection that was supposed to serve as a store of
sermon exemplars was Alexander Neckam's *De naturis rerum*. In this work,
however, humans appear in a peculiar and particularly interesting position,
right in the middle of the chapter about quadrupeds, or terrestrial animals.
They come after the wild beasts, but before the first domestic animals, the
dogs that, significantly, are described as their most loyal companions.[61] This
sequence makes it particularly difficult to imagine that Neckham was thinking
in terms of any schematic distinction between humans and animals.

The fundamental influence of genre and context upon an author's conceptual approach is very effectively illustrated within the twenty-six volumes *De
animalibus* (On animals) written by the Dominican scholar Albertus Magnus
(d. 1280). The first nineteen of these are thoroughly grounded in Aristotelian
thought.[62] Yet at the conclusion of this comprehensive and sophisticated reworking of Aristotle's zoology, Albertus felt compelled to append five more
books that compiled knowledge about animals in more familiar encyclopedic
form, species by species, in alphabetical order. Although he was repelled by
the method because of its unscholarly nature, Albertus was nevertheless aware
that a large part of his audience would be expecting nothing else: "... we will
append just such a tract at the end of our book since we feel we are under
obligation to both the learned and the unlearned alike, and since we feel that
when things are related individually and with attention to detail, they better instruct the rustic masses."[63] Clearly, Albertus could turn his mind from
cutting-edge philosophy to his pastoral obligations within a single work. In
sermons and exemplars, he knew there was no place for Aristotelian discussions of the blood vessels or reproductive organs of animals. To make the
information about animals he was providing more user friendly, he therefore took care also to present it in the accustomed encyclopedic manner. The
eminent theologian had no problem in adapting the form and content of his
presentation to the diverse expectations of the different audiences for whom
his text was compiled.

The depth of knowledge of animals assembled in the books of Albertus
Magnus is no less remarkable than his systematic approach. It reveals the mind
of a fascinating scholar at work, who grasped every opportunity to regale the
reader with details that demonstrate he took just as serious an interest in observing nature as he did in presenting the perfect philosophical system. For
example, he made extensive efforts to verify what his textbooks could tell him
about the size of whales by confirming how many cartloads of matter they
would account for when chopped up:

The ancients write that this fish occupies four *jugera* of land at the widest part of its belly. We have never been able to verify this from any of the fishermen who have seen many of them on many occasions. But what we have verified is that at its largest, and when divided into flesh and bones, it comprises 300 cartloads. Such large ones are rarely captured, but frequently there are ones brought among us which are between two hundred and one hundred fifty cartloads, a little more or less.[64]

Albertus likes to refer in similar style to personal experience whenever he doubts his sources' details. He had clearly acquired some of his knowledge in his youth, long before he received his first theological education. So when he explained how hunters with dogs "collaborated" with birds of prey to catch birds, he reported some practices he recalled from his childhood:

Now I myself have experience of this sort with respect to falcons when I was a lad. Whenever I led my dogs into the field (they are called 'bird-dogs' because they know how to find birds), falcons would follow me to the field, flying above me in the air, and they would strike the birds which the dogs had put to flight. These birds came back to earth trembling and allowed themselves to be picked up in our hands. At the end of the hunt we gave one to each falcon and then they left us.[65]

He continued to observe nature throughout his life, on his frequent travels as well as at home: "Thus, I experienced in my country home above the Danube, where there are many holes in the walls and stones, that every year, after the autumnal equinox, fish gather together there."[66]

His personal experience of and abiding interest in nature encouraged Albertus to question the knowledge he found in his textual authorities, Aristotle included. He often did so by experiment. To see whether Aristotle was correct in claiming that moles were blind and had black liquid under the skin where the eyes should be, Albertus tried dissection: "When I delicately cut into the mole I found nothing at all of the dark of the eye or of the matter of eyes. I found rather some flesh that was moister than it is elsewhere. Now this was a freshly caught mole, so much so that it was still squirming." The mole had no eyes, but no black liquid in their place either.[67] Albertus also dipped a scorpion in oil, put it under a glass container, and waited to see how long it took for the creature to die—twenty-two days. He put a spider on a hot grill to test the common view that animals of a "very cold complexion" did not burn; the common view turned out to be wrong.[68]

Despite the grisly and often cruel nature of Albertus's experiments, his immense intellectual curiosity about animals is palpable and found more positive expression in care for their correct treatment. This may be limited to the animals that mattered most to him—the birds of prey and dogs that were used for hunting—but here he shows a genuine concern for the creatures' well-being. When Albertus describes the signs of illness in a goshawk he shows every sign of casting a medical eye over the bird and diagnosing from the outward appearance of the patient:

> When this bird is sick, its feathers and wings fairly bristle and its wings droop as well. It also calls a good deal due to its feeling of languor. It is a sign of its being indisposed if it vomits out its food undigested and if it does this rather often. For this then signifies that it has a defect in its stomach and crop. However, it also sometimes suffers from fullness as does a human. At such time it has dull vision, a heavy and slow flight, and does not desire food, wishing rather to sleep a good deal and to rest. It allows prey presented to it to get away and sits on the earth. When recalled with food to its master's hand, it does not return quickly and when called does not pay heed to one's calling.[69]

In such descriptions of the symptoms of illness Albertus Magnus follows his customary practice by quoting from appropriate textual authorities—in this case hunting manuals—while relying equally on his own expertise or that of other specialists. He does the same when he describes the various cures: "In this section, then, which we have set forth on healing, we have especially followed the expertise of William, the falconer of King Roger, adding a few things of our own."[70] Or again: "These, then, are the things which we have said about the cures of falcons following the experience of prudent people. The wise falconer, however, may add to or subtract from these in time as a result of experience as he sees expedient, given the complexion of his bird. For experience is the best teacher in such matter."[71]

Since the boundaries created by language and discourse in the Middle Ages pose such formidable obstacles to the modern historian who tries to investigate medieval attitudes to animals, Albertus Magnus's works are an especially valuable source of insights into the concern of medieval people for animals. They are, of course, by no means unique; it is undoubtedly the case, for example, that household pets could be much cared for.[72] Such writings show not only that medieval Europeans had feelings for animals, but also that they had no doubt that animals themselves had feelings, an issue that became subject to considerable debate in later centuries, despite such studies as Darwin's *The Expression of Emotions in Man and Animals* (1872). In the medieval period, by contrast, philosophers and theologians were in agreement that humans and animals shared the capacity for emotion, the significant qualitative distinctions notwithstanding. Bestiaries are full of examples of animals' feelings: camels "become unrestrained with lust" and hate horses, tigresses can be "goaded by rage," and lions "cannot become angry toward men, unless … hurt."[73] Apes are described as lunatics, as "they rejoice with the new moon, grow sad with the waning and darkening," while dogs "love their masters."[74] (See Figure 0.5 for the depiction of an ape on the margins of a manuscript.) Of course, the animals in bestiaries are being presented as exemplars for humans; the feelings attributed to them do not necessarily reflect the level of sensibility of which people thought them capable. But numerous examples of similar type also exist outside the exemplary literature. The feelings of dogs for their masters are so frequently written about in the medieval period that they can appear stereotypical. However, if this was in some sense a mere commonplace, it was none imposed by the dominant Christian discourse. The image of the dog in scriptural references is consistently unfavorable across about forty passages such as: "Like a dog that returns to his vomit is a fool who repeats his folly" (Proverbs 26:11) or "[D]ogs are around me; a company of evildoers encircle me" (Psalm 22:16). Yet the longest stories incorporated by Alexander Neckam into his encyclopedia of animals are about greyhounds eager to win their owners' appreciation.[75] It is no coincidence that, as we have seen, he placed them directly alongside humans in his taxonomy.

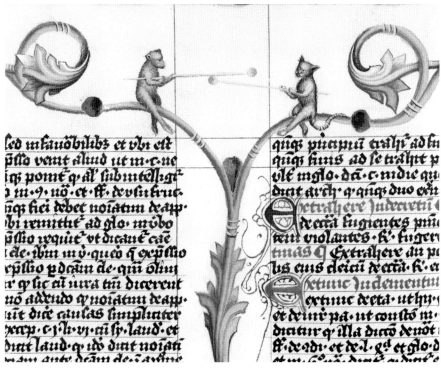

FIGURE 0.5: *Ape and cat.* Ulrich von Albeck, *Promptuarium iuris,* 1429, Chorherrenstift Seckau, Universitätsbibliothek Graz, MS 23, I, fol. 313v. © Institut für Realienkunden—ÖAW.

Dogs, therefore, are one of the clearest illustrations of how wrong it would be to conclude that medieval perceptions of animals were simply based on their biblical status. Dogs had become invaluable for humans in many ways, whether in assisting them in hunting or guarding the flocks, or in entertaining them as pets. Their high value is documented in law codes.[76] The great emotions that humans could feel for their dogs are reflected in poems and romances, as for example in Tristan's affinity with his hunting dog Husdent, while the courageous greyhound Guinefort could even be turned into an object of religious devotion.[77] In all this, as in other ways, the exegetical approaches of the earlier medieval period were being supplemented and superseded by experience. In the eyes of humans, animals had evolved into more complex beasts in the later Middle Ages.

CHAPTER ONE

Good Creation and Demonic Illusions

The Medieval Universe of Creatures

SOPHIE PAGE

HUMANS AND ANIMALS

Of living creatures many are the kinds
Throughout the world—unnumbered, since no man
Can count their multitudes, nor rightly learn
The ways of their wild nature; wide they roam,
These beasts and birds, as far as ocean sets
A limit to the earth.[1]

Medieval people acknowledged that the diversity and multitude of animals in the physical world presented a challenge to human knowledge and understanding. Attitudes to this mysterious world of creatures began to change in the twelfth and thirteenth centuries, as translations of Aristotle's *De animalibus* (a nineteen-book compendium of the *De generatione animalium, De partibus animalium,* and *Historia animalium*) suggested new ways of thinking about animals, and medieval travelers returned with knowledge of extraordinary and exotic beasts. Religious and philosophical approaches to animals were not isolated from lived experience, but how people used animals—their economic significance—and how they thought about them—their place in the belief system—did not necessarily coincide. Medieval theologians emphasized the differences between humans and animals, especially the superiority of human rationality and the belief that human souls would have an afterlife whereas animals' souls would not. They expressed unease about the mixing of animal and human bodies and went to great lengths to deny that human consumption of animals affected human identity in this world or that animal consumption of humans affected successful bodily resurrection in the next. This emphasis on separate human and animal identity and the apparent exclusion of animals from the Christian sacred sphere has led Western European society to be distinguished from other cultures for its rejection of the idea that animals can be people.[2] But the ecclesiastical authorities' notions of the correct interpretation of animal symbols or use of animal bodies did not always prevail, and attitudes to animals that contradicted the apparently stringent medieval policing of the border between human and animal can be found among all social groups.

An intellectual and aesthetic fascination with animal–human hybrids and metamorphosis is found throughout medieval culture, and cases of the perceived mixing of species provoked responses of wonder and pity. Discussing the ox man of Wicklow, the supposed offspring of human–animal intercourse, the cleric Gerald of Wales described how he had a human body but hooves instead of hands and feet, his eyes were huge and round like an ox, and he made a lowing sound instead of using human speech.[3] At first situated on the animal side of the species barrier, the ox man followed the other calves with his bovine mother but later was transferred to the society of his human father. He was eventually killed by some local youths, and Gerald comments with compassion that he did not deserve their cruelty. Animals endowed with human qualities in the Middle Ages included satyrs and werewolves who sought Christian blessings or salvation, and a greyhound that was honored as a saint. The opposite phenomenon, of a human who assimilated animal qualities while retaining human identity, is described in Icelandic sagas, heraldic treatises, and magical texts. This process will be referred to as beast identification.

Medieval exploration of the continuity and merging of animal and human identities occurred alongside attempts to view animals in relative isolation from their relationships with humans; that is, in their own environments, in relationship only with each other and with God. Observation of animals to learn about their characteristics and habits was influenced by the pragmatic concerns of husbandry and hunting, by Aristotle's emphasis on studying nature, and by curiosity about the secrets of the world. Some of the earliest nonallegorical images of animals in naturalistic environments are found in illustrated copies of the *Livre de Chasse* (1387–1389) of Gaston Phebus, Comte de Foix. (See Figure 1.1.) Hunters are instructed by this manual to study their prey, and manuscript images depict them in the act of hidden surveillance, perched in trees, and behind animal decoys. Illustrations accompanying chapters on each species *et de toute sa nature* show the animals fighting, mating, eating, climbing trees, and feeding

FIGURE 1.1: *Wolves*. Gaston Phebus, Hunting Manual (fifteenth century), Bibliothèque Mazarine, Paris. © The Bridgeman Art Library.

their young. These images had the pragmatic function of species identification and also expressed the idea that humans had power over animal prey through knowledge of their natures and habits. Yet they also seem to uphold the view of the English natural philosopher Adelard of Bath (1070–1160) that each creature "has an inborn wish to exist," they love to exist "with a natural desire."[4]

One of the most extraordinary medieval representations of the curious observer of nature is the image of Alexander the Great being lowered into the sea in a diving bell. Here the powerful military ruler—exemplified in the Middle Ages as a despoiler of nature's secrets—is shown risking his life to investigate the hidden realms of the physical world. (See Figure 1.2.) Enthusiasm for marine exploration was not only a literary topos. Nicholas Pipe, a diver and *maris sedulus explorator* in the employ of King Roger II of Sicily, was said to spend so much time at the bottom of the sea that he became a friendly and familiar figure to sea creatures (*Hic a marinis beluis quasi notus ac familiaris*).[5] Alexander

FIGURE 1.2: *Alexander the Great's descent into the sea.* BnF, Paris, MS Français 9342, fol. 182r.

is shown observing strange kinds of aquatic humans at the boundaries of the physical world. At another limit of the known world, far to the east of Christian Europe, the explorer Marco Polo reported that there were men with dog heads and tails.[6] Ambiguous beings, such as the animalic humans of Alexander and Marco Polo, are more easily situated in barely accessible realms. Yet it was a striking aspect of medieval culture that monstrous creatures and hybrids were not only discovered and projected into unknown and almost inaccessible regions but also placed at the heart of Christian culture—on the walls of cathedrals and the margins of religious manuscripts.

ANIMALS IN THE CHRISTIAN WORLD VIEW

Medieval theologians placed animals below humans in the hierarchy of creation, excluded them from the afterlife,[7] and viewed them with suspicion relative to the sacred sphere because of their previous associations with pagan worship.[8] According to the book of Genesis, the creatures of land and sea were intended by

God to be under man's control and to provide him with benefits, but following Adam's disobedience to God man was punished by the disobedience of the animals that should have been subject to him. Fierce, poisonous, biting, and stinging creatures were inflicted upon man, and fear, violence, and disharmony entered the relationship between humans and animals.[9] In the Garden of Eden, the diet was vegetarian and man did not kill animals,[10] but in the postlapsarian world it was permissible to kill animals because they lacked reason and were therefore excluded from the community of justice. The harmony in the Garden of Eden remained an ideal evoked in certain literary genres and magical texts, however, because the voluntary submission of wild animals (especially lions and wolves) was now interpreted as a special sign of holiness and the favor of God.

Hermits, saints, questing heroes, and penitents who entered the forests and wilderness of hagiographical and romance narratives attracted the companionship of wild animals, thus signaling their prelapsarian purity. These stories showed animals responding to and being attracted by the spiritual aspect of man. The theme of the saintly healing of animals—most famously exemplified by Saint Jerome's removal of a thorn from a lion's paw—is also significant because it associated compassion toward wild animals with exemplary figures in medieval culture. Augustine argued that God took care of individual species, although this may have been partly to reassure medieval farmers that he protected the domestic animals on which medieval agriculture depended.[11] In return, animals had a duty to praise God, an idea taken up most expressively in the medieval biographies of Saint Francis. He is said to have told the birds in a famous sermon: "My brothers, you have a great obligation to praise your Creator. He clothed you with feathers and gave you wings to fly, appointing the clear air as your home, and he looks after you without any effort on your part."[12] (See Figure 1.3.) In this sermon Saint Francis extended his evangelical mission to all creation and expressed the idea that animals lived not only for humans but also for God.

A few medieval texts drew animals even closer within the Christian scheme of salvation by describing sympathetic humanized creatures who sought Christian mercy from holy men. In his *Topographica hibernica*, Gerald of Wales described two unfortunate natives of Ossory who were cursed by a saint to endure the shapes of wolves for seven years.[13] When the male werewolf requested the last sacrament from a priest for his dying female companion, the priest reluctantly agreed, because humans in animal form might still be worthy of salvation. The story of the satyr who met with Saint Antony in the desert and expressed a desire for the mercy of Christ is more ambiguous, as this creature—half man, half goat, and with horns on its head—was normally classified as a beast.[14] (See Figure 1.4.) John of Mandeville uses the story to give a Christian and exotic aspect to the Egyptian desert landscape of his fourteenth-century travel narrative. He has the satyr petition the hermit "to pray to God

FIGURE 1.3: *Giotto, Saint Francis of Assisi preaching to the birds.* Musée du Louvre, Paris.

for me, that He who came from Heaven to earth for the salvation of man's soul, and who was born of a maiden, and suffered bitter Passion, through whom we all live and move and have our being, may have mercy on me."[15]

At the conclusion of his sympathetic portrayal of the satyr John of Mandeville notes that "the head of that beast, with the horns, is still kept at Alexandria as a marvellous thing."[16] In his mid-thirteenth century *De animalibus*, modeled on Aristotle's works on animals, Albertus Magnus also records that specimens have been killed and their bodies preserved in salt and taken to Constantinople. Albertus appears uneasy about the satyr's human characteristics and classifies it as a monstrous creature that occasionally walks erect and submits to domestication (*De animalibus*, bk. 22, tract 2, chap. 1, 93). But stories of the collecting of satyr bodies as marvelous objects were not necessarily intended to convey revulsion at their strangeness. Monstrous beings always had the potential to be seen a positive expression of the wondrous diversity of God's creation, and this

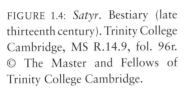

FIGURE 1.4: *Satyr*. Bestiary (late thirteenth century). Trinity College Cambridge, MS R.14.9, fol. 96r. © The Master and Fellows of Trinity College Cambridge.

was particularly true of human races with animal characteristics, which were potentially redeemable and could even represent a missionary triumph. The Cynocephali, or dog-headed men, were a particular focus of Christian interest. At one extreme they were represented as cruel cannibal idolators, but at the other, one cynocephalus became the remarkable Saint Christopher.[17]

ANIMALS AS RELIGIOUS SYMBOLS

Medieval Christians used symbols as a bridge between their experience of the physical world and longing for the invisible one. Symbols revealed the divine—a gathering of visible forms for the showing of invisible ones—and incited movement toward God through contemplation.[18] In the medieval cosmos God spoke to man in symbols, an interaction that worked on the one hand through the analogy or dissimilarity of visible and invisible things, and on the other through the participation of all physical things in their creator. Thus the use of animal symbols depended on the view that every living thing had some resemblance to God and that the physical world was an expression of the thought of God, from which his teaching could be uncovered. The significance of this approach to Creation is shown by the popularity of the bestiary, a genre based on the principle that the characteristics of animals had been determined by God to serve as a guide to moral conduct and to reinforce biblical teachings. Bestiaries provided complex readings of the animal world that combined abstract ideas and legitimate observations about animal habits with interpretations of their moral significance. It was unnecessary for the didactic purpose of bestiaries that they presented accurate natural history, but recognizable animal characteristics made the moral message memorable and striking. For example, the warning cackle of the goose when it saw strangers approaching was compared to prudent men who looked out for their own safety.

A second approach to animal symbols was centered on the question of how to interpret and represent sacred forms. In the Bible, God is described by means of the images of a lion, panther, leopard, bear, eagle, dove, and worm, and angels are given the form of the lion, ox, eagle, and horse. One of the most influential writers on biblical symbolism in medieval western thought was Pseudo-Dionysius (late fifth to early sixth centuries), who argued in his *De coelesti hierarchia* that sacred things could be made manifest through incongruous images (*dissimilia symbola*); that is, images bearing no likeness to what was symbolized. In his discussion of the animal figures attributed by scripture to the intelligent beings of heaven, Pseudo-Dionysius admitted that "perhaps people will think the super celestial regions are filled with leonine and equine hosts, or with a mooing prayer of praise."[19] But he argued that such symbolism did not wrong the divine powers. It hid holy truths from the masses by means of incomprehensible and divine enigmas (*per incomprehensiblia et divina aenigmata*) that resulted in less danger of the image actually being taken for the divine reality it represented, and hence of idolatry. In his explanation of the forms of angels Pseudo-Dionysius expressed a more positive interpretation of creation: all matter kept "some echo of intelligible beauty," therefore "all the feelings and all the various parts of the irrational animals uplift us to immaterial conceptions and to the unifying powers of the heavenly beings."[20]

Biblical animal imagery resulted in some strange medieval iconographical traditions, such as the motif of evangelists with the heads of their symbolic animals. This originated in the four animal-faced cherubim in the prophet Ezekiel's vision. (See Figure 1.5.) It was acceptable to interpret the deliberate use of animal characteristics in pagan religious images; the twelfth-century philosopher William of Conches thought "the ancients … gave Mercury a dog-image, for the dog is an intelligent animal, to focus on Mercury's shrewdness, for he is the god of cunning and shrewdness."[21] But churchmen advocated caution in the use and interpretation of animal symbols for God, particularly in contexts where images were likely to have a pedagogical role. William Durandus, a thirteenth-century bishop of Mende in France, explained how to use the symbol of the lamb in his discussion of the pedagogical value of art: "A holy lamb must not be principally depicted on the cross. But there is no objection when Christ had been represented as a man to paint a lamb in a lower or less prominent part of the picture, since he is the one true lamb who 'takes away the sins of the world'."[22]

Animal images in the Bible were considered symbols for inspiration rather than literal representations. As Augustine's influential treatise on the interpretation of sacred scripture pointed out, however, it was useful to know the nature of an animal indicated by a figurative reference: "the well-known fact about the snake, that it offers its whole body to assailants in place of its head, marvellously illustrates the meaning of the Lord's injunction to be as wise as serpents,[23] which means that in place of our head, which is Christ, we should offer our body to persecutors."[24] It was important to be open to the multiple significations of a single animal. The Bible told how a serpent in the Garden of Eden seduced Eve (Genesis 3:1–15), how God sent serpents as a punishment

FIGURE 1.5: *Ezekiel's vision*. Initial, Winchester Cathedral. © The Bridgeman Art Library.

(Deuteronomy 32:24), and how the serpent placed on a pole by Moses to cure the Israelites (Numbers 21:8–9) prefigured Christ on the Cross (John 3:14). The illustration for Psalm 65 in the Eadwine Psalter (fol. 109v) shows how complex the depiction of animals could be within a single image accompanying a biblical text.[25] (See Figure 1.6.) God is represented trampling on a lion and serpent (Psalm 91:13: "thou shalt tread upon the lion and adder"), an ox and sheep are shown being led to sacrifice, and pastoral animals are depicted on a hill outside the celestial city (Psalm 65:13: "the pastures are clothed with flocks").[26] Framing the whole composition and indicating its celestial setting is a band of zodiac signs, including several represented by animal symbols. Below this image the initial of the psalm contains a small naked figure, the human soul, struggling within interlaced foliage that terminates in three dragon heads. This initial and the depiction of God subduing the lion and serpent are examples of the ways animal symbols were used to dramatize the contest between good and evil.

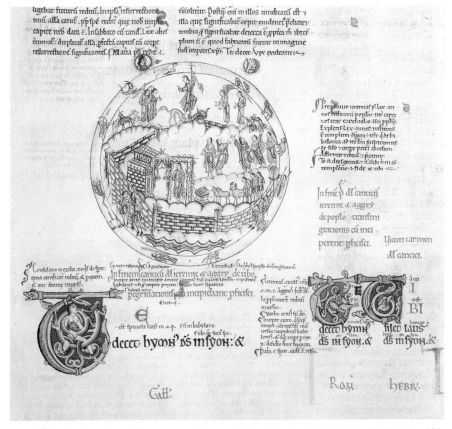

FIGURE 1.6: *Yahweh standing on an adder and a lion.* Psalm 65, Eadwine Psalter (twelfth century), Trinity College Cambridge, MS R.17.1, fol. 109v. © The Master and Fellows of Trinity College Cambridge.

Medieval animal imagery was vibrant and flexible. On a symbolic level animals could be found on either side of the spiritual struggle that constituted man's existence on earth, and they could help or hinder his chances of salvation. Romanesque art often placed the divine–human and animalic–demonic spheres in opposition, for example, representing a human hero engaged in fierce, intimate combat with an animal monster in a stylized forest setting. The contest between good and evil could also be represented by the human form of Christ combating demonic forces with animalic shapes, or solely by animal images, such as the battle between the divine animal (lamb) and the diabolical animal (dragon). Pairs of animals designated as enemies in the bestiary tradition, such as the panther and dragon, the elephant and crocodile, and the stork and serpent were also used to symbolize this contest. Still further variants were possible: in the romance tradition and hagiographical narratives animals joined forces with saints and virtuous knights against their human and monstrous adversaries, such as the famous pairing of the knight Yvain and a lion he had rescued from a dragon.[27] Finally, the human–animal–demonic could be merged in opposition to the divine sphere, as demonstrated by late medieval depictions of a female-headed serpent in the garden of Eden and the striking sculpture of Eve at Autun, which is sensuously serpentine. (See Figure 1.7.) Using animal images in these contexts placed them at the center of the Christian sacred sphere, in which superficially they appear to be absent.

One of the most significant exclusions of real animals from the Christian sacred sphere was the rejection of animal sacrifices to God. Jesus's crucifixion was understood as the perfect sacrifice that annulled the need for the animal

FIGURE 1.7: *Eve*. Relief from the Cathedral Saint Lazare de Autun (1130), Autun, Musée Rolin. © S. Prost.

sacrifices mentioned in the Old Testament, and the dominant paradigm of sacrifice in Christian culture was human self-sacrifice. Animal sacrifice retained
a certain symbolic importance, since Christ was said to have been offered
for mankind as a sacrificial ox or lamb, and the ox symbolism of the gospel
author Luke was explained with reference to the ox as an animal fit for the
priest's sacrifice.[28] The illustration for Psalm 65 depicts sheep and an ox being
led to sacrifice in the heavenly city symbolizing thanksgiving for the divine
bounty of waters. Self-sacrifice had some limited application to animals, as
they could act as channels for divine action in the world. The sculptures of
oxen placed on the summit of the west front of Laon Cathedral (ca. 1190–
1195) evoke the animal of a local legend that had miraculously appeared to
haul the heavy stones required to build an earlier cathedral.[29] When animal
sacrifice was encountered by travelers in the East it retained some of the positive associations of Old Testament tradition and contemporary symbolism.
Marco Polo's response to animal sacrifice depends on the context in which
he places it. He describes how idolators in the province of Tangut (Kan-su in
northwest China) sacrificed sheep with solemn devotion to ensure the protection of their children and to honor idols in sacred places he calls by the
approving Christian terms abbeys and monasteries.[30] By contrast the sacrifice
of sheep in the province of Kara-jang (Yün-nan in western China) is said to
be the work of magicians, "conjurers of devils and guardians of idols," who
declared that spirits inhabiting an invalid's body would only be propitiated by
the sacrifices of sheep.[31]

The symbolic meaning of animals and the daily experience of working with
them both influenced medieval attitudes to animals. Some animals, like the sheep
or lamb and ox, had religious and economic significance, whereas others like the
lion and serpent were prominent as symbols but not agricultural assets. Gerald of
Wales's *Topographica hibernica* shows how a range of approaches to the natural
world might be harmoniously combined. His descriptions of Irish animals include close natural observation, assessment of economic value, and explanation
of symbolic importance. The reader learns, for example, how an osprey catches
fish, that Irish pigs are poor specimens ("small, badly formed and inclined to
run away") but Irish falcons are first rate, and why the unusual reproduction of
barnacle geese should convince unbelievers of the truth of the Virgin birth.

Images of animals need to be read in terms of their artistic genealogy as well
as their religious symbolism. The theme of the struggle between two animals or
a man and beast was an ancient motif transmitted to Western medieval artists
on Eastern textiles, and didactic interpretations rather than purely decorative
functions can be difficult to justify. The appropriateness of some animal and
hybrid images in a religious context was certainly questioned by Bernard of
Clairvaux in his *Apologia:* "What are the filthy apes doing there [the monastic
cloister]? The fierce lions? The monstrous centaurs? The creatures, part man

and part beast? The striped tigers?"[32] So startling were these and other monstrous and hybrid figures that, in his opinion, monks were distracted from their spiritual reading and stopped to wonder at them rather than meditating upon the law of God.

Animal images remained a universal and accessible language in the Middle Ages in spite or because of their combination of didactic opacity with aesthetic power. They were a vivid point of departure from which to explore the relationships of humans to each other, to their physical world, and to God. The power of animal images as mediators in human relations with the cosmic order derived in part simply from their perceived physical power as apotropaic motifs to keep demonic forces at bay.[33] But they could also carry complex allegorical meanings that served to summarize and stimulate the mystical process of the soul's ascent toward God. The miniature of the *Palma contemplationis* in the *Rothschild Canticles* (ca. 1300), an arboreal allegory based ultimately on a verse in the Song of Songs, was conceived as a series of seven steps toward spiritual perfection, with a bird or birdlike creature characterizing each spiritual stage.[34] Contemplative viewing and reading begins with a peacock on the first branch symbolizing the soul in meditation with itself, and moves upward to the final branch that has a phoenix in flames, representing the state of spiritual rapture or ecstasy. Understanding the meanings of this image would have required knowledge of the Bible and devotional literature.

Animal symbols and their religious meanings were disseminated into secular contexts and adapted to the needs and interests of the laity. In the thirteenth century friars popularized theological and scientific approaches to animals in works such as Alexander Neckham's *De naturis rerum* (ca. 1200), Bartholomaeus Anglicus's *De proprietatibus rerum* (ca. 1240) and Thomas of Cantimpré's *Liber de natura rerum* (1230–1245). These and other medieval encyclopedias aimed to bring all spheres of human knowledge within a hierarchical structure that emphasized the goodness and harmony of God's creation. At the same time, the beginning of a shift toward naturalistic art was signaled by the appearance of the sculpted leaves of arum, plantain, and fern on the capitals of churches and found exquisite expression in the individuated bird species of Giotto's painting of Saint Francis at the end of the century. (See Figure 1.3.) Struggling animals and hybrid monsters continued to adorn cathedral walls and manuscript margins and to illustrate accounts of the fauna of distant lands, while the decorative animals of the eastern heraldic style found popularity in devices on the arms of the nobility of medieval Europe.

ANIMAL SYMBOLISM IN SECULAR CONTEXTS

In many human societies participation in nonhuman animality indicates social preeminence and power, while the possession of zoomorphic attributes

FIGURE 1.8: *White hart*. Wilton Diptych, reverse, right wing, National Gallery, London.

expresses an individual's ability to transcend the categories of ordinary existence and to mediate between ordinary and extraordinary domains.[35] The most
explicit expression in medieval Christian culture of such participation was the
ancient Scandinavian *fylgja,* or "fetch," a pagan concept that appears in the
Icelandic sagas, texts by Christian authors of the thirteenth and fourteenth centuries but set in the pagan past.[36] This guardian spirit or projection of the soul
(a term for which the pagans had no precise equivalent) often took an animal
form determined by a human's character and status or others' perception of
it: thus the king's fetch took the form of a lion, the brave hero's a bear or bull,
and his enemy's, a wolf. The mediating role of the fetch was signified by its appearance in dreams and its function as an omen of death. Particularly powerful
heroes or practitioners of magic could also send their fetches on shape-journeys
(*hamrfarir*) as fierce animals to do battle while their human bodies lay in a
state of sleep or trance. The *Saga of Hjalmther and Olvir* has a particularly
dramatic representation of its protagonists doing battle at sea in the forms of a
whale, a walrus, and a dolphin.[37] In the medieval romances of Western Europe
figures with shape-shifting abilities like Merlin and Nectanebus had social preeminence and supernatural powers but were morally ambiguous.[38] Some literary werewolves, such as Bisclavret in Marie de France's lai of this name, and
the enchanted Spanish Prince Alfonso in the medieval romance *Guillaume de
Palerme,* were sympathetically portrayed. But shape-shifting, even for ostensi-
bly chivalrous purposes, tended to have dangerous consequences. In the lai of
Melion (ca. 1200) the hero uses a magic ring to turn himself into a wolf in order
to catch a giant stag for his wife, but she betrays him and keeps the ring to make
his transformation permanent so she can elope with her lover.

The concept of the fetch or shape-shifter merged human and animal identity
in ways that were discomforting for medieval Christians outside of a literary
context. Participation in nonhuman animality generally had negative connotations, as Eve's assimilation of serpentine qualities in the Autun relief and
the fear of shape-shifting witches and werewolves illustrate. A positive role
for such participation was found in the heraldic devices that twelfth-century
knights started bearing on their shields in tournament and battle and that were
subsequently found in numerous late medieval contexts from clothing and
horse harnesses to domestic interiors and objects and ritual performances. By
the early thirteenth century, heraldry had become a complex symbolic language
with its own system and classification, and heraldic badges acted as symbols
of individual identity and membership of a family, the class of knighthood, or
a political faction.

Knights identified with the properties or characteristics of their heraldic
animals and with the virtues those animals symbolized. This symbolism
largely originated in bestiaries. The physical characteristics of heraldic animals
were often deliberately exaggerated to emphasize qualities appropriate to

knighthood. In his treatise *De insigniis et armis* (1350s) Bartolo di Sassoferrato advised that a ferocious animal like a lion should be depicted in an upright pose with gnashing jaws, while to express the energy of a horse it should be portrayed partly rearing up as if it were running or leaping.[39] Did the bearers of such devices think that they would be endowed with the qualities possessed by real animals? Evidence from practical treatises on animal parts and from literary works equating an individual's character and skills with the properties of his animal heraldic device suggest that this was possible. Recipes on the use of animal parts in works of magic, natural philosophy, and the encyclopedic tradition offered such advice as wearing a wolf's eye or items made from the skin of a lion to induce boldness and guarantee victory.[40]

Chivalric literature used animal heraldic devices to draw attention to the particular attributes of heroes and villains in ways that resemble the Icelandic saga presentation of heroic characteristics through the choice of animal fetches.[41] Heraldic treatises encouraged identification with the animal symbol because associations between bearer and device flattered patrons and expressed aspirations to the ideals of chivalric culture. In the case of saints and kings, an association with a particular animal or its symbolic meaning was a useful way to emphasize individual over group identity.[42] Richard II of England favored the badge of the white hart, an animal of unusual and marvelous coloring that signaled the special identity of the king and his ability to mediate between ordinary and extraordinary domains: whiteness was a sign of the hounds of the dead and the steeds of fairies.[43] Although hunting white harts portended a dangerous encounter in medieval romance literature, Richard's hart is a beast already captured and therefore chained and passive.[44] (See Figure 1.8.)

Johannes de Bado Aureo's *Tractatus de armis* (1382–1384), written at the request of Anne of Bohemia, Richard II's wife, emphasized correspondences between the personal characteristics of an armiger and the elements of his coat of arms. In late-fourteenth-century England the same authority was responsible for designing and assigning coats of arms, and during his discussion of the heraldic symbol of the dog, Bado Aureo says that when a man makes a petition for arms it is important to know his habits.[45] This point was particularly pertinent to the symbol of the dog, since Bado Aureo says that it represents a loyal man who would never desert his master and would even be willing to die for him. Nicholas Upton's *De studio militari* (ca. 1446) also took the view that the bearer ought to hold an animal device that corresponded to his character and abilities; for instance, a person with excellent eyesight should hold a lynx, and a man called Pike should bear the fish of that name.[46] Animal symbols could even be suitable for an entire people (*natio*)—Upton says that the Irish have the boar on their arms because they are very fierce—and reflect personal physical characteristics, such as a hunchback (the camel), or infertility (the ox).

Upton often describes the characteristics of heraldic beasts according to the formula "the first person to bear such-and-such as animal on his arms was. ...." For example, the first bearer of the lamb was meek, lovely, and courteous, while the bearer of the hart was musical, wise, and cautious. This reference to the original bearer of a heraldic symbol suited the fashion for exotic genealogical myths that appeared after a widespread shift to patrilineal inheritance among noble families in the twelfth and thirteenth centuries. The Germanic and Scandinavian pagan tradition of fierce animal forebears and family names[47] merged with the medieval romance tradition to produce otherworldly (and more delicate) beast ancestors, such as the serpentine or fish-tailed fairy Mélusine adopted by the dynasty of Lusignan as their founder and the Knight of the Swan linked to the Bouillon family. Placing the adoption of these ancestors in the context of the rising knightly class, Le Goff argues that Mélusine and the supernatural gifts at her disposal were "l'incarnation symbolique et magique de leur ambition sociale."[48] Here the serpent woman forebear has positive connotations of social preeminence and mediation between realms in contrast to the Eve of Autun.

In the later Middle Ages, complex representations of coats of arms incorporating emblematic and naturalistic animals and fabulous creatures became more common. The coat of arms of Jacques d'Armagnac, duke of Nemours (ca. 1433–1477), combines a shield bearing symbols of the *lion rampant* with more naturalistically depicted mermaid and wildmen shield supporters and a *lion dormant*. (See Figure 1.9.) The supporters allude to the fashion for exotic semihuman forebears—wildmen were very popular from the late fourteenth century as symbols of hardiness, strength, and virility. The lion at the foot of the shield is represented according to the bestiary description of the lion sleeping with open eyes, an image evoking constant vigilance, and allegorically, Christ being spiritually alive after the Crucifixion. Its presence in the coat of arms may reflect the duke's avid readership of Arthurian romances in which the lion was presented as a suitable companion for the chivalric knight. Real animals could also act as symbols of identity in a period when the possession of a menagerie was beginning to be a mark of status: the bears of Jean, Duc de Berry (1340–1416) traveled with him from castle to castle and became a special emblem of his.[49] Many Italian communes kept lions in captivity as living symbols of multiple significance: power, fertility, near-regal status, allegiance to the Guelph party, and (in Venice) the special protection of Saint Mark.[50] When a city's lions mated and gave birth it was an occasion for public curiosity and pride.

Animals gave meaning and status to other kinds of territories. The diversity of their appearance and use by humans made them vivid signifiers for unknown regions, and they represented a level of profitability and exoticism that could express the attraction or otherwise of travel, alliance, trade, and conquest. In Marco Polo's *Travels* animals are signifiers for each new land he describes, especially by their exotic differences of color, size, and beauty, and

FIGURE 1.9: *Coat of Arms of Jacques d'Armagnac (ca. 1433–1477)*. Musée Condé, Chantilly, MS 860/401, fol. 7r. © The Bridgeman Art Library.

he has a particular aesthetic appreciation of gentle, harmless animals such as giraffes and parrots. The realm of Quilon (Coilum) in India, with its black lions, scarlet and blue parrots, and handsome peacocks, is described in particularly heightened terms: "Everything there is different from what it is with us and excels both in size and beauty."[51] Gerald of Wales's Ireland is also represented as being rich in desirable animals—tasty fish, courageous falcons, numerous cranes and swans, marvelous barnacle geese, plump stags, and copious wild boar—including several species he says are not found elsewhere. Together with its lack of poisonous creatures (pt. I, 21–24), temperate climate (pt. I, 26), wonders and miracles (pt. II), and primitive people (pt. III, 93), Ireland is represented as a country apt for conquest and settlement by Gerald's patron, Henry II.

As indicators of status, animal symbols were used to raise or lower an individual's place in the social hierarchy. The success of an animal symbol in asserting individual identity can partly be measured by its future popularity as an image through which loyalty or rejection could be expressed. Richard II's white hart was used by the anonymous author of *Richard the Redeless* (1399–1400) to satirize the King's followers through beast allegory, while the Edward IV roll (ca. 1461)[52] displays the white hart conspicuously in order to present Edward as the legitimate heir to the throne. According to an author's or owner's sympathies, therefore, a specific animal emblem could be used to assign negative or positive status. Animal devices might be inherited or chosen, but they were also invested in the ritual of becoming a knight, an elevation of status that was a revelation of nobility. In the mid-fourteenth century romance *Octavian*, Florent's true noble identity is made clear to his adopted parents, Paris burghers, when he compulsively purchases a falcon and a snow-white war horse (lines 652–735). Animal symbolism was also used to express a sense of identity and status by nonnoble individuals and social groupings such as guilds, confraternities, and urban quarters, particularly during significant ritual processions, pageants, and carnivals.[53] The fables of Reynard the Fox were popular sources of animal exemplars on these occasions, partly because they were not explicitly associated with the clerical and noble genres of bestiary and heraldry.

Animals were used to symbolically demonstrate the degraded status of criminals, cuckolds, and Jews in punitive and anti-Semitic rituals and executions such as the backward ride on an ass or the upside-down hanging with a dog or wolf.[54] This form of degraded participation with symbolic nonhuman animality appears to have been more frequently expressed through image rather than action. Punitive images had the advantages of acting against a person who had physically escaped and alluding to a whole group of people rather than just an individual (such as the Jews or a political faction). They could be removed or maintained according to changing circumstances and enabled extreme symbolic expression. Defamatory images (*pittura infamante*) were particularly popular for shaming so-called public enemies in the late medieval communes of northern Italy where *fama* had acute social implications among the newly empowered merchant classes.[55] In 1377 the governing body of Florence ordered that defamatory images of Ridolfo Varano, a *condottiere* who had deserted Florentine service for that of the Pope, be painted onto the Bargello and other public buildings. Ridolfo was depicted upside down on the gallows with a siren on his left side and a basilisk on his right. These symbols of evil voice and vision respectively were vivid signifiers for the horrific crime of treachery.

Rituals that assigned animal symbols to individuals provided a temporary revelation of true identity. Writers of heraldic treatises went further when they asserted parallels between animal devices and human bearers, but because they adapted their beast identification from the world of nature described in bestiaries and encyclopedias they linked the devices of their noble readership to an ordered creation, the work of a good, omnipotent God. Noble characters, abilities, ancestors, and even names and personal histories were linked to the world of creatures and their symbolic virtues, and hence to God. In this context beast identification was acceptable because it was primarily expressed through animal images and symbolic virtues rather than engagement with actual animal bodies.

ANIMALS AND BELIEF

Medieval people thought that animals could act as channels of supernatural power in the physical world, helping saints or punishing sinners according to God's command. The actions of a wolf in different narratives of the life of Saint Edmund reveal how nature and divine will could be represented working together. All versions of the life describe how a wolf guarded the martyr's head against other wild animals until it could be recovered by his human followers.

Ælfric's *Passio Sancti Eadmundi* (before 1002) related that the wolf was greedy and hungry but did not dare to eat the head because of God's command to guard it (*grædig and hungrig and for gode ne dorste þæs heafdes abyrian*).[56] An anonymous Anglo-Norman work, *La Passiun de Seint Edmund* (ca. 1200), described how the wolf remained with the martyr's head, grieving for the saint's death. But when the head had been reunited with its body by Saint Edmund's followers, the wolf "went back to the woods where it had long dwelt. It did not want to give up its own nature; and so it went off of its own free will" ("Ne volt estre desnaturé; Pur ço s'en vait tut de sun gré").[57] Although the wolf had temporarily repressed its own nature and even expressed grief as a human would, once the divine will had been achieved it returned to its natural state.

In late medieval Europe both the dominant religion, Christianity, and the dominant philosophical current, Aristotelianism, promoted a separation between animals and the supernatural realm. God was accessible through contemplation of his creation but not through the physical manipulation of animals or animal parts, such as animal sacrifice. Animals like Saint Edmund's wolf were only temporarily transformed by their contact with the supernatural, and only God (sometimes acting through special humans like saints) and his angels could legitimately intervene to make animals behave against natural laws. Explaining the passage in Genesis 2:18–23 where the animals were brought together for Adam to name, Aquinas said: "Now an angel is naturally higher than man. Therefore certain things in regard to animals could be done by angels, that could not be done by man; for instance, the rapid gathering together of all the animals."[58]

Attitudes toward animals that challenged these mainstream views and therefore came under critique from ecclesiastical authorities can be loosely grouped under four headings: idolatry, heresy, divination, and magic and sacrifice. Idolatry was the belief that an individual animal or a particular species was worthy of reverence or worship. Heresy included perceptions of animals that detracted from the orthodox position on the goodness and order of God's creation. Divination required the belief that patterns in nature (such as animal sounds or movements) could be interpreted and used for human benefit. Magic and sacrifice involved the ritual manipulation of animals or animal parts to gain access to supernatural powers. While none of these beliefs and practices was ever held or performed by a significant majority of medieval people, they reveal some of the diverse ways in which beliefs about the supernatural influenced attitudes toward animals and how practical experience of animals influenced belief.

Idolatry

The story of Saint Guinefort, the holy greyhound, outlined the dangers perceived by ecclesiastical authorities when admiration for the exceptional behavior of an animal was translated into reverence for a miraculous individual. Of all animals, dogs were most noted for their strong emotional attachments to humans, sometimes even sacrificing their own life for their master. There were commendatory stories of dogs who tried to revive a dead master, died of grief after his death, or attacked his murderer. In the case of Saint Guinefort, however, the preacher Stephen de Bourbon (d. 1262) was horrified by the reverence that peasants of Lyon paid to a greyhound they believed had been mistakenly killed after protecting its master's baby from a snake.[59] At the beginning of Stephen's account, he classifies the rituals he uncovered at the site of the cult as idolatry. He says that local women performed rituals at the place of the greyhound's death to make local fauns take back their sick changeling children and return the real, healthy ones. The supposed changelings were abandoned by their mothers as part of the ritual, leaving them prey to a passing wolf, or as one peasant woman puts it, the devil in disguise (*lupus vel diabolus in forma eius*). The unnaturalness of reverence for an animal led Stephen to interpret the peasants' idolatry as the worship of demons rather than a real animal. This analysis had contemporary parallels: in the late twelfth and early thirteenth century it became common to associate heretics and Jews with worship of the devil in the form of a monstrous cat.[60]

In late medieval Europe the worship of animals was largely relegated to the pagan past or the heretical and non-Christian fringes of orthodoxy and the known world. The use of animals as religious symbols introduced some ambiguity, however, because the popular image of the Lamb of God, Agnus Dei, was a focus for worship in many forms: the Lamb of Crucifixion portrayed with its blood pouring into a chalice, the Lamb of Resurrection carrying a triumphant banner, the monstrous Apocalyptic Lamb with its attribute of the Book with seven seals and the Lamb as Christ accompanied by his disciples, depicted as sheep. The anxiety surrounding misuse or misinterpretation of the image of the Lamb of God is suggested by William Durandus's comments on its correct portrayal and William of Auvergne's defense of the orthodoxy of wax images of this subject (discussed subsequently). The prevalence of certain animal symbols in Christian culture did not necessarily influence people's attitudes to real animals, but a transference of attitudes can sometimes be detected.

Marco Polo's thirteenth-century encounter with ox worship in Maabar (Coromandel Coast, India), for example, seems to have been influenced by the positive status, both economic and religious, of the ox in Christian culture. He describes the custom of soldiers wearing ox hair as a protective amulet because of the sanctity of the ox, and he mentions the yogi who lived austere lives of abstinence and worshipped the ox. Although he categorizes this worship as idolatry, Marco Polo says that the yogi anoint their bodies with burned and powdered cow dung "with great reverence, no less than Christians display in their use of holy water."[61] By contrast, references to ox worship in John of

Mandeville's *Travels* are negative, associating this practice with hybrid monstrosity. He relates that in India the sacred cow is worshipped in a form half ox and half man. Other worshippers of the ox are the cannibal dog heads, who in one manuscript illustration are shown genuflecting before an idol like the biblical golden calf, thus drawing biblical past and exotic present together.[62]

Heresy

The repression of religious groups and movements categorized as heretical by the Catholic Church put a range of beliefs under scrutiny, including some that reveal contradictions and ambiguity in medieval attitudes to animals. The inquisition register of Jacques Fournier, bishop of Pamiers (1318–1325), included many confessions of Cathars who believed in metempsychosis and were therefore reluctant to kill animals who might be reincarnated souls. Beatrix de Ecclesia said that a Cathar priest (*sacerdotes*) had told her that spirits reincarnated in animals had just as much reason and understanding as those in human bodies (*eque bene racionabiles spiritus et scientes*), the only difference being that they were unable to speak.[63] Spirits in both kinds of body retained the memory of previous incarnations,[64] thus erasing almost all distinctions between animals and humans except their outward forms. But this similarity of approach to animal and human bodies was the result of a very pessimistic view of the world, in which physical bodies were thought to be the creation of an evil god, and spirits' incarnation within them a punishment for sin.

The late medieval confrontation between the Catholic Church and dualist Cathars resulted in an increased orthodox emphasis on the goodness and order of God's creation. According to this view animals were the creation of a good, omnipotent God. Therefore if an animal or species behaved with particular ferocity toward humans it was because God willed that either a real animal or a demon in the form of an animal acted as an instrument of divine justice. When animals caused severe physical or economic suffering, however, this concept was hard to adhere to. The peasant Arnaud Cogal of Lordat told the authorities investigating heresy in Pamiers that he was unable to accept that a good God had created such an evil animal as the wolf, but believed that the first wolf had emerged into being by itself.[65] Arnaud's belief was problematic because of the diminution in God's omnipotence implied by the existence of a self-created and inherently evil animal, but he convinced the authorities that it reflected his own experience of a wolf's slaughter of his livestock rather than contact with dualist heretics.

The belief that certain beings—Fates, magicians, witches—could turn themselves or other people into animals also cast doubt on God's unique role as creator. Like a number of other suspect beliefs in the late Middle Ages it was initially ridiculed as a foolish delusion, notably in the influential *Canon episcopi* (ca. 900) and Burchard of Worms' *Corrector* (1010–1012) where it was situated under unbelief and assigned a minor ten-day penance of bread and water.[66] But following an increase in the circulation of learned magic texts, especially those of Arabic and Jewish origin, and changes in demonology, thirteenth-century critics of magical operations began to assert that the transformations proposed in these texts could actually happen through natural or demonic causes. Theologians argued that there was no actual species transformation of man to beast or hybrid—only God could create new beings in the physical world—but an apparent transformation was produced by demonic manipulation of certain natural seeds and processes or the deception of men's senses by means of phantoms.[67]

These changes in medieval attitudes to shape-shifting influenced early constructions of witchcraft. The *Malleus maleficarum* (1486), perhaps the most famous of the witchcraft manuals, explained how witches could change men into beasts with the assistance of demons and specifically tackled the apparent contradiction of this proposition in the *Canon episcopi*.[68] The *Malleus* also argued that the devil could possess wolves or cause people to imagine they were wolves, although here Albertus Magnus's *De animalibus* is cited on the point that some very dangerous and aggressive wolves were simply real animals acting out of starvation or natural ferocity (*De animalibus*, bk. 22, chap. 68). The insistence by the *Malleus* that demons could possess real wolves rather than just assuming their forms is an exception to the usual perceptions of limited demonic power over animals but is unsurprising in view of the belief in demonic possession of humans. That a witchcraft manual makes frequent reference to the *De animalibus* indicates the need for its authors to extricate demonic from real animals to make their point.

Confusion between the categories "real animal" and "demonic animal" was probably exacerbated by bestiary moralization as well as real predation: the bestiary allegory of the wolf presented it as the devil, who saw humankind as his prey and circled the sheepfold of the faithful. But the *Malleus maleficarum* also expresses the beginning of a crisis in philosophy and demonology: an increasing conceptual difficulty in distinguishing what was real and what was demonic illusion.[69] It was thought that lesser supernatural beings—demons and ghosts—took physical forms, including those of animals and monstrous animalic hybrids, to interact with humans. Numerous medieval accounts of the appearance of demons in the shape of animals survive. Caesarius of Heisterbach's *Dialogus miraculorum* (ca. 1230) relates the suffering of sinful monks and nuns plagued by demons in the shape of fawning cats, huge toads, grunting pigs, hideous dogs, mocking apes, and black oxes.[70] These demonic animals could only be seen by those with special vision and were used by Caesarius to exemplify particular sins. For example demon hogs fed on the husks of half-heartedly spoken psalms and demon toads squatted before monks weary of prayer.

Ghosts appearing in animal form are rarer, but two of the twelve ghost stories copied into a manuscript of Byland Abbey in about 1400 describe spirits taking on the forms of animals (*quasi equus* and *quasi corvus*) as an initial stage before they could communicate in human shape. In the second of these stories the spirit met by the tailor Snowball successively takes the form of a crow, a dog, a goat, and a cadaverous man.[71] Another story in the Byland Abbey collection refers to actual animal ghosts: Richard Rountre encounters a crowd of the dead accompanied by their *mortuaria,* the horses, sheep, cattle, and other animals that were offered to the church at the time of their funerals.[72] These supernatural animals are presented in a neutral fashion, but later medieval authors would argue that it was mainly evil spirits that appeared in animal form. Jacobus de Clusa (d. 1465) claimed in his treatise on spirits, *De animabus exutis a corporibus,* that a good spirit would have the appearance as a person, whereas an evil spirit took the form of a lion, bear, frog, snake, black cat, or shadow.[73]

In this context, while it was sometimes difficult to perceive the difference between a real living animal and a demon or spirit in the shape of one, the essential core of belief in a good and ordered creation was preserved by classifying all that was disordered, evil, or inappropriately mixed as demonic. The increasingly popular dichotomy between demonic forms and the good creation can be seen in various late medieval artistic developments. Some mid-thirteenth century Apocalypses depict animals in the scenes of the events of the Apocalypse beside the monstrous demonic beings. The small rabbit in the foreground of an image of the dragon, the Beast, and the animalic false prophet in the Metz Apocalypse (ca. 1250–1255) serves to distinguish the monstrous and evil beings from the good Creation.[74] It is arguable that although the late medieval cosmos was very rich in supernatural animal forms it was isolating the real animal of God's creation in a way that was beneficent to the studies of natural science. The suspicion of churchmen was no longer focused on the worship of real animals but on relations with demons in the forms of animals. A few unnatural animals and animalic humans fell on the positive side of the supernatural spectrum, as examples like Saint Christopher and the animal companions of saints attest. Another significant exception was the interpretation of creatures that were extraordinary by virtue of their appearance or behavior as a divine sign.

Divination

Divination is the art of identifying and interpreting meaningful patterns and signs in nature, including the sounds, movements, and appearances of animals and the parts of their bodies. Ancient forms of animal divination such as predictions from the flights of birds or the entrails of animals were maintained in medieval taxonomies of magic but no longer widely practiced as divinatory systems. They remained a point of reference, however, for clerical suspicion of belief in natural omens, which seemed to express a lack of trust in God and divine providence. John of Salisbury used examples from classical texts in his *Policraticus* (1159) to build up an ironic picture of the chaos that would result if humans tried to act upon all the multiple and contradictory omens supposedly found in the behavior of birds and beasts. He interposes his own amusing points of advice: hares are better met with on the table than the road; goats should be avoided because they butt; and having a dog at your heel is most comforting—even the angel who accompanied Tobias did not scorn it.[75] In the medieval cosmos, the interpretation of signs in nature could not be dismissed altogether, as natural signs such as birds engaged in nest building were useful to predict seasonal change, and signs that violated the customary course of nature's laws might represent a forewarning from God. Churchmen were much less suspicious of the significance of animals that were recognizably outside the order of nature, because the category of natural marvel evoked the wonder and diversity of God's creation. When Gerald of Wales reported that a fish of unusual size and quality with three gold teeth was found at Carlingford in Ulster, he suggested that it prefigured the conquest of Ireland.[76]

Ecclesiastical authorities tried to communicate the spiritual dangers of divination to the laity. In his work for priests receiving confession, Burchard of Worms condemned predictions about journeys and lodging according to the flight and sounds of the crow, cock, and a bird called *muriceps* (mouse-catcher) as well as predictions of an invalid's chances of recovery according to whether insects and worms were found under a stone.[77] This kind of superstition was considered unbelief by Burchard because those who relied on animal sounds and movement did not trust in God, their own faith, and the sign of the cross to protect them. In his treatise for preachers, Stephen de Bourbon ridiculed divination as a vain cult of devilish delusions by which the stupid rather than the wicked were seduced. Nevertheless, it could have serious repercussions: Stephen related how an old woman failed to receive the last rites because she heard a crow on May Day and believed that it predicted she would have five more years of life.[78] In another of Stephen's anecdotes he tells how a king mocked his advisors for relying on the "prattling" of irrational, short-lived crows for their serious military decisions.[79] Yet the translation of Arabic and Greco-Roman divinatory texts in the twelfth and thirteenth centuries introduced works that defended their efficacy with complex theories of cosmic harmony. For example, treatises on scapulimancy (divination using a sheep's shoulder bone) suggested that the bones had absorbed knowledge from the heavens where God placed all the secrets of the world. These secrets descended to earth in rain that provided nourishment for grass, and the sheep that ate the grass then absorbed them into their shoulder blades.[80]

Magic and Sacrifice

The mainstream Christian belief that animals were put on earth for the use of man implied not only that the life of animals belonged to humans but that the very design of their bodies was intended for human use. Bartholomaeus Anglicus argued that every part of an animal's body was valuable, and his popular work *De proprietatibus rerum* (1242–1247) outlined the many benefits of food, clothing, and medicine that animal parts and substances provided. The chapter on the ox, for example, described diverse vessels, tools, and instruments that could be made from ox horn, including armor, lanterns, combs, hunters' horns, and paint holders.[81] Authors of medieval encyclopedias did not find it incongruous to draw the pragmatic and contemplative together. In his prologue Bartholomaeus asserted the Dionysian idea that the properties of material things could be used, with guidance, to ascend to the contemplation of invisible things. A fourteenth-century copy of the French translation by Jean Cordichon illustrates some of the real and mythological animals he included in his discussion, with the dog, represented by an elegant greyhound, taking central place. (See Figure 1.10.) The use of animal parts, objects, and substances was integral to medieval attitudes to animals. They were discussed

FIGURE 1.10: *Mammals.* Jean Cordichon, *Le Livre des Propriétés des Choses*, Bibliothéque Municipale, Reims, MS 993, fol. 254v. © The Bridgeman Art Library.

in such diverse genres as bestiaries, encyclopedias, natural history texts, medical works, and even heraldic manuals. Common animal parts and substances were promoted in collections of cheap remedies for the poor such as the *Thesaurus pauperum* (1272) of Petrus Hispanus, while the more exotic—ostrich eggs, crocodile skeletons, and so-called unicorn horns, toadstones, and griffin claws—were collected by the wealthy as natural marvels and repositories of occult power.

Although Christian belief and economic demand promoted the exploitation of animal bodies, not all uses of animals and animal parts were viewed favorably. Some were treated by authorities as superstitious, involving improper ritual without recourse to divine protection. It was from this position that the 1075 Council of London forbade the hanging up of animal bones to ward off cattle plague.[82] Attitudes to the uses of animal parts depended very much on context, however. In Albertus Magnus's discussion of the wolf in his work of natural philosophy he states that burying a wolf's head in a dovecote or a wolf's tail at the entrance to a farm will ward off predators (*De animalibus*, bk. 22, track 2, chap. 1, 68). In the fifteenth century similar practices were incorporated into conceptions of witchcraft. The *Malleus maleficarum* refers to a woman burned at Regensburg who had confessed to burying the bones of animals "in the name of the Devil and all the other devils" under a stable door to bewitch horses and cattle.[83] Operations were categorized as magic by ecclesiastical authorities when they stood outside mainstream scientific theories of cause and effect and of appropriate relations with supernatural powers. The operations of learned magic texts were, however, related to two mainstream theories of natural philosophy and theology: the idea that some natural objects had the power to influence spirits, and the notion that spirits were able to speed up natural processes and provide knowledge of hidden properties in nature.

In late medieval Europe, as in other times and places, supernatural assistance was sought for curing sick animals, attracting desirable animals such as bees and birds, and repelling those classed as vermin and predators like mice, snakes, and wolves. The means to access these supernatural benefits varied from those generally viewed as licit—prayers, charms, blessings, and curses—to others classed as magical, superstitious, or idolatrous. Medieval people drew on the powers of patron saints of animals, the connections between animals and celestial influences, and words and images that were thought to have power over particular species. Magic texts offered the means for anyone to beguile wild beasts without possessing the exceptional holiness of a saint, virtue of a chivalric hero, or talent of Orpheus. The *Liber de quattuor confectionibus*, a magic text of Arabic origin, for example, was devoted to the capturing of animals belonging to the four categories of wolves, wild beasts, birds, and reptiles, "so that their spirits incline toward you and their nature is offered to you without hindrance" ("ut inclinentur tibi spiritus eorum et ingeratur ad te natura eorum absque impedimentis").[84] Its claim that the four recipes were given to Adam by the angel Gabriel associates the magic text with prelapsarian dominance over nature.

The first preparation (*confectio*) of this text is for attracting wolves and consists of a mixture of the blood, fat, gall and brains of a horse, wolf, black cat, raven, vulture, eagle, goat, hen, ass, fox, pig, and hare, as well as snake skin and various plant substances. The practitioner draws the wolf to him through knowledge of correct celestial times, suffumigations, and the recitation of a prayer provided by the text. Then he gives it the *confectio* to eat, which completely subjects the animal to him. The operations of this text were probably too messy and expensive to have invited much practical interest but they attest to a desire to dominate wild animals, and perhaps also a sense of prelapsarian loss, evoked in an instruction that the practitioner may either kill or tame the wolf once it is in his power. The theologian and bishop of Paris, William of Auvergne, absolved this text of impiety, interpreting its recipes as an alternative to the hunt that used the natural persuasive force of words (the prayer).[85] A harsh critic of magic, William was nevertheless keen to distinguish texts relying on natural powers that he classified as licit natural magic from operations relying on demonic assistance.

The use of words of power to influence animals is found in many Christian charms, performative speech acts directed at specific medical and social needs that drew upon medieval perceptions of the instrumental power of sacred words and texts. The mid-eleventh century manuscript of the Vitellius psalter recommends singing the *Tersanctus* hymn over sick cattle and Psalms 51 and 68 and the Athanasian creed over those with lung disease.[86] A contemporary manuscript (Cambridge, Corpus Christi College 41), has Anglo-Saxon charms in its margins for catching a swarm of bees and finding lost cattle. After invoking Saint Helena and Christ on the cross one of the charms expresses concern over the welfare of the speaker's cattle: "So I expect to find them, not have them gone far away, and to know where they are, not to have them harmed; and to care for them, not have them led off."[87] Charms for influencing animals continued to be popular throughout the Middle Ages. A breve (portable charm) on the flyleaf of a compilation of legal texts (ca. 1300) gives instructions for using Christian formulas that will rid a granary of mice.[88] A veterinary charm in a fifteenth-century medical miscellany gives a cure for a lame horse that call upon the aid of Christ and St. Stephen. The horse's color, owner, and injured leg are specified.[89]

Images of animals acting as channels of celestial or supernatural assistance were also acceptable to ecclesiastical authorities if their power was thought to come from natural properties or, ultimately, from God. William of Auvergne defended the legitimacy of wax images of lambs that had been blessed by the pope to protect against lightning, arguing that the effect was achieved

by God himself.[90] In the fourteenth century associations of the Black Death
with poisonous air led to an increase in the popularity of gems engraved with
the astrological images of the scorpion and the serpent bearer.[91] These were
thought to draw down the natural celestial influences of the constellations
Scorpio and Ophiuchus. In magic texts the sculpted images of animals were
used to represent the species of animal that the operator wanted to influence
and to symbolize the emotions it was desirable to stir up in human victims.
The *Liber lune*, a work translated from Arabic into Latin in the twelfth century, includes both types. An experiment for putting the doves of an enemy to
flight instructed the magical practitioner to make an image of a dove and fill
its stomach with mustard before burying it; the mustard in the image is said
to repel the real birds.[92] Another experiment uses the images of a dog and a
wolf to arouse hatred between two people and draws on physical as well as
symbolic antagonism: one of the images should be buried in an eastern place,
facing east; the other in a western place, facing west.[93] This ritual constructs a
form of beast identification between two animals known for their ferocity and
mutual animosity and the two human victims. According to the *Liber lune*, its
magical images drew power from the mansions of the moon and the spiritual
relationship between God and wild animals. This power was transferred into
the image by making it at an appropriate time. The potency of these objects
therefore lay in a view of the universe parallel to that of Pseudo-Dionysius in
which animal images were effective (as symbols or as magical instruments)
because animals participated—however distantly—in their creator and the celestial realm.

Some uses of words to influence animals, and of animal images to influence
humans, were acceptable even if similar practices could be condemned if they
were found in a suspicious text or context. The ritual killing of animals also
had some legitimate contexts: animals were sometimes killed in public rituals
where they acted as symbolic bearers of the guilt of individuals or the community.[94] The private ritual killing or sacrifice of animals, was, however, almost
universally interpreted as an idolatrous offering to demons. The performance
of animal sacrifices to mediate with the cosmic order can be found in works of
Arabic magic translated into Latin, where it is usually associated with a natural
transforming power or the drawing down of planetary forces and spirits. For
example, the *Picatrix*, translated into Latin in 1256–1258, advised sacrificing
doves to Venus, sheep to the moon and cows to Saturn to harness celestial
powers.[95] Al-kindi's *De radiis*, a text of Arabic origin that dealt with the theoretical underpinnings of magic, proposed a theory of cosmological harmony
to explain why the ceremonial killing of animals was effective and natural.[96]
He argued that because animals had a similitude with the world, when they
died against the course of nature by the ritual action of man, the matter of the
world was changed in a way which rendered it more malleable to alteration.

According to al-Kindi, therefore, sacrifices had a natural transforming power, rather than being intended to honor spirits and gain their assistance.

Christian authors of nigromantic texts, which explicitly drew upon the powers of demons, were influenced by the Arabic tradition but used animal sacrifice primarily as an instrument to entice, pacify, and compel demons.[97] While the sacrifice of animals formed part of the stereotypical construction of witchcraft and devil worship, other sources attest to its practice. *Les Grandes Chroniques de France* record that in 1323 some monks of the Cistercian abbey of Sarcelles were found guilty of hiring a necromancer to recover some stolen money. The necromancer had buried a black cat in a chest at a crossroads, intending to use its flayed skin to summon a demon named Berich.[98] Works of magic by Christian authors usually advocated the use of small sacrificial animals such as doves, hoopoes, and cats that suited the personal, secretive nature of magical rituals in medieval Europe. The sacrifice of an animal was thought to release the occult properties of its body (such as the power of hoopoe blood to attract demons), to bind a celestial spirit to the physical world with earthly matter, and to pacify an unwilling or malevolent spirit with an offering. Although demonic magic was a very marginal practice in medieval culture it nonetheless attests to a continuing interest in this means of using animals as mediators between humans and the cosmic order.

CONCLUSION

Christianity excluded real animals from a dominant place in religion: it was forbidden to worship them and to use their bodies in rituals of communication with God. This exclusion of animals from the center of religion strengthened their symbolic use because it was less ambiguous. As the created beings of a good God, however, animals possessed an "echo of intelligible beauty" in the words of Pseudo-Dionysius and were therefore good to think with. Animals acted as mediators in human relations with the cosmic order in three significant ways. Firstly, they provided symbols of visible things that revealed the invisible: for example, an aspect of Christ, the spiritual struggle of human existence, or models of abstract virtues. Secondly, they acted as instruments of divine will: for example, by protecting the body of a saint from hunger or other wild animals and by providing companionship so that the saint's spiritual purpose was unrestricted. Thirdly, God permitted demons, and to a lesser extent ghosts, to take animal forms in order to interact with humans.

The medieval position that God could make animals act against their nature but demons could only assume their forms is an important aspect of medieval attitudes to animals. Animals were not worshipped as sources of beneficent power but nor were they reviled as sources of malevolent power. Their bodies were associated with the good creator God, and with rare exceptions only illusory forms of animals were linked to malign forces in the cosmos. Context was important in interpretations of beings as animals or demons. The wolf's natural ferocity to man, as exhibited by the animal that attacked Arnaud Cogal's flock, was interpreted as a just punishment for human disobedience in the Garden of Eden. In the context of rituals perceived as suspect by churchmen like Stephen de Bourbon, wolves were more likely to be categorized as demons. Suspicion also fell on animals whose appearance or behavior seemed unnatural, such as the *quasi corvus* encountered by the tailor Snowball or the horse of a Catalan knight that gave intelligent political advice.[99] After the twelfth-century renaissance, medieval philosophy bound real animals to the laws of nature.[100] Not all animals categorized as acting unnaturally were assumed to be demons or divine instruments, but those that fell outside these categories could be punished to draw attention to their malevolent singularity. Thus animals involved in acts of bestiality were executed in spite of being viewed as innocent parties in the crime, and domestic animals that killed humans were killed or even put on trial (at least in the genre of literary test cases for would-be lawyers).

The boundaries between God, animals, and demons were thus relatively firm in medieval culture. Images of animals could be used or interpreted wrongly in relation to the divine, and demonic appearances could be deceiving, but there was no actual merging of bodies. The border between humans and animals was more fluid and hence a site of anxiety, although problematic transformations were similarly viewed as taking place at the level of appearance only. Identification with beasts occurred in medieval secular culture because animals possessed desirable (and undesirable) physical and allegorical qualities that were widely disseminated through the bestiary and encyclopedic traditions, a symbolic mapping of the universe of creatures that was transferable and popular. The same qualities were sought or manipulated in illicit magic rituals that often used real animals rather than images (that is, sacrifice rather than contemplation) to mediate between humans and the cosmic order. In literary and heraldic contexts, identification—if not actual merging—with animals was used positively to express power and delineate the characteristics of heroes or ordinary knights. Human–animal hybrids and shape-shifters were also positive figures of power in images, literature, and genealogy. Outside these contexts the overlap with the equally unstable forms of demonic beings was too great and they were assigned negative meanings, although wonder and pity occasionally prevailed. The forms of demons were of endless monstrous variety, but the reach and plenitude of God's good Creation also extended to the diversity and multitude of real and imagined animals.

CHAPTER TWO

Medieval Hunting

AN SMETS AND BAUDOUIN VAN DEN ABEELE

THE DIFFERENT FORMS OF HUNTING

Medieval society cannot be studied without dealing with hunting. At various levels, hunting played a decisive role, whether as a pastime, a social display, a school of skill and knowledge, or a necessity. While it is not always possible to make a clear distinction between the hunt of the rich versus the hunt of the poor, as they all existed under various forms, one can observe some differences between the hunting habits of separate social groups. First of all, the poor simply could not afford the dogs or birds needed for the more aristocratic ways of hunting, neither could they afford the staff needed to train these animals and to take care of them, nor could they devote sufficient time to this. Training a falcon was time-consuming; one needed several days in order to induce it to accept the proximity of man before training it daily to the lure and gradually accessing to free flight. Second of all, the reasons for hunting were also different: whereas the animals caught in traps could end up on the table of the less fortunate, game constituted less than 5 percent of the meat prepared in the kitchens of noblemen. For these people, hunting was more of a free time exercise, but also a social activity, involving a whole company of men and also of women, especially in the case of hawking.

Hawking or Falconry

Most scholars agree that falconry, or more generally hunting with birds of prey, was introduced to the medieval West by Germanic tribes around the fifth century.[1] Hunting with birds was especially popular from the period of the crusades until the end of the Middle Ages. (See Figure 2.1.) Falconry became an indication of social prestige, requiring wealth and staff: no less than thirty falconers and varlets were appointed for this at the court of Philip the Good in 1446. Hunting with birds can be done with different kinds of diurnal birds of prey, especially falcons, but also with other raptors such as the sparrow hawk and the goshawk.[2] During the Middle Ages, the latter birds were often used in Germanic countries, whereas falcons were preferred in Latin Europe, especially the peregrine falcon and the gyrfalcon. These two families of birds hunt in different ways: falcons ascend high up in the sky before catching their prey by diving or stooping, whereas hawks follow their prey at a low altitude. This difference also has its consequences for the hunting field: falcons were generally preferred for hunting in the open country or by river sides, whereas hawks were used when hunting in the bush or near to the wood.

Birds of prey were trained to catch river birds or field birds. Among the river birds, the crane and the heron were the most prestigious quarry, flown by the highly prized gerfalcons or saker falcons, even if other species, such as ducks and small waders, were more current. Commonly flown field birds include the partridge, the pheasant, and even crows and magpies, whereas the smaller merlins and sparrow hawks would catch larks or thrushes. Goshawks might also be trained to catch rabbits or hares.

FIGURE 2.1: *Hawker.* Month of May, thirteenth century, Cathedral of Münster. © B. Van den Abeele.

One of the factors that probably contributed to the success of hawking during the late Middle Ages was the fact that this form of hunting was open to both men and women, whereas venery was a more masculine activity, although various exceptions can be documented. Browsing through a sample of hawking scenes in medieval art, the presence of women is at any rate conspicuous. (See Figure 2.5.) According to hunting treatises, the most appropriate bird for a woman was a sparrow hawk, some of them actually being called *éperviers à dames,* because after catching the lark they brought it back to the lady.

Venery

Venery or hunting with hounds was practiced throughout the Middle Ages, either on horse, with free-running hounds, or on foot, the dogs being retained by the leash. Different kinds of dogs were chosen by the hunters. The greyhound was used to seize and pull down a running quarry as soon as it had reached it; such was also the role of the large so-called alaunt or alant, sometimes provided with heavy studded collars or a sort of body armor; mastiffs, usually reserved to guard flocks and houses, might also be used, although they were less valued; finally the running hound or *chien courant* was reserved to *par force* hunting or *chasse à courre,* in order to track and follow the hart; these medium-size hounds formed a pack of at least twelve and sometimes up to fifty dogs.[3]

In France and in England, the most prestigious hunt was that of the stag or, to a lesser degree, the deer. The *par force* hunting of a hart followed very strict rules: the quest of the finest hart by a huntsman with a silent lymer was followed by his report to the assembly, where the master of game and the whole company would decide how to begin the chase; packs of hounds were posted in different places, or relays, before being released on seeing the hart; the pursuit itself, accompanied by precise indications blown on hunting horns, may last for hours, until the hart was exhausted, turned at bay, and surrounded by the hounds; the hunters gathered around it, blowing their horn to the bay or abay, and finally the hart was killed with a sword. The most intricate ceremonial was that of the unmaking or braking with special hunting cutlery, in an order evoked at length by the treatises; all this ended up in the *curee* (hence the English word "quarry"), the ritual rewarding of the hounds on the emptied skin of the animal, where bread, blood, and chopped intestines were devoured by the pack, while the hunters continued blowing their horns.[4]

From Carolingian times onward, the boar hunt was considered to be the most dangerous and martial form of hunting, a sort of man-to-man combat with a ferocious and fearless animal, whose tusks might strike a hunter to death in one moment. The boar was the perfect antithesis to the timid and elegant stag, and the archetype of the black animals, according to the French treatises. In his *Livres du roy Modus et de la royne Ratio,* Henri de Ferrières distinguishes between the red animals, or *bestes rouges,* also called *bestes douces* (hart, deer, fallow buck, roebuck, hare), and the fierce and nocive black animals, *bestes noires, bestes mordans, bestes puans* (boar, sow, wolf, fox, and otter). Although it was gradually less favored in France, the boar hunt continued to be highly valued in the Iberian Peninsula and in Germany.[5] Harmful and uneatable animals such as foxes and wolves were sometimes hunted by mounted noblemen, but they could also be trapped or killed by professional hunters (e.g., *louvetiers*) or during collective beats organized by landlords or villages. In the Alps and the Pyrenean Mountains, chamois and ibex might be hunted, using crossbows or specially developed javelins, which are shown on various late medieval depictions. (See Figure 2.9.)

During the late Middle Ages, royal and baronial deer parks were greatly developed in England and Scotland, which secured permanent possession of game. For example, the house of the Percy, earls of Northumberland, had a total of 4,471 deer in twenty-one parks in 1512.[6] This produced a changing attitude in aristocratic hunting, enabling great landlords to organize spectacular hunting parties. In Germany, these conspicuous massacres or *Schaujagden* continued during the Renaissance and Baroque periods and were depicted by artists such as Lucas Cranach.

Archery

With the hunting method of archery, the animal auxiliaries are replaced by weapons. Archery is a technique that was used during the whole medieval period, both for big game, where archers were helped by their dogs (usually the relatively small *brachetus,* or brachet) to localize or to follow the prey, and for smaller prey, like birds or rabbits.[7]

Two types of arms were generally used, namely, the bow and the crossbow, the latter being a typical medieval weapon. The first crossbows had a bow of wood, which was replaced in the thirteenth century by a bow composed of different layers of horn and, later still, by a bow of steel.[8] For shooting at small game, such as rabbits and birds, archers might use blunted arrows or *boujons,* with a rounded end in order just to knock down the prey without damaging it. Being accessible to almost everyone, archery is a way of hunting requiring fewer resources than falconry or venery, and, as a consequence, it played a more important role in providing the table. Whereas a *par force* hunt involving dozens of hunters and a large pack of hounds would result in the taking of one deer, a small group of six men and one brachet, such as described by Guicennas in the mid-thirteenth century, might come home with three deer.[9]

Trapping Birds and Quadrupeds

Another way of hunting is using material auxiliaries such as nets and traps. Although these methods were considered to be deprived of any prestige, they were a very common activity, of which the practical knowledge was essentially shared and transmitted orally. For this reason, hunting with traps, nets, and lime is less well documented than the hunting techniques described in the previous section.[10] (See Figure 2.2.) Different methods were developed to catch the prey, from the use of baits or calling birds to attract the prey to the making of pits or the use of nets to catch the animals. There are some regional differences between these techniques: to master the prey, the Germans preferred to work with hedges or permanent enclosures, whereas in France and in the Mediterranean countries, the hunters more often used nets.

This form of hunting could have a direct utilitarian purpose, to catch harmful animals such as boars destroying the crops or wolves attacking the flocks.

FIGURE 2.2: *Device for trapping birds. Livres du Roy Modus,* copied in 1379, BnF, Paris, MS Français 12399, fol. 87r.

It served also for small game or birds, in order to fill the kitchen larders. Birds might be a nuisance for the fields, hence their hunting was seen as an agricultural necessity. Especially in Flanders and Brabant, nets were used for catching birds of prey, which were sold to the courts or exported abroad for the use of hawking. These specialized trappers crossed Europe on foot, wearing a cadge formed by four wooden perches arranged in a rectangle with four short fixed legs; the carrier stood in the center of the frame, supporting it with shoulder straps and steadying it with his hands; six to twelve falcons could thus be carried on the perches of the cadge.[11]

SOURCES FOR A HISTORY OF MEDIEVAL HUNTING

Treatises on hunting are our foremost source for the knowledge of hunting techniques, for objects related to it, and for therapeutics applied to the falcons or hounds. On the whole, however, they remain mainly theoretical, explaining how one should behave properly in order to have excellent birds and dogs, how one keeps them in good health, and how to hunt with them. There are many aspects escaping the attention of the authors of these treatises, such as the social dimension and the cultural image on the whole. These topics have to be studied through various other means.

For the early Middle Ages, the most detailed historical evidence comes either from archaeological findings or from legislative texts. In tombs dating from the sixth to the eighth century in Northern Europe (Denmark, Sweden) and in Germany (Thuringia, Saxony), archaeologists have found remains of goshawks, sparrow hawks, and peregrine falcons associated with dogs. These were most probably trained birds of prey that were inhumed or cremated together with their owners.[12] The laws of the various Germanic tribes, which were written down during the same period, establish fines for stealing hawks or falcons, or for killing hunting dogs.[13] The Welsh *Laws of Court* attributed to Hywel the Good (tenth century) provide precise data on the office of the falconers at court,[14] while other forms of hunting (deer, bee, salmon, bear, "climber," woodcock, fox, hare, and roe) are evoked in the Welsh *Nine Huntings,* whose sixteenth-century manuscripts reflect medieval practice.[15] Similar and at times more detailed data are found in the *Leyes Palatinas* of James III, king of Mallorca (1324–1349). There we find chapters on the head falconer (*falconarius maior*), his subordinate falconers, and the keeper of the hunting dogs, explaining the duties, the rights, and the expenses of these servants.[16]

From the twelfth century onward, governmental records are a generous source, but they have been too little used in this respect. Detailed inquiries have been carried out by R. Oggins on the English royal sources[17] and by C. Niedermann on documents related to the Burgundian court of Philip the Good (d. 1467).[18] Important findings were published by J. Bover from thirteenth- and

fourteenth-century records of the kingdom of Mallorca,[19] by D. Dalby from
the official accounts contained in the Prussian *Marienburger Tresslerbuch* (ca.
1400),[20] and by G. Malacarne from the Gonzaga archives in Mantua.[21] G.
Hoffmann has studied the trade of falcons from Northern Europe during the
late Middle Ages, where one can observe the important role played by the
Teutonic Knights, who controlled the capture and trade of the highly prized
gerfalcons. These birds were even used as diplomatic gifts to various rulers.[22]
The passion of kings for hawking is most clearly shown by the example of King
Edward I (1272–1307), whose reign was the most brilliant period of medieval
English royal falconry. The Wardrobe Accounts show a steady increase of the
amounts spent on royal falconry from 1274 onward, with a peak of £1,002
in 1285–1286. On various occasions, Edward vigorously acted to preserve the
quality of his hawking, either by sending precise orders to his sheriffs or by
severely punishing offenses, such as the destruction of royal eyries (nests of
hawks) or the theft of falcons. Messengers brought him the first heads of cranes
taken by his falcons, and gifts of birds were part of the royal diplomacy.[23]

Narrative sources, for example, annals and chronicles, provide vivid depictions of the passion of sovereigns for hunting, such as the Carolingian rulers
in their forests of the Ardennes and the Vosges. Chroniclers recorded dramatic
events, such as the death of rulers while hunting boars or stags or even during
hawking parties, from Louis III of France (882) to Mary of Burgundy (1482).
They mention gifts of hounds and hawks, or large displays of courtly hunting, even in times of military sieges. It is interesting to note, for example, that
the Emperor Frederick II (1194–1250) lost a decisive battle at Parma (1248)
because he had left his camp to go out hawking exactly at the time when the
besieged made a forceful attack.[24]

As to sources endowed with a more cultural dimension, such as literary fiction and poetry, manuscript illumination, monumental painting and sculpture,
ornamental artifacts, and furniture, motifs of hunting are ubiquitous, which
testifies the preeminent position of hunting in the cultural and social codes of
the ruling classes. Special sections shall be devoted to this subsequently.

TREATISES ON HUNTING

Much research has been carried out recently on falconry treatises and, to a
lesser degree, on texts concerning venery, especially in Latin, French, Spanish,
and German.[25] For the other hunting forms and the other languages, some lacu-
nae remain, as unknown texts or copies might still be hidden in manuscripts.

As a hunting treatise, we consider a didactic writing on hunting or its
auxiliaries—quadruped or bird of prey—written in Latin or in the vernacular
and generally intended for a public of practitioners. Although there existed
some treatises in classical Greece and Rome, they were largely ignored during

the Middle Ages, hence a proper cynegetic tradition developed anew and became a typical medieval genre.

Latin Treatises

No less than thirty-three Latin hunting texts are known, which are preserved in seventy manuscripts.[26] Most of them deal with falconry, and the oldest ones are all collections of remedies to cure the hawk: for example, what to do when a hawk gets a cold or is wounded after having been bitten by another animal. Among these texts are the Anonymous of Vercelli (mid–tenth century), the *Liber accipitrum* by Grimaldus (probably written at the end of the eleventh century),[27] and the numerous treatises of the twelfth century, such as the *De avibus tractatus* by Adelard of Bath[28] and the anonymous texts *Dancus rex*, *Guillelmus falconarius*, and the *Epistola Aquile, Symachi et Theodotionis ad Ptolomeum*. These rather short treatises occupy a fundamental place in the tradition of falconry literature because their remedies were frequently copied during the following centuries.

The thirteenth century witnessed an important cynegetic activity at the court of the Emperor Frederick II of Hohenstaufen, who ordered a translation of the oriental works *Moamin* and *Ghatrif*, the first of which deals both with birds of prey and dogs. But the emperor is also himself the author of a treatise that can be considered to be the quantitative and qualitative apex of the Latin cynegetic tradition: the *De arte venandi cum avibus*.[29] After a grandiloquent prologue, the first book is a sort of general ornithology about the habits, the migration, the reproduction, and the anatomy of birds. Books II and III explain which falcons are used in hunting, as well as their furniture, care, manning, and training to the lure. Book IV deals with the most spectacular hunt, the crane hawking with a gerfalcon or with a cast of two or three birds; book IV treats heron hawking with saker falcons; and book VI deals with duck hawking with peregrines. This comprehensive hawking manual has no equivalent in medieval times and, curiously enough, it has exerted no influence on later treatises whose principal subject has remained the care of the various illnesses of birds.

Almost at the same moment as Frederick II was writing his work, Albertus Magnus, or Albert the Great, wrote his *De falconibus*, which he later included in his encyclopedic work *De animalibus* (ca. 1260–1270). As for the later treatises, there are compilations based on recipe collections from the twelfth century, as well as some original works such as the *Liber falconum* attributed to a certain Archibernardus. This work is the only versified treatise on hunting written in Latin, and it deals in 321 hexameters with the species of falcons, their diet, and their illnesses.

Generally, the subjects dealt with in the treatises from the thirteenth century onward belong to the following fields: ornithological information, cynegetic information, hygienic data, veterinary information, and miscellaneous data. However, not all the treatises present all these categories, which can, furthermore, overlap.

As to venery, the number of Latin treatises is very small. There is only one text on big game, the *De arte bersandi* by a German knight named Guicennas, which can be dated to the middle of the thirteenth century. Guicennas describes in detail the hunt with bow or crossbow, with the help of a brachet to find the deer, and of a few horsemen dressed in green tunic, who quietly tried to induce the animal to move toward the bowmen. The hound had also to locate the wounded deer, following a track of blood through the forest. Besides this, there are also some texts concerning the care of dogs,[30] of which the oldest is the *Practica canum,* a small text on the care and cure of hounds. This text was one of the primary sources of the more elaborate *De canibus* by Albertus Magnus, a long chapter about hounds included in his *De animalibus.*[31]

Popular forms of hunting (archery and trapping) are even less documented. For archery related to big game, one should mention again the *De arte bersandi,* but there are no independent treatises dealing with the other forms. However, in his *Ruralium commodorum libri XII,* an encyclopedia on agriculture written in Bologna around 1305, Petrus de Crescentiis devotes his tenth book to different kinds of hunting: falconry (chapters 1–15), catching birds (chapters 16–20), trapping quadrupeds (chapter 21–26), trapping mice (chapter 27), and fishing (chapters 28–30).[32]

Vernacular Treatises

Vernacular hunting treatises appear from the thirteenth century onward. The first of these are translations and compilations: all the important Latin treatises from the twelfth and the thirteenth centuries were translated in one or several languages. But vernacular treatises soon developed in a more original way, at first in Spanish and in French, during the second quarter of the fourteenth century. These vernacular works share some new characteristics. They have a stronger regional mark, alluding to specific habits observed in France or England, or to places known for their abundance of game in Spain, for example. Several authors are of a higher social status, such as the count of Foix Gaston Phebus or Edward, duke of York. Their texts have a more elaborate literary style, adapted for a courtly audience, which explains also why a significant number of manuscripts are illustrated with vivid illuminations, having been commissioned by aristocratic patrons.[33]

French Hunting Literature
For the French field, we know of forty-seven texts from the thirteenth to the fifteenth century, which are preserved in 179 manuscripts.[34] Eleven of the

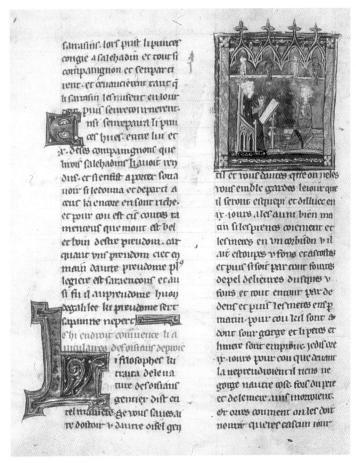

FIGURE 2.3: *Opening page: Aviculaires*. Bibliothèque Municipale de Lyon, MS 867, fol. 216v. © Bibliothèque municipale de Lyon, Didier Nicole.

forty-seven French hunting treatises are translations.[35] Among the translated texts are several therapeutic collections of the twelfth century, but also larger works as Albertus Magnus's *De falconibus*[36] and Frederick II's *De arte venandi cum avibus*. The oldest original texts are written in Occitan, Anglo-Norman, or Franco-Italian. (See Figure 2.3.) From the fourteenth century onward, original French works appear, of which the best known are the *Livres du roy Modus et de la royne Ratio* by Henri de Ferrières (1360–1379), the *Roman des deduis* by Gace de la Buigne (before 1377), and the *Livre de Chasse* by Gaston Phebus (1387–1389). The success of these three well-elaborated masterpieces, preserved in dozens of manuscripts, often lavishly illustrated, has cast a shadow over later works, even if some of them, such as the *Fauconnerie* by Artelouche de Alagona and the *Livre de faulconnerie* by Jean de Francières, certainly deserve to be studied.

Looking at the content, we notice that thirty-three texts deal with falconry; seven with venery, of which the oldest one is the Picardian *Chace dou
cerf*; one with archery (*La fachon de tirer de l'arc a main* at the end of the fifteenth century);[37] and seven with different kinds of hunting, this last category
containing, among others, the three well-known works of the fourteenth century cited previously. Moreover, Henri de Ferrières is also the first author of a
debate between falconry and venery. Two ladies, named *la dame a l'oysel* and
la dame des chiens, try to convince each other that falconry, respectively venery, is the most noble, agreeable, and valuable form of hunting, before bringing their contest to the count of Tancarville, who is acting as a kind of courtly
judge. This theme was developed at length by Gace de la Buigne in his *Roman
des deduis*, and was also used by Guillaume Crétin and Robert du Herlin.[38]

Iberian Hunting Literature

The Iberian tradition starts in the thirteenth century: it is an early tradition,
of which, however, the creativity seems to decline by the end of the fourteenth
century. This tradition contains twenty-eight texts in Catalan, Spanish, and Portuguese, which came to us in seventy-one manuscripts.[39] The Catalan texts are
essentially veterinary works about the care of falcons or hawks, whereas the later
Spanish and Portuguese treatises are more elaborated. As it is the case in other
traditions, the first vernacular texts of this region are translations, whereas original works appear in the fourteenth century. The major Spanish falconry texts are
the *Libro de la caza* by Juan Manuel and the *Libro de la caça de las aves* by Pero
López de Ayala, and, for venery, the *Libro de la montería* by King Alfonso. The
most important Portuguese text is the *Livro de falcoaria* by Pero Menino.

Italian Hunting Literature

The Italian tradition is also quite rich (twenty-seven texts preserved in sixty
manuscripts), but, unfortunately, relatively little research has been done on the
entirety of this tradition, which is limited to hawking texts.[40] The first original
text, by Petrus de l'Astore, probably dates from the beginning of the fourteenth
century: it is a bilingual Latin–Italian text concerning the care of falcons. At the
same time, the first translations of Latin works were made. However, other original works only appear in the fifteenth century and did not get a wide diffusion.

English Hunting Literature

Eleven English texts preserved in forty-seven manuscripts or printed editions
are known of.[41] If one considers the Anglo-Norman texts as belonging to this
field, it is an early tradition, but the treatises in Middle English only appear in
the fifteenth century. First of all, there are some translations from Latin and
from French treatises: the *Master of Game*, by Edward, second duke of York
(ca. 1406–1413), contains the sections on venery from the *Livre de chasse* by

FIGURE 2.4: *Hart hunt. Master of Game* (fifteenth century). The Bodleian Library, University of Oxford, MS Bodl. 546, fol. 86v.

Gaston Phebus. (See Figure 2.4.) *L'art de venerie* by William Twiti has even been translated several times in English.

As for hawking, the *Booke of Hawkyng after Prince Edward* combines some indications on the taming of hawks with a more developed therapeutic part, which is based on different Latin sources, through their reworking by Albertus Magnus. It is the most important source text for an anonymous *Tractatus de hawkyng* [sic], and also for the hawking part of the *Boke of St. Albans* (1486). In these texts, the authors pay more attention to the goshawk than to the falcon. This is also the case in the original texts of the fifteenth century: the *Percy Poem on Falconry* and three anonymous, essentially therapeutic texts.

German Hunting Literature

While the first conserved German manuscripts go back to the fifteenth century, the redaction of certain works can be situated in the fourteenth century.[42] This is probably the case for the text known as the *Ältere Deutsche Habichtslehre*, dealing with the taming and the care of both the goshawk and the greyhound. This treatise was reworked into a second version and even translated into Latin. It is also one of the sources for the *Beizbüchlein* at the beginning of the fifteenth century, which was printed in 1480 at Augsburg and is thus the oldest printed hunting text. The translation of the hunting sections by Petrus de Crescentiis probably dates from the end of the fourteenth century and a more recent translation of the same work, as well as translations of the treatise by Albertus Magnus, were made in the fifteenth century in Heidelberg by Heinrich

Münsinger. Finally, there is also a short German text on hunting hares and bird catching in the middle of the fifteenth century.

Dutch Hunting Literature

There are two known falconry treatises in Middle Dutch: an abridged version of the Latin text by Thomas de Cantimpré, in the encyclopedia *Der naturen bloeme* by Jacob van Maerlant, and an anonymous treatise, probably written in Brabant in the second half of the fifteenth century, dealing with the taming of goshawks and sparrow hawks, their diseases, and their molting. There is also a sixteenth-century treatise preserved in another single manuscript.[43]

LITERARY IMAGE

Medieval vernacular literature is pervaded by images and scenes of hunting, being partly written by, and largely directed toward an aristocratic audience.[44] Those listening to *chansons de geste* loved to hear about knights involved in dramatic hunting parties, opening up toward new adventures. They appreciated hunting metaphors of love and pursuit. An inquiry limited to French literature before 1350, for example, brought to light a corpus of about 1,030 quotations or episodes related to hawking.[45] Similar work has been carried out for hunting motifs in English and Germanic texts,[46] whereas for Italian and Spanish literature, this remains a desideratum: there are several articles about hunting motifs in various poems in Spanish (e.g., *Poema de mio Cid, Cantigas de Santa Maria, Conde Lucanor*) and Italian (e.g., Dante and Boccacio), but no thorough study has been devoted to this.[47] While speaking of the image of hunting in medieval literature, two different registers have to be distinguished. Either the motif is presented as a reality, as an element in the narrative, or it is developed as the image of something else, as a metaphor, a comparison, or a symbol.

As an element of reality, the presence of game, or the frequency of nesting falcons and hawks, enhance the quality of a resort. Mastering the hunting skills is part of the hero's education or is a quality of a protagonist, as is testified by the figure of Tristan in the stories of Beroul and Gotfried of Stasbourg. Exiled into the forest, Tristan has to hunt in order to survive with Yseut. He invents the unerring bow, the *arc qui ne faut,* a sort of bow trap, and teaches his brachet to hunt silently. In his encounter with Cornish huntsmen depicted by Gottfried, he is a master of game, teaching the incredulous onlookers how to unmake the hart according to the elaborate courtly ritual. These romances have installed Tristan as an archetypal hunter.[48] On a more general scale, by carrying a falcon on the hand, a knight or a lady is depicted most favorably, and in some contexts, the bird becomes an attribute of the lover. Carried by a messenger, it is a sign of his peaceful intentions, because hawking was an activity that implied no use of weapons. Hunting episodes are most frequent in epic

and romance, and they often introduce new adventures.[49] Going out to pursue
the hart or the boar, men are confronted to the haphazards of the forest. The
chasse du blanc cerf, the hunt of the white hart, in Chrétien de Troyes' *Erec et
Enide* is a prelude to the first adventure for Erec,[50] and hunting develops as a
kind of leitmotif in this romance. Such is the case also in *Sir Gawain and the
Green Knight,* its hunting scenes being the most developed in Middle English
literature. A. Rooney has shown how the three accurately depicted hunts (deer,
boar, and fox) are crucial to the themes of love and death in the poem, operat-
ing on several levels: entertaining, aesthetic, and symbolic.[51] As valuable and
beautiful gifts, sometimes as objects of contest, hounds and hawks also play
an important role in the interaction between protagonists. Furthermore, they
serve as prizes for tournaments or beauty contests, as in Chrétien's *Erec et
Enide,* Renaut de Beaujeu's *Le bel inconnu* (The handsome stranger), and the
anonymous *Durmart le Gallois.*

Romances and other texts also depict different kinds of dogs. In Old French
literature, for example, the greyhound is mentioned in the *Roman de Thebes*
and *Partonopeus de Blois,* among other works; the running hounds appear in,
among others, the *Lais* by Marie de France and the brachet in the romance
of *Tristan* by Béroul, the *Roman de Rou* by Wace, and the *Lai de Guigemar*
by Marie de France.[52] The very deep affection toward a hound is splendidly
depicted in Beroul's *Tristan:* the hero has fled into the forest with Yseut, when
he is rejoined by his brachet Husdent, who has followed his tracks. By baying,
the dog betrays his master, so Tristan prepares to kill him, but Yseut suggests
another way. Husdent will be taught to hunt silently, and thus the dog becomes
an ally instead of a menace.[53]

As an image, hunting animals or game are most frequent and serve a vast
range of meanings. In English texts, "literary similes assume a society familiar
with all aspects of falconry,"[54] and the same is true in Old French texts. Comparing women's eyes to those of a falcon is a commonplace in descriptions of
feminine beauty, and the Sarrasin ruler Balans, in the *Chanson d'Aspremont,* is
as elegant as a falcon who has just molted or renewed his plumage. A jousting
warrior is readily compared to a falcon stooping at his quarry, his eagerness to
win is similar to that of the bird pursuing a heron (*Enfances Ogier*), his horse is
as swift as a sparrow hawk (*Chanson de Roland*), and the defeated enemy is flee-
ing as the lark before the hawk (*Chanson d'Antioche*). The most innovative and
varied hawking images occur when depicting feelings or situations of love, which
is encouraged by a general symbolism linking love and birds. (See Figure 2.5.)
A gifted poet such as Chrétien develops the feelings of Erec and Enide at their
first love night by the metaphor of the hart longing for the fountain, and of the
sparrow hawk flying to the lure. As is shown in this case, images taken from the
hart hunt also occur.[55] They even develop into special poems, such as the *Jagd*
(Hunt), by the Bavarian poet Hadamar von Laber, which is a complex hunting

FIGURE 2.5: *Couple with a hawk.* Anjou Bible (ca. 1340), Maurits Sabbe Library, Faculty of Theology, K.U. Leuven, MS 1, fol. 278r.

allegory of the pursuit and the haphazards of love.[56] Old French debates about the different kinds of love, such as the *Jugement d'amours* or the *Fablel du Dieu amours,* make use of hawking and hunting images, and the long poem *Dit de l'Alerion* by Guillaume de Machaut is a lengthy allegorical development about the conquest and the training of hunting birds, related to a sort of *art d'amour.*

As for the hounds used in hunting, and for dogs in general, their status is more ambiguous in medieval literature. Latin bestiaries, for example, show a neutral or slightly positive view, whereas the French bestiaries focus more on the vices of this animal. Encyclopedias show the same ambiguity: the encyclopedists of the thirteenth century are rather neutral, but the authors of the moralized encyclopedias generally do not hide their antipathy, reserving more space for the dog's vices, such as ferocity or greed, than for its virtues, for example, loyalty. These differences may be due to the sources the authors used, as especially biblical images carried over to Christian texts charged dogs with mainly negative stereotypes.[57]

RELIGION

Dealing with medieval culture, one cannot escape wondering about the position of the Church toward hunting. The official attitude has always been very critical, especially toward the exercise of hunting by members of the clergy.[58] From the early sixth century onward, councils have repeatedly legislated against it. Flying hawks and wandering around with dogs was seen as worldly and vain.

FIGURE 2.6: *Wheel of the evil monastery with an abbot carrying a hawk.*
Hugh of Fouilloy, *De rota verae et falsae religionis* (fourteenth century),
Stiftsbibliothek Melk, MS 737, fol. 100r.

Nevertheless, numerous records testify that the clergy, especially bishops, did
indulge in hunting, even to the point that certain treatises on hunting were
written by clerics, such as Albertus Magnus, Egidius de Aquino, or Gace de
la Buigne. (See Figure 2.6.) Some authoritative writers have ridiculed hunting
in general: in his *Polycraticus*, John of Salisbury (1115–1180) has devoted an
entire chapter to this topic, and his example was followed late by the human-
ists Poggio Bracciolini (*Facetiae*), Sebastian Brant (*Narrenschiff*), and Erasmus
of Rotterdam (*Encomion moriae*).

Hawking has however been employed as a metaphor for the elevation of
the soul,[59] such as in a poem by San Juan de la Cruz,[60] or even for the love
of Christ: in a fifteenth-century poem Christ is said to win back sinners to
grace by showing them his wounds, as a falconer lures back his hawk by offering it meat.[61] Several saints are depicted with a falcon on their hand, such
as Bavo in Belgium, Gengoult and Thibaut in France, Julian the Hospitaler in

France and Spain, and Tryphon in eastern Europe. Saint's lives include hunting anecdotes, such as the appearance of a cruciferous stag to saint Eustace, a legend that was later transferred to Hubertus, patron saint of hunters whose cult was developed at Saint-Hubert in the Ardennes. In fact, the image of the stag has been pervaded with religious symbolism since early Christian times.[62] A suggestive image is certainly that of the resemblance between the ten antlers and the Ten Commandments, as is illustrated in certain manuscripts of the *Livres du roy Modus* of Henri de Ferrières.

More often, however, preaching manuals and moral literature show negative examples, the hunter being at times a symbol for the devil, as is the case in the *Contes moralisés* of the English Franciscan Nicole Bozon (ca. 1320).[63] Hunting itself is sometimes seen as a battle of the devil forces against the souls of Christians, whereby the devil and his helpers use different kinds of traps, an idea that is well developed in the allegoric passages of the *Livres du roy Modus*,[64] but also in nontechnical texts, such as the *Trinity College Homily* or *The Parson's Tale* by Chaucer.[65]

ICONOGRAPHY

In all periods, hunting has been a rich artistic theme, and the Middle Ages are no exception.[66] Miniatures in manuscripts are by far the richest source for our topic, and it is hardly possible to make comprehensive inquiries in this field. Both hawking and hunting with dogs provide endless series of representations, which are either purely decorative or charged with some meaning or symbolism.

The most detailed images occur in the miniatures accompanying hunting treatises in luxury manuscripts. The best-known Latin example is the Vatican codex of Frederick II's *De arte venandi cum avibus* (Palatinus Latinus 1071, between 1250 and 1266).[67] Every page of this magnificent copy is decorated with marginal illustrations of birds, objects, and falconers, which provide a sort of parallel discourse to the text.[68] Among Latin hunting manuscripts this is exceptional as only few illuminated manuscripts have been transmitted.[69] French treatises, on the other hand, have often been illustrated, some of them even being designed from the outset as illustrated texts. This is the case for the *Livres du Roy Modus* of Henri de Ferrières and the *Livre de chasse* of Gaston Phebus;[70] the most original features of these codices are the miniatures showing various trappings and nets, a subject barely treated by other texts. Among the 179 surviving manuscripts of French hunting treatises, no less than sixty-two are illustrated, whereas this is the case only for ten of the seventy known Latin manuscripts. In all languages, the figures are eighty-three manuscripts with miniatures on a total of 454 listed copies.[71]

Hunting images occur not only in treatises, they abound in all types of manuscripts. As marginal decoration, the image of the stag pursued by dogs is frequent on opening pages of psalters and bibles, where it might allude to the dangers of evil. Hounds and hawks also abound on opening pages of prestigious manuscripts, where a court is depicted during the act of presenting the codex to its committent.[72] One encounters hunting attributes in portraits of princes or noblemen, or even complete hunting scenes, as in the famous *Codex Manesse,* where hunting is one of the most frequent themes.[73] Hunting episodes in romances, such as the hunt of the white hart in *Erec et Enide* of Chrétien de Troyes, gave welcome inspiration to artists. The motif escapes also from a text-bound relationship and pervades marginal decoration from the latter half of the thirteenth century onward.[74] There it is just part of the decorative repertoire, without any necessary double meaning. Whole cycles are known, for example, in the Queen Mary Psalter (London, BL, MS Royal 2 B V II) and in the Taymouth Hours (London, BL, MS Yates Thompson, 13). The lower margins of the former are occupied by high-grade drawing, where no less than thirty-two hunting scenes are depicted, including some rare motifs, such as a fowler trapping partridges with a clap net (fol. 112), ladies hunting rabbits by introducing a ferret into their holes (fol. 155) and by beating them with clubs (fol. 156), and two men digging out foxes (fol. 175). As Kurt Lindner has shown, the borders of Queen Mary's Psalter provide a faithful picture of English hunting techniques around 1300.[75] One of the most frequent examples of hunting imagery occurs in illustrated calendars, usually for the month of May. (See Figure 2.7.) It is very often a falconer, either on foot or mounted, sometimes in the company of a woman, riding or sitting in a blooming landscape. But there are calendars where several months are devoted to hunting, depending probably on the preferences of the patron.[76] Falconry is associated with youth in the cycles of the Ages of Man, and with love in a substantial number of illuminations.[77] Some personifications wear a falcon on the hand, such as, most predictably, Nobility, or, in a less obvious association, Soberness or Hope.[78] However, negative connotations occur as well, where the falcon is seen as an incarnation of worldly vanity, *superbia,* envy, hatred, and *luxuria.*[79]

All these motifs also appear in other artistic expressions, sometimes in much more detail. Tapestries provide large-scale depictions of hunting, as for example the famous *Devonshire Hunting Tapestries* (London, Victoria and Albert Museum) or the *Chasses de Maximilien* (Paris, Musée du Louvre). The Devonshire set, woven in Arras or Tournai circa 1425–1450, comprises four twenty-eight- to thirty-six-feet-wide hangings, depicting the full range of courtly hunting activities in Burgundian times: deer hunting, boar and bear hunting, falconry, otter hunting, and swan catching.[80] (See Figure 2.8.) The second set, mistakenly connected with the emperor Maximilian I (1459–1519) but woven in Brussels between 1531 and 1533, is a complete calendar cycle of twelve large tapestries, each month devoted to an aspect of hunting, mostly hart and boar. The last scene—for February—shows the hunters paying a respectful visit

FIGURE 2.7: *Hawker*. Month of May, Italian Book of Hours (fifteenth century). Bibliothèque municipale d'Avignon, MS 111, fol. 6r.

to a king and queen in a place recalling the Brussels ducal palace of Coudenberg. An inscription in Latin woven on the upper part shows that the rulers are King Modus and Queen Ratio: thus a Renaissance artist has paid a spectacular tribute to one of the best medieval hunting treatises, composed by Henri de Ferrières about 150 years earlier.[81] Hunting motifs had in fact become a genre in Flemish and French tapestry production during the fifteenth century, many of them being mentioned in inventories and descriptions of treasuries. In this context, one should also mention the famous late medieval unicorn tapestries that are now on show at The Cloisters Museum in New York, and their conjunction of real hunters and a fabulous animal.

A similar corpus can be assembled with wall paintings, where earlier examples have been preserved. Northern Italy and Tyrol host a remarkably rich cynegetic iconography in castles and churches, from the early stag hunt in Hocheppan (ca. 1210) to Churburg castle at the end of the fifteenth century.[82]

FIGURE 2.8: *Hawker. Devonshire Hunting Tapestries,* Arras or Tournai (ca. 1425–1450), Victoria and Albert Museum, London.

Among many instances, a very instructive cycle is located in Torre dell'Aquila at the archbishop's palace in Trento, where the various months occupy high landscape paintings, with numerous hawking and hunting details (ca. 1400). A few years later, Roncolo or Runkelstein castle, near Bolzano, was decorated with courtly scenes, among which a rare chamois hunt, the unmaking of the bear, hawkers, and even a fishing party. (See Figure 2.9.) One should also mention the magnificent months of the Ferrara Palazzo di Schifanoia (ca. 1470), where Duke Borso d'Este and his courtiers are repeatedly shown with a falcon on the glove; no less than thirty-three birds of prey are represented. The hunt is a sort of continuous line in this complex cycle, as a metaphor for chivalric virtues embodied by the duke.[83]

Stained glass windows add further examples, mainly through hagiographical or biblical motifs, such as the Saint Eustace window at Chartres cathedral showing a *par force* hunt, the parable of the prodigal son at Bourges, where the son leaves his family boasting with a falcon on the hand, or scenes with

FIGURE 2.9: *Chamois and ibex hunting.* Castel Roncolo/Runkelstein, ca. 1405–1410.
© B. Van den Abeele.

Esau as a hunter. Examples appear in monumental sculpture, either in wood
(e.g., misericords, caskets) or in stone (e.g., the month of May as a falconer on
Gothic doorways). On a smaller scale, courtly scenes on ivory objects (mirror
coverings, boxes, knife handles, etc.) show dozens of hunting scenes or persons
with falcons and hounds. Even purses and garments can be adorned with this
iconography, but their survival rate is much lower.

In the same way as for literary images, one might distinguish between narrative and symbolic uses, but these categories are at times impeding, especially
given the lack of a textual basis. One has to beware of searching a priori for
hidden meanings in cases where the scene is solely decorative. In general, the
two major symbolic meanings of hounds and hawks are high status and world-
liness. In ecclesiastical context, hunting is more often represented as a worldly
vanity, for example, in scenes depicting the encounter between the Three Living and the Three Dead, where corpses stand up to remind three princes of the
idleness of their present state. In secular art, on the other hand, hunting iconography has a more neutral status. Working for upper-class commissioners,
artists often depicted hunting scenes as a natural element of courteous life.

Throughout various cultural expressions, hunting shows as a major source
of inspiration for poets and for artists during the high and late Middle Ages.
Authors, artists, and patrons shared a common experience of wildlife and pursuit, as well as a familiarity with both the animal auxiliaries and those that were
hunted. Hunting is therefore one of the most generously documented aspects of
the interrelationship between man and animal during the Middle Ages.

CHAPTER THREE

From Forest to Farm and Town

Domestic Animals from ca. 1000 to ca. 1450

ESTHER PASCUA

In medieval times, high ecclesiastic culture established a sharp distinction between cultural spaces such as the cloister, monastery, garden, village, and castle and the unknown and threatening wilderness beyond, that is, the forest, mountains, and seas. In contrast, medieval authors drew no dividing line between the worlds of domestic and wild animals. Beasts were of a mixed and changing nature, sometimes domestic, sometimes wild, and this is how they appear in bestiaries and encyclopedias.[1] This is in part because there was probably no period, other than human prehistory, in which animals and humans shared space, food, famines, work, and weather conditions more intensely than the Middle Ages. Wherever one looked, there were animals: the forests, fields and farms, towns, fairs and markets, and the household itself.

In this chapter I scrutinize what we now consider domestic and farm animals such as cows, oxen, horses, sheep, goats, pigs, fowl, and rabbits, and cats and dogs. The system of domestication in the Middle Ages made a clear distinction between animals according to their physical proximity to human beings and their role as working or edible animals. Domesticated herbivores were eaten, except in the case of the horse, but domesticated carnivores were not.[2] The closest animals were those living in the house, which were not eaten. This group includes those animals that helped men hunt, such as dogs. Next came those that lived on the farmstead and were eaten such as geese, hens, chickens, and rabbits. A further step down were those working and grazing in the fields: oxen, horses, cows, and sheep. Those living in the forest were closer to the status of wild animals, such as the pig. Of course, animals' position in these concentric circles changed over time. The pig, for example, initially roamed in the forest, but later moved to the pigsty close to the house. The cat was considered a nuisance little better than vermin and became a luxury kept in the home only in the Late Middle Ages.

Much changed during the Middle Ages and the animal world was certainly no exception. The general trend between the eleventh and fifteenth centuries brought animals from the forest to the farm and from the farm to the urban market and slaughterhouse. Even the horse, a valued being initially used exclusively for military purposes, passed to the manor in the thirteenth century, first for harrowing and later plowing, then to the town as packhorse or cart horse. The first attempts to select breeds were an expression of the increasing economic competition and specialization of these centuries. These changes reflect deeper transformations in medieval society and economy. For our purposes, it is crucial to keep in mind the cycle of growth and crisis marking the eleventh to fifteenth centuries. Up to the thirteenth century, Europe experienced a massive expansion of cereal production, encroaching upon large parts of the once extensive forests. In the fourteenth and fifteenth centuries, this system suffered a major setback and recurrent crises. The pace of recovery differed in every region. Nonetheless, the main features of the previous economic expansion, such as increased urbanization, integrated markets, technological advances, and specialization persisted. The proportion of cereal fields, forest, marshland, and pasture changed forever. The status and management of animals and their position in the productive system changed in line with this. From the roaming pig to large flocks of sheep, from the docile ox to the erratic horse, from a diet based on cereals and dairy products to the production of wool for the international market and meat for the urban market, humans and animals would soon feel the force of commercialization.

IN THE FOREST: ROAMING PROPERTY

When animals appear in hagiography, they are used mainly to evoke the saint's holiness by underlining his extraordinary, supernatural relationship with wild animals. However, there are some instances of saints dealing with domestic animals. One is the story of Saint Robert, a hermit who settled at Knaresborough (Yorkshire) around 1173. We are told that Saint Robert was offered a cow that had been living wild in the forest of Knaresborough and was thus too vicious to handle. Robert's special powers enabled him to tame her with a single touch.[3] The scenario portrayed here reflects the life lived by many if not most animals until well into the twelfth century. They lived in between the peasant village and the forest and would have been considered semiwild animals by a present-day observer.

Horses and hogs are the best example of this semidomesticated status. Up to the twelfth century, a large proportion of swine roamed the forests, feeding on beech nuts and acorns. This system was called "denbera" in Saxon charters and "pannage" in Norman ones. Horses were mainly kept in the village or on the farm, but mares were often released into the forest during pregnancy, when they could not be used as draft animals. The newborn foal was left in the forest until he could be put to good use.[4] (See Figure 3.1 for a depiction of a horse with foals.) Cattle and sheep spent most of their time outdoors. Indeed, during their summer sojourn in mountain passes and after the lambing season they required nocturnal protection from the numerous predators still living in European forests, such as bears, wolves, wild cats, and foxes.

This special way of keeping animals between the farm and the forest is more than just a primitive practice characteristic of backward rural societies. The economy of the early Middle Ages was mixed: agriculture and livestock raising were combined in order to meet the needs of the peasant communities and ecclesiastic and lay aristocracy of the time. This was an economy featuring a small degree of specialization and, as a consequence, they kept a diverse range

FIGURE 3.1: *Horses*. Ulrich von Lilienfeld, *Concordantiae caritatis* (fourteenth century), Stift Lilienfeld, MS 171, fol. 146v. © Institut für Realienkunden—ÖAW.

of animals such as sheep, cattle, pigs, horses, and fowls. This economy used living animals and the full range of their products: manure, milk, wool, butter, cream, and cheese. In addition, they were used to transport goods, people, or even mail in certain circumstances. Animals were killed at the end of their productive lives, and their meat, tallow, hides, hair, feathers, marrow, hooves, and bones were all put to good use.

For modern people, a cow provides milk, butter, cream, cheese, and beef. The cow's role as producer of milk was first explored in the Middle Ages. Cows were used as draft animals in this period, even when pregnant. This they often were, as people strove to produce a sufficient number of oxen. The sheep was in fact the main producer of milk, which rather than wool was its most valued product. They also produced manure. Folds were moved daily so that as large an area as possible could benefit from their dung, urine, and the warmth of their bodies each night.[5]

Growing animals using exclusively forest or natural pasture had several consequences. First, most animals grazed together in common spaces, pointing to the existence of communal ties. Second, this system opened up major opportunities for domesticated and wild species to mix genetically, one reason why the physiognomy of some of the former differed so greatly from that of their modern counterparts. Third, as the fattening and growth of livestock was based on pastures, medieval animals were smaller than today. Large breeds of cattle, sheep, and pigs disappeared along with the Romans, as did their methods of animal breeding; the keeping of animals became rudimentary.[6] The size of domestic animals reached its lowest point by the tenth to thirteenth centuries. By then, a female pig weighed in at between 30 and 40 to 70 and 80 kilograms, a third of the modern figure, and the average height of cattle was 110 centimeters as compared with Roman bovines of 130–150 centimeters. The size of sheep is more difficult to determine but probably fell to the Iron Age level, below 59 centimeters. Even the horse, the animal least affected by domestication in terms of its physical appearance, became smaller. Apart from poor feeding, early and frequent mating and harnessing and wars contributed to their small size.[7] A fourth consequence of the medieval livestock raising system was that animals lived longer, should they escape natural disasters or war. Due to the slow growth process, they were killed late to maximize their meat yield and secondary products. However, during the winter months (mid-October to May in northern Europe, December to February in the Mediterranean) it was so difficult to keep and feed animals that there is some evidence that in some regions they were culled before the period of harsh weather commenced. Otherwise, the pig was killed in its second to fourth year; the sheep when it was four to five years old, and the cow, ox, or horse around the age of ten.[8]

Fowl (hens, chickens, ducks, and geese) clearly had an important place in the diet of both peasant and lord as they are the bones most commonly represented in archeological remains. In Anglo-Saxon times, there were twice as many chickens as geese, but by the tenth to eleventh centuries the latter had become increasingly important, a state of affairs that persisted until ca. 1500.[9]

However, the most popular animal of all was the pig. This animal, useless alive, was the most important source of meat and fat, particularly in central and northern Europe, in this early period.[10] (See Figure 3.2.) Pigs require very little attention. They are versatile in their feeding habits and can be reared on very poor quality land. In captivity, they do not need any food during the night. Their flesh was well suited to preservation, in contrast to beef and mutton, which became tough and dry on salting. The pig featured in both peasant and lordly houses, particularly in France, Germany, and Italy.[11] So important were they that villages had swineherds who collected animals from households in the morning. The pigs roamed the forest in a semiwild manner until needed, to the point of crossbreeding with wild types.[12] This is one reason why the physiognomy of the medieval pig was far from that of its modern counterpart. In the Middle Ages, the pig had an elongated facial profile, little different from that of the wild boar. It was also long legged, long snouted, razor backed, dark brown, half the size of the wild boar, and bristly.[13] A similar breed still lives in the *dehesas*, the wood pasture forests of southwest Spain, herded among evergreen oaks and cork oaks. Historical documents describe the role of the forests as a source of food for the pig in autumn and winter, primarily acorns and beech nuts (referred to as "mast"), supplemented with berries and roots of bracken. The *Domesday Book* (1089) tends to classify English woods according to their pig-holding capacity; the better ones presumably being those containing the largest proportion of oak and beech trees. The truffle-finding pig is probably a specialization of this time, when pigs were regularly driven into the woods and truffles were still plentiful.

The right to drive pigs through woods was a privilege requiring payment in kind or cash. In Anglo-Saxon England hogs could feed in the forest during the four months from August 29 to December 31. October was the most important month. The rent was paid at the start of the season, usually Michaelmas (September 29). Due to the lack of winter food, many animals were killed and salted down in early winter. However, in some regions of France, the *pannage* season was extended up to the appearance of the first leaves of spring or even as late as Saint George's Day, April 23. Maybe some areas of common pasture were set aside for the purpose of feeding these animals. In England, the importance of the pig peaked in the aftermath of the Norman Conquest (1066) and in France, Germany, and Spain a century later, at the end of the twelfth century. The decline of the pig economy was bound up with the restriction of pannage, as lords and kings increased their control of the forest, the felling of forest to make way for arable crops and the rise in importance of the sheep and charcoal economy. In England, where this happened first, access to

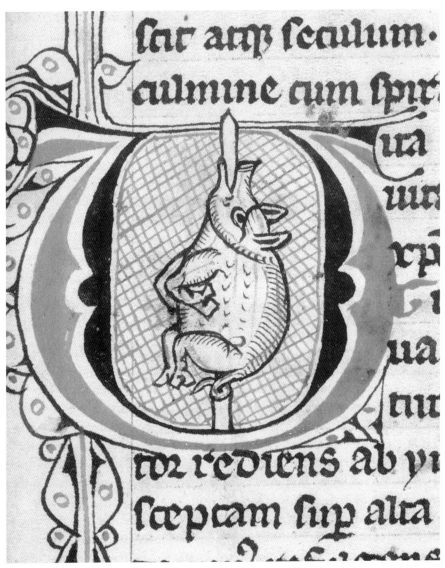

FIGURE 3.2: *Sucking pig*. Initial, Breviary, Chorherrenstift Seckau, Universitätsbibliothek Graz, MS 789, fol. 383r. © Institut für Realienkunden—ÖAW.

woodland was restricted for a period of between six and eight weeks during October and November, from Michaelmas to Martinmas (from September 29 to November 11). Laws prohibiting the knocking of acorns and mast off trees with sticks were common in the thirteenth century.[14] The pig eventually became part of a larger economy based on other animals but continued to play an important role in the peasant household.

Goats and sheep made up the mixed herds typical of the Mediterranean environment. In Italy and Spain, a clear boundary existed between the area of cattle, straddling the northern fringes, and the central and southern regions of sheep and goats. Goats tended to disappear from the northern latitudes early. In Santa Giulia di Padua (Italy) at the beginning of the tenth century, cattle made up 9.4 percent of the animals; pigs, 44.6 percent; sheep, 40.9 percent; goats, 3.7 percent; and horses, only 1.1 percent.[15] However, geographical generalizations about the distribution of sheep in Europe fail to capture regional nuances. From the tenth to thirteenth centuries in Germany and Hungary the proportion of animals in neighboring areas differed markedly. In Hungarian villages of the Great Plain, in addition to the ubiquity of cattle and horses, animal keeping was characterized by the outnumbering of pigs by sheep and goats. The Magyars, once a nomadic people, retained the proportion of species typical of their formerly nomadic domestic fauna. These villages differed from Germanic or Slavic settlements of the same period, in which cattle and pigs alternated as the most frequent domestic animals, leaving sheep and goats and especially horses far behind. In Slavic areas during the period of the Magyar conquest pigs were very common, sometimes outnumbering cattle. Horses were missing entirely.[16]

Underlining this lack of geographical determinants is the fact that the two regions in Europe in which sheep were herded earliest were England and Castile, one an Atlantic, the other a Mediterranean region. For England, we have extraordinary evidence: the *Domesday Book* and manorial records, which provide figures unique in Europe for such an early period. We have less evidence for Castile but there are clear signs of the institutional development that allowed such a change in the scale of production to take place. Both regions were to compete intensely to supply the wool market in the late Middle Ages.

The *Domesday Book* furnishes us with eleventh-century figures for demesne livestock for two regions, East Anglia and the southwest of England, although the same probably applied to tenants' holdings. Livestock was made up of the following animals: sheep (63 percent), pigs (17 percent), goats (5 percent), cattle (10–15 percent) and horses (1 percent).[17] (See Figure 3.3.) Bone remains do not chime entirely with this picture, the predominance of sheep over cattle being less striking. Sheep account for 45 percent of animals, with 30 percent cattle and 20 percent pigs. In towns and castles, cattle bones are as common as those of sheep.[18] A study of the southwest suggests that cattle made up between 40 and 50 percent of total animals, sheep 30 to 50 percent, and pigs 20 percent.[19] Sheep, cattle, and pig bones constitute the bulk of remains in this area.

Castile has been a pastoral region since prehistoric times, albeit featuring different animals. Occasional vertical transhumance, involving movement from the mountains to the valleys and coast, appeared in Asturias and Galicia in the early Middle Ages. Mentions of *montaticum,* a toll on the use of a village's pasture imposed since the early tenth century, the existence of common grazing areas and some privileges granted to ecclesiastic houses are symptoms of

FIGURE 3.3: *Flock*. Initial, Psalter, Heiligenkreuz, Stiftsbibliothek, MS 66, fol. 67v. © Institut für Realienkunden—ÖAW.

a hidden reality.[20] This was still a mixed farming system of peasant communities. In the eleventh century the estates of generously endowed Benedictine monasteries expanded; they began moving their animals over 100 kilometers from the Cantabrian Mountains to the valley of the Duero River in order to produce wool for the nascent local towns. This medium-distance transhumance could be practiced only by landowners with property at either extremity of summer and winter pasture. In England and Castile, the association between sheep flocks, ecclesiastical and urban owners as well as town markets was to dominate the relationship between animals and human communities over the coming centuries.

ON THE FARM: ANIMALS IN AN EXPANSIONARY CROP ECONOMY

In England in 1086, everybody plowed with a team of oxen. By 1272 in many regions people employed horses, the overall quantity of pastoral land had diminished, pigs were less important than cattle, and goats had virtually disappeared.[21] Extraordinary sources are available for England for the period 1089–1300, furnishing us with an excellent insight into a phenomenon general across Europe: the emergence of the so-called manorial or seigneurial system. This was the articulation of a productive system comprising two interconnected socio-economic units: the lordly estate and the peasant village. With marked regional and local variation, manorial cultivation organized the countryside around the arable land surrounded by meadows, the commons on which villagers held grazing rights, and beyond them the wasteland, or woods and forests. This system produced the most astonishing expansion of arable land ever seen in Western Europe. Crops occupied all low-lying land and fertile valleys.

Indeed, it is no coincidence that several small carnivores specialized in preying on rodents and storage grain pests entered the human environment during this period: the cat, ferret, and mongoose.[22] However, this economic development had consequences infinitely more far reaching than the spread of new species. The expansion of arable land and the contraction of forest forced manorial animals to roam on the shrinking commons and wasteland and increasingly on the stubble of cultivated fields after harvest. This neglect of livestock in the twelfth to thirteenth centuries may explain the deterioration in the size of animals during a phase of economic growth. It has been argued that smaller cattle and sheep with more modest food requirements would have survived better on the remaining grazing land.[23] Zooarchaeology is clear on this point: cows, oxen, pigs, and sheep failed to grow larger during the central centuries of the Middle Ages. Cattle were still of Iron Age proportions, not dissimilar to feral breeds.[24] The size of medieval horses increased only with the breeding experiments of the late Middle Ages, intended to improve the war horse.[25]

The reduction in pasture, meadows, and number of animals brought competition for dung, the usual way to fertilize the expanding fields. Lords had unrestricted right to the manure of their own herds, but they also had a *jus faldae*, the right to fold the manorial sheep and cattle on their own land. The manorial shepherd moved his master's fold from place to place within the demesne. Cattle markets and fairs were also used to fertilize the ground. Even the dung on village streets was reserved for the lord's use. Large dove houses, sometimes holding hundreds of birds and therefore producing a valuable amount of dung, became one of the most hated symbols of the lord's position and the subjection of the villagers. No peasant was allowed to kill these birds, however harmful to his crops. The peasants faced a vicious circle: they could keep only a few animals given the difficulty of feeding them during the winter and thus lacked fertilizer to cultivate their land.[26] Up to the early fourteenth century, a lively traffic in dung flowed from London to country estates along the Thames.[27]

Poultry and dairy products were the mainstay of the peasant household in terms of animal protein. Most homes probably had a chicken, in light of the number of eggs peasants usually handed over as rent. Walter of Henley, who wrote one of the most important treatises on husbandry in the thirteenth century, tells us that a hen ought to lay 180 eggs a year, one every two days. Another contemporary treatise, *Husbandry,* estimates 115 eggs and seven chicks per year. Geese were fairly common, so much so at times that they required the presence of a village gooseherd.[28]

The three animals most associated with the new economy were the ox, horse, and sheep. For generations, the ox was the dominant draft animal throughout Europe. Usually consisting of teams of eight animals, oxen were owned by lords or held in common by the entire peasant community. Most were yoked when they were about four years old and worked for four to eight years. Oxen and horses in stalls cost four times as much to feed than in the summer. The ox was a healthy animal. Its dung was valued as manure and fuel, and when an animal died every part of it was put to good use: the meat and marrow were eaten; the horns, bones, and hide were used to make shoes, windows, parchment, weapons, and clothing; the fat for tallow (for lighting); and the hooves for gelatin and glue. Peasants usually salted the flesh of the ox down at Martinmas to provide stores for the winter. Oxen were worth some thirteen shillings on average in the thirteenth to fourteenth centuries, while cows and bulls fetched about ten shillings per head.[29]

Thirteenth-century treatises on husbandry made all these points clear in their defense of the ox as a draft animal. Oxen were cheaper to feed than horses. According to their estimations, winter feed cost three shillings and four pence for an ox and nine shillings and two pence for a horse. When their working life ended, they could be fattened on grass for a summer and sold for meat. Due to the Church ban on eating horse meat, horses' value lay solely in the use of their hide to make leather, hair to make rope, and meat to provide food for dogs. Oxen manure was also considerably more valuable than that of horses and less expensive to buy. The authors mention the cost of shoeing horses, which seemingly did not apply to oxen.[30] Walter of Henley, though, saw some benefit in mixed

FIGURE 3.4: *Month of April* (ca. 1405–1410), Castello Buonconsiglio, Trento. © Institut für Realienkunden—ÖAW.

teams. The oxen and the horse would produce more draft power together, though their differing speeds required an experienced plowman.[31] (See Figure 3.4.)

The horse in the early Middle Ages provides a marvelous example of how different social classes used animals in different ways. This is apparent in their names. Horses for the rich were usually classified as destriers, great horses, coursers, and palfreys. For the middle groups, the common terms were rounciers, sumpters, hackneys, pads, and hobbies. For the peasant and workers, cart horses, stots, and affers were low-status animals used in harrowing and plowing.[32] Horse bones rarely represent more than 1 percent of identified bones from archeological sites. Because horse meat was not consumed, horse bones found at excavations tend to be relatively intact; rarely do they bear evidence of butchery other than cut marks associated with skinning.[33]

The working horse was a small, inelegant animal generally too weak to cope with the heavy plough.[34] Medieval authors mention that domesticated horses suffered from disorders more frequently than wild horses because of worms caused by eating inappropriate food such as bread, bran, and oats, which they were unable to combat by feeding them various herbs.[35] Oxen lick themselves a great deal and are subject to hairballs but suffer from far fewer diseases and pathological conditions than horses, which are particularly susceptible to colic.[36] The additional stress suffered by equids as a result of their use for riding or draft caused some vertebrae to become ankylosed or fused. Similar lesions sometimes occurred on the hooves. The ankle bones had a tendency to become ankylosed as a result of arthritic irritation and inflammation. The nail attached to the back of the hoof when horses were shod was an additional source of trouble, affecting blood supply, creating contracted heels and a deformed hoof. Animal skeletons do not allow us to identify which uses an animal may have been put to.[37] However, a horse's reproductive life extends, on average, from about four to twenty years of age. Heavily used, overworked or maltreated animals may not survive so long. The age of the six individuals from a London site (LUD82) demonstrated this because it varied from seven to fourteen and a half years, one late Saxon animal (IRO80) being seven to eight years old when it was slaughtered.[38]

Despite its disadvantages, the horse caught up with the oxen as a draft animal from around the fourteenth century on for three reasons. First, as cows became increasingly valuable as a source of milk, more cattle were diverted to dairying, thus creating a demand for horses. Second, the improvements in horse traction and shoeing outweighed those in ox traction.[39] Third, murrain, a recurrent disease of the early fourteenth century, had a greater impact on oxen than on horses, making the latter profitable. Nonetheless, integrating horses with oxen in a mixed team was a slow process and only in modern times did horses supersede oxen. This change started earlier in France, in the mid-thirteenth century, before taking hold in England, particularly in agriculturally advanced counties such as Norfolk. This failed to occur to any great extent in most Mediterranean regions such as Spain and Italy.[40]

The relevance of the sheep in an economic system in which pasture was shrinking may have been due to regions' relative specialization in different economic activities. All over Europe pastoral regions emerged in every upland area not suitable for cultivation. The Scottish Highlands, Wales, Yorkshire, Wiltshire, the South Downs, and the Pennines in England; the Cantabrian Mountains, Pyrenees, Iberian Mountains, and the Central Plateau in Spain; the Apennines in Italy; the Alps; the Central Plateau in France; the Bohemian Mountains; the Carpathians; and the Dinaric Alps were among the main regions producing vast herds of animals for the market to satisfy the needs of the lowland areas. Two main economic protagonists underpinned the increase in the size of flocks and their yields: monasteries and towns.

The sheep was the most common medieval farm animal as well as the most versatile. It produced milk, meat, tallow, manure, skin for parchments, and wool.

Wool became its most valuable product only gradually, attaining this status by the thirteenth century.[41] In earlier times, manorial accounts indicate that milking was a common practice on large ecclesiastic estates. According to the estimations of thirteenth-century agriculturalists, in the Middle Ages cows and sheep yielded less butter and cheese than at the present.[42] These writers held a variety of opinions about the milking of ewes and the weaning of lambs. They were all aware that milking ewes for a lengthy period could lead to rejection of the ram and reduce lambs' resistance to disease. The treatises recommend that one stop milking around Lammas (August 13). Practices could however vary greatly from one estate or manor to another. There are instances of manors that had to buy milk back for weak lambs. Given the state of malnutrition, parasitic infestation, and veterinary attention at the time, these practices no doubt underlay many diseases, but we lack information on this.[43] Records for lambing percentages are similarly unavailable. It is however safe to assume a figure of no more than 50 percent. Sterility and abortion were not major problems.

Zooarchaeology in England has shown that the number of sheep increased in the thirteenth century. At four English medieval urban sites (London, Exeter, Lincoln, and King's Lynn, covering the period AD 55–ca. 1500), sheep, cattle, and pigs form the major part of the faunal remains. At Exeter and Lincoln, the number of sheep bones increased relative to those of cattle and pigs, from 35–50 percent to 50–60 percent, from the fourteenth century on. The age at which sheep were slaughtered in King's Lynn had risen by the thirteenth century, and in Exeter by postmedieval times. This suggests an emphasis on secondary products, probably wool rather than milk. There is little direct evidence of this, but important English towns such as Lincoln and the county of Devon experienced a boom in the wool industry.[44] In addition, we have some evidence hinting at selective breeding to produce a better quality of wool. In 1190, estate officials of the see of Winchester improved the quality of their flocks in this way. The wool of Lindsey is mentioned in the surviving pipe-roll of 1208–1209, which records the introduction of forty Lindsey rams to the manors of Clere, Fanham, and Knoyle; there were already at least six at Downton. For years, Downton clip and Lindsey wool were sold at higher than average prices.[45] Accounts by Flemish and Italian merchants in the fourteenth century mentioned variation in the quality of sheep. Some of the rams imported at this early stage probably came from Cistercian monasteries on the continent, which sent them to daughter houses. Ralph Neville, Bishop of Chichester, obtained sheep from the abbeys of Vaudey and Bordesley and brought a monk over from Vaudey to advise on the management of his Sussex flock.[46] Cistercian monasteries in Yorkshire managed to establish a reputation for good quality sheep in the Low Countries and Italy. Their wool was far superior to that produced by villages.

In Spain, sheep transhumance became the most important economic activity during the late Middle Ages. This was associated with a specific breed rich in wool fiber: the Merino sheep. As twelfth-century *fueros* or municipal codes show, horses, mares, asses, oxen, cows, pigs, goats, ducks, hens, and wild cockerel were among the animals common in the frontier towns of Spain. However, sheep became increasingly important, and the economy of these towns came to be dominated by booty and sheep-based pastoralism. Every citizen of the *concejo* (frontier town) had the right to use its grazing land. They had to pay only for use of the *dehesa*, the grass enclosure for draft animals: one ram for every 100 sheep.[47] Sheep rearing matured in the thirteenth century when, following the conquest of the main Muslim towns, the southern meseta became a safe region.[48] Local associations of sheep breeders called *mestas* organized the first circuits of sheep migration and the allocation of stray stock. We know very little of this early period. In 1273, King Alfonso X of Castile granted a series of privileges to members of the *mestas*, creating a unique organization covering the whole kingdom. The inhabitants of the northern towns of Leon, Soria, Segovia, and Cuenca, the owners of the flocks, emerged as its main protagonists.[49] During the same period in the Kingdom of Aragon, shepherds' brotherhoods were founded in several towns in the Ebro River basin, such as the *Casa de Ganaderos* of Zaragoza, with the support of the king, to promote the settlement of Christians in the region.

All these associations created circuits of transhumance entailing movement from the uplands to the lowlands and corresponding to what were known as *cañadas* in Castile, *cabañeras* in Aragon, and *carratges* in Catalonia. These were complex networks of routes that peppered the landscape of the entire Peninsula with churches, watering holes, resting places, pens, and huts. Three million sheep were involved in this unceasing flow from north to south.[50] The many brotherhoods and associations produced massive amounts of information on their members' conflicts with the representatives of the towns they passed by over the course of their long-distance migration; farmers who illegally cultivated sheep paths; shepherds' battle with wolves; the care of dogs (usually mastiffs); the complicated business of mating sheep; the long journey to winter pastures; the lambing that took place there; and the shearing of the sheep on the way back home, a social event in its own right. The Laws of the Mesta also featured instructions on flock management and dealing with disease. The most important ailments were mange and agalaxia (gout), small pox, bacterial anthrax, and foot rot. They also included rules on keeping sick stock separate, animal reproduction, selective breeding, tail cutting, and the compulsory branding of animals.[51]

This refined management of flocks ultimately produced a unique breed with an unprecedented wool yield. The Merino is an Ammon's horn wool sheep and may well be one of the descendants of the Mesopotamian wool sheep of this type. It is a breed content with poor and dry pasture, such as that typical of the Mediterranean region. Its mutton quality is poor, but the breed copes very well with a hostile environment. The Merino can walk long distances.[52] The transhumance regime was a response to a challenging environment, allowing sheep to benefit from the lush grasses produced by the autumn and spring rains in ecologically complementary regions. The system had a profound effect upon individual animals, causing the fleece to grow heavier, longer and coarser. The origin of the merino has been subject to particularly intense debate since the publication of an article by Sabatino Lopez in 1947 that argued that the Genoese facilitated the import of the breed from North Africa to Spain in the fourteenth century for commercial reasons. Some Spanish historiography places its origins in the Iberian Peninsula itself. Recent works claim that it resulted from the repeated mixing of breeds native to Spain and from Africa from the twelfth to fourteenth centuries.[53]

The profitability of the sheep sidelined the pig, which had been so important in the early Middle Ages. The pig became residual, feeding on the fallows, wasteland, and in the monastic woodland, the area around its owner's house, and urban yards.[54] Its unpopularity during these centuries may have been a consequence of the damage it could do to crops with its grubbing and to the sheep's increased importance as a farm animal. The steppe landscape on which sheep grazed contrasted with the forest domain of the pig; the self-sufficient peasant often had different interest that the owner of large herds of sheep.[55]

These central centuries of the Middle Ages saw the arrival of a newcomer, the domestic rabbit, a genuine product of the era. The wild rabbit was confined to the Iberian Peninsula in postglacial times. Only when the steppes of northern Europe were opened up did the wild rabbit begin to spread slowly, first to southern France and then to central Europe and Britain.[56] In Roman times, it was kept in *leporaria* (warrens). Medieval monks were probably the first to domesticate the rabbit as an alternative source of food for the fast at Lent because unborn or newly born rabbits, called *laurices*, were regarded as fish. Between the sixth and tenth centuries French monasteries pioneered the breeding of rabbits above ground. Princes's interest in rabbits as game and their ability to escape from captivity, despite the fact that they were often introduced to islands, facilitated the species's spread. Both factors contributed to the frequent genetic mixing of wild and domestic rabbits, endowing them with brown and black fur for a lengthy period.[57]

Rabbits arrived in Britain in 1176, during a period when a number of other animals were introduced as game for the entertainment of the aristocracy: the pheasant, peafowl, partridge, and fallow deer.[58] These were first recorded in central Europe in 1423.[59] The scarcity of the rabbit in northern Europe in the late thirteenth and fourteenth centuries is reflected in the high cost of its meat, which was four or five times that of chicken. It was consumed by the aristocracy. By postmedieval times, judging by the number of bones at archeological sites, the rabbit had replaced the hare as an important element in the diet of the general population.[60] In France it even became a pest, upsetting peasants by eating crops.

IN THE TOWN: ANIMALS IN A TIME OF CRISIS

The late Middle Ages, rather than a phase of economic growth, were one of
hardship and crises. The productive system was beset by a number of problems, while the climate worsened, causing a series of bad harvests, plagues, and
pest attacks. Animals were affected by these crises in both grain-farming and
pastoral areas, with northern Europe suffering more than the warmer Mediterranean region. The best-known early epidemics occurred during the period
1315–1319. However, the problems began in the decade of 1270–1280. From
England to Castile, chroniclers mention declining crop yields and monasteries,
particularly Cistercian, unable to produce the amount of wool contracted with
merchants. Large manors went bankrupt, a sign of an economy in collapse.
The flocks of the Bishop of Winchester, which exceeded 27,000 sheep in 1272,
numbered fewer than 9,000 in 1278 and yet fewer in 1280.[61]

Animals' nightmare was called murrain (from Latin *mori,* to die). The exact
meaning of the word is unclear. It may refer to scab, though this was also
called scabies or clausik by contemporaries and was not fatal. In 1283, Dun-
stable Priory reported that many of its sheep had died from a disease brought
on by torrential summer rain. It added that the sheep in the manor of Meon
had suffered seven years of scab. The disease was described as "voreliis and
pokes," which may refer to sheep pox, *variola ovina.*[62] Seneschaucy and Walter of Henley issued dire warnings about liver fluke, an infestation of parasitic
worms, another disease typical of wet springs and summers. So dangerous
could this illness be, and so common in heathland and moorland, that they
recommended preventative cullings, dissecting the sheep to look for traces of
the disease.[63] Walter refers to *vermes* or worms, both of which caused the sheep
hoof to rot. Later fourteenth-century Winchester accounts refer to *rubeus mor-
bus* but mention no symptoms.[64] These accounts suggest that several diseases
were at work here, to fatal effect.

At the turn of the fourteenth century, working animals were in poor physical
condition. (See Figure 3.5 for an example of working animals.) Yet the worst
was still to come. The terrible weather of 1315–1317 laid the foundation for
endemic murrains that affected bovines and sheep from Ireland to Germany.
Horses were less susceptible to murrain, unlike oxen, whose reduced numbers
meant that land went uncultivated.[65] Rinderpest or anthrax appeared. Affected
animals manifested discharge from the nose, mouth, and eye succeeded by emis-
sion of a foul stench, diarrhea, dehydration, and death. Years of damp weather
caused hay to rot, severely cutting animals' food supply. A second terrible winter in 1317–1318 made this situation even worse. Malnutrition and parasitic
worms made animals prone to the fatal murrain that arrived in 1319–1322,
which mainly affected sheep.[66] Reference to catastrophic animal mortality and
ruined crops in every monastic cartulary suggests rates of mortality in oxen of

FIGURE 3.5: *Month of September* (ca. 1405–1410), Castello Buonconsiglio, Trento. © Institut für Realienkunden—ÖAW.

between 25 and 50 percent and between 50 and 70 percent in sheep, far higher than human mortality during the period of the Black Death. Drought struck in 1325–1326. Floods in 1327 caused further hardship. In 1360 reference was still being made to murrain in horses and sheep.[67]

It is a paradox that animals' size increased during the fourteenth and fifteenth centuries. The environmental changes, contraction of arable land, and decline in the number of animals eventually produced good, abundant pastures for those remaining. After the Black Death, wool production was still more profitable and less labor intensive than agriculture, and the larger estates created after the mid-fourteenth century were devoted to grass. Enclosed pasture provided the opportunity for controlled breeding and large estates inaugurated a systematic policy of selecting breeding stock. The introduction of crop rotation, which included fodder plants as well as improved techniques for hay making and storage, solved the problem of feeding the animals in the winter.

Pig size appears to have increased in the Middle Ages in the southwest of Spain, central Italy, and Bavaria, while in the north of Germany pigs grew smaller during this period.[68] In excavations of fourteenth to fifteenth century London, Armitage found a number of long-horned cattle, suggesting larger body size. Despite controversy among researchers, it seems that oxen also increased in size. Late medieval bone and horn finds from Kirkstall Abbey in Yorkshire and Baynard's Castle in London show a significant increase in cattle size over that of Anglo-Saxon times and earlier.[69] This was probably due to the import of breeds from France.[70]

The evolution of horses is yet more striking. The size of war horses increased dramatically to produce the heavier and taller *magnus equus* or *grant chival* of seventeen to eighteen hands in the fourteenth century. This horse was highly prized and imported at great expense; its breeding was encouraged and export banned. Somehow these genes influenced working horses. Archeofauna all over Europe hint at an increase in size from thirteen or fourteen to fifteen hands.[71]

There is an explanation for these paradoxical developments: the takeoff of urban markets. Despite the crises that swept all Europe, the key developments set in motion by the economic growth of the central centuries of the Middle Ages persisted: urbanization, market integration, and regional specialization. Meat consumption boomed in the mid-fourteenth century, replacing a diet based on cereal and dairy products. In towns, however, the chief source of meat was no longer the pig but the cow. Consumption of ovines and pigs was now restricted largely to the countryside. The diet of thirteenth-century peasants consisted mainly of bread and dairy produce, that is, cheese and milk, which together accounted for four-fifths of the calorific value of all food consumed. Fowl was the main source of meat in France, and pork was the main source of meat in Britain and Germany. In the fourteenth and fifteenth centuries, animal protein accounted for 40 percent of total food. The common diet was based on mutton and goat in the Mediterranean region, Italy, and Spain; fresh beef in Hungary, the Low Countries, and Sweden, and pork in France and Germany. Beef and mutton remained paramount in Britain, where ovine livestock predominated, though less so than in the south of Europe.[72] Quantities of dairy produce declined over the long term. In aristocratic households and the town, a combination of fowl, wild birds, and rabbit predominated, while the pig remained important in the countryside. Harvest workers were given the meat of old animals such as bulls, oxen, cows, hens, and sheep of no further use to the manor. The domestic hen became the fauna most frequently found in the peasant household during this period.[73]

The provision of urban butchers became a major item on the agenda of every council; supplying the town and jurisdiction over grazing land for animals were at the heart of village legislation.[74] The distribution of animals differed: in towns cattle, horses, fowls, pigs, and cats dominated, while cattle, pigs, dogs, sheep, and goats did so in the countryside. Regions gradually specialized as meat suppliers: the needs of England were met by Scotland, Wales, and southern England; those of Venice, Austria, Moravia, Bohemia, and Swabia by Hungary; the southern towns of Spain were supplied by northern Castile and the Pyrenees, while central and northern Italy supplied the northern towns.[75] Cattle droving became a major activity among the inhabitants of the Scottish Galloways and Wales, who brought cattle to fairs and sales all over the Lake District. Using old drove paths, these drovers traveled to England selling cattle for slaughter at major towns such as Manchester, Birmingham, and London.[76] In Spain, the routes of transhumance stretching from north to south created a comprehensive network of markets. The long journeys involved posed immense challenges for the animals. Only certain breeds and age groups could survive such conditions. In modern England, hornless cattle were favored by drovers as distinct from those used for draft purposes.[77]

The semidomestic forest pig now tended to be housed for longer periods and fed on household refuse. Some wooded regions persisted in bringing up pigs, but on treeless estates the large majority would keep only the number that could survive on stubble and waste. Pigs kept in towns were frequently allowed to scavenge for food during the day and were fattened on peas, beans, dairy, and brewery waste.[78] Even monasteries tended to develop a sty management system, feeding hogs for the consumption of the monks on grain and legumes.[79] This change in pig keeping helped develop types of pig more suited to an indoor existence and aided pigs' adaptation to an urban environment. The sty pig was to develop into a larger, fat animal white in color. In post medieval times, fat bacon again became an important source of meat for the single peasant family too poor to buy other types of animal protein.

The burgeoning towns were the center of political, cultural, and economic life in the late Middle Ages; their central role in production and consumption attracted people and dragged animals. One animal whose fate was profoundly entangled with that of the towns was the horse; from noble horses to cart horses or packhorses, they became a common sight there. City dwellers spent much time transporting foodstuffs and goods to, from, and around the city. For London, recent research has confirmed the increasing value of cart horses in the period between 1250 and 1400. These usually formed teams of two or three; they were a major contributor to London's traffic, blocking bridges and streets, and were frequently involved in accidents with pedestrians.[80] Carrying by cart was twice as effective as the use of packhorses. The recommended load for a pack animal seems to have been between 100 and 150 kilograms; a cart of three horses could manage around 700 kilograms.[81] These carts and horses could be hired for the carrying of foodstuffs and other materials, usually on the basis of the distance traveled.[82] Horses' value varied a great deal. The lead horse cost ten shillings, the shaft horse, six shillings, and the trace horse only four shillings. In the late Middle Ages, horses were traded on a spectacular scale. The Gonzaga dynasty of Mantua, which bred horses from 1329 on, had agents in Spain, Frisia, North Africa, Sardinia, England, Ireland, France, and Italy. Dealers across Europe congregated in special horse fairs and markets held outside towns. Some of the most important were held in Hungary, Cologne and Frankfurt (Germany), Genoa (Italy), Medina del Campo (Spain), and Antwerp (Low Countries).[83]

The abundance of animals in towns inspired specific municipal legislation intended to regulate related industries and the keeping of animals. This often involved moving all activities producing unhygienic conditions, smelly waste, or noise to the outskirts of the town. These urban by-laws usually prohibited the throwing of dung or other filth into the streets from butchers or fishmongers and burying animals inside the walls of the town. The feeding of mules and oxen on the street and the keeping of pigs or large numbers of cattle in

houses were also forbidden.[84] The large number of domestic animals roaming
the cities and streets were a genuine danger and often aroused fears. Dogs
could carry rabies and other diseases, pigs could attack and devour children,
while packhorses and carts ran people over and caused accidents.[85] In towns,
particularly in Italy and the Iberian Peninsula, veterinary medicine emerged
for the first time as a practice and in the form of theoretical treatises. Indeed,
important fourteenth- and fifteenth-century towns engaged the services of the
alvetarius for one to five years. This figure was to progressively substitute the
farrier (Latin *ferrarius,* French *feroun* or *ferrour*), who formerly tended not
only to shoe horses but also treated injuries and diseases.[86]

At the opposite extreme of this world lay the noble country household.
During these centuries, it was defined as a space contrasting sharply with the
rustic farm and noisy town. England epitomizes this tendency. One of the earliest English etiquette books produced in Angevin times, the *Urbanus* (Civilized
man) by Daniel of Beccles, is concerned chiefly with helping lords avoid rustic-
ity. This treatise suggests keeping the seigneurial hall as free as possible of pigs
and cats, although riding horses, hunting dogs, and hawks were acceptable.[87]
Working, hunting, and luxury animals all came to enjoy a distinct status. This
flagged the owners' status and underlined the contrast between two spaces, the
manor house and the farm. Exotic animals found their way into the houses of
the mercantile middle classes, high ecclesiastics, and nobility.

It is in this context that certain animals emerged as something similar to
the modern pet, lacking functional use and forming part of the inner circle of
the family. Given how sentiments have changed over time, we must be wary of
imposing our own attitudes to animals on the past. What were the true feelings of the oxen owners who cared about their animals' health and feeding or
the Spanish hunting foresters who proudly described the deeds of their dogs
or shepherds who knew their sheep by name? Their concern may have been
largely utilitarian. There is however one animal, the dog, with which human
beings in the Middle Ages formed genuine bonds. We are fortunate enough to
have evidence of this.

Zooarcheology cannot identify breeds in dogs, but size can easily be distinguished. At the end of the Middle Ages, some dogs were so small that they
can only have been lapdogs.[88] Many medieval authors such as Gerard of Wales
or Gervase of Tilbury praised the fidelity of dogs as the companions of human
beings. (See Figure 3.6 for a dog being trained.) In the real world, men and
women of the baronial class frequently had birds and other animals at their
side. Dogs and puppies were often to be found snuffling around tables.[89] Medieval nuns and monks also kept pet animals, sometimes in religious houses,
a practice frequently decried by bishops carrying out inspections within their
dioceses. Abbesses, abbots, and bishops themselves might have kept animals,
as might their patrons and visitors, some of whom stayed in monasteries for

FIGURE 3.6: *Dog.* Ulrich von Lilienfeld, *Concordantiae caritatis* (fourteenth century), Stift Lilienfeld, MS 171, fol. 167v. © Institut für Realienkunden—ÖAW.

a time.[90] The Council of Vienne (1311) complained that many ministers entered church "bringing hawks with them or causing them to be brought and leading hunting dogs."[91] Indeed, some monks of noble stock, reluctant to give up their habits, continued to hunt, upon taking up holy orders. Inspections tended to result in complaints about the money spent on food for these animals rather than the sisters or brothers. Repeated condemnations and the many exceptions made demonstrate that such practices were difficult to stamp out.[92]

If the dog was at one end of the spectrum, the cat was at the other.[93] Animals become pets when they have no utility and no cultural or religious prejudice exist against them. In the Middle Ages, both factors prevented the cat from becoming an adored member of the human household. Ecclesiastics found cats repugnant due to their negative symbolic connotations: evil, death, the devil, witchcraft, and heresy, not to mention the strong sexual associations. Cats, moreover, were expected to control pests in churches, cathedrals, and towns as it is shown by the cat holes that can be found in some cathedrals all over Europe. They were considered low animals and were also unpopular in baronial households. They appeared in the houses of the lesser folk as useful predators. Cats became pets only in the sixteenth century, when they were imported as precious and exotic animals.

It has been claimed that the cat arrived in Western Europe with returning Crusaders. Yet cat remains appear in ninth- to eleventh-century sites in most French towns (Paris, Douai), military fortresses (Trelleborg), trading centers (Haithabu), and abbeys (Villiers-Le-Sec) as they did also in Spanish Muslim towns and castles.[94] The bones generally suggest young cats, small and with some pathologies; they were probably semiwild. Some medieval authors, such as Thomas of Cantimpré, Vincent of Beauvais, Albert the Great, and Jérome Cardan advised cutting off the cat's ears or hair to keep it attached to the house and afraid of the rain outside.[95] In the thirteenth century cats proliferated in towns; they were far from being seen as precious. In thirteenth-century Castile and Aragon villages', money compensation for killing or stealing a cat were low. Cats' skulls are often found in the refuse pits of medieval towns and castles but seldom occur in villages.[96] In towns, cat fur became a commodity. Jacques de Vitry mentions that it was sold by students in Paris. The early fourteenth-century Ordinances of Ipswich give a price of four pence for 1000 furs and one penny for twelve wild cat furs. The fourteenth-century Statute of Rome condemned those who sold cat furs while making them out to be fox furs. Monks seeking low-quality furs in order to adhere to their orders' regulations on dressing were among the consumers of these furs. The industrial exploitation of cats explains the extraordinary concentration of cat bones at some archaeological sites.[97] The fourteenth century saw the first attempts to select breeds. Cats brought from Syria and the Levant to Italy were imported to France, England, and Spain. These cats were considered more beautiful than common cats, those with black or striped fur coming in for particular praise. In the sixteenth century the cat became a familiar pet.

As the Middle Ages drew to a close, working animals were more confined to specific spaces than before, their lives controlled more tightly by human beings. Their fate was determined by the profitability of their activities and products. The division into pets, domestic animals, and wild animals had truly taken hold.

CHAPTER FOUR

Animals in Medieval Sports, Entertainment, and Menageries

LISA J. KISER

In John Trevisa's translation (1398–1399) of Bartholomaeus Anglicus's magisterial encyclopedia of natural history, *De proprietatibus rerum,* we learn that there are four purposes for animals. Some beasts, writes Trevisa, provide humans with food, such as sheep and deer; some offer service to humans, such as horses, asses, oxen, and camels; some bring proper humility to humans, such as fleas, lions, tigers, and bears; and some are for "mannys merthe, as apes and marmusettes and popingayes."[1] In other words, to Trevisa and his Latin authority of a century before, the divinely ordained role of some animals was to supply amusement for their human counterparts. Indeed, we shall see that apes, marmosets, and popinjays were hardly the only kinds of animals pressed into service as entertainers for medieval people, for virtually every common European animal—and a large number of exotic imported species as well—took some part, large or small, in games, spectacles, menageries, performances, tournaments, and displays. Between 1000 and 1400, the period of time this chapter will cover, medieval Europeans not only witnessed animal-centered entertainment inherited from the classical and early medieval worlds, but they also added many of their own. Some of these forms of entertainment had regional distributions (certain kinds of horse racing, for example, were largely found in Italy, and ritualized bullfighting had its greatest prominence in

Spain); some had strong affiliations with certain social classes (private menageries were maintained by the wealthy, for example) or with specific genders and ages (boys were the primary participants in cockfighting games). Nonetheless, animal entertainers in general would have played a large part in every medieval person's experience, for their variety and wide distribution insured that everyone would have seen them at some time in their lives.

Unfortunately, evidence documenting some kinds of animal entertainment is scarce from this period. At times, the only evidence we have are entries in account rolls, cryptically noting payment for some form of entertainment about which nothing is said. At other times, we only have records from ecclesiastical sources that criticize, and prohibit, the game or the pastime. And finally, sometimes we need to turn to literary texts to augment our information, in spite of the fact that literature, though rich in cultural attitudes, is sometimes unreliable as historical record. In short, records from this period are complex, as well as sparse, with strengths and weaknesses we must carefully assess.

Games, spectacles, and other entertainments are expressions of the cultures and social groups that create them, and our focus here is on the multiple, culturally various, ways in which medieval people included animals in their amusements. Because the social status of those involved in these games and spectacles is perhaps the most significant determinant of the forms such entertainments took and the cultural meanings they exhibit, this analysis gives special emphasis to the ways in which specific cultural practices of play were deeply tied to late medieval class-based social organization. Even those games and pastimes that the medieval world had inherited from classical antiquity reflected, in their new medieval contexts, characteristic medieval attitudes about the social superiority or inferiority of the audiences, the participants, and even the animals themselves.

This chapter begins with the private keeping of menageries and the public display of animals by the medieval royalty and aristocracy. Then it discusses games and spectacles typical of the royal and noble classes, before moving to town and village entertainment, much of it traditionally labeled popular and much of it overtly imitative, or possibly even parodic, of that of the nobility. In the course of its cultural analysis, however, this chapter attempts, as much as possible, to maintain a strong focus on the medieval animal participants themselves, for, as Robert Delort has observed in 1984, animals have histories, too, and those histories have only begun to be recorded.

MENAGERIES

The history of menageries in Roman antiquity is richly documented, as is the widespread Roman practice of organizing public games and spectacles involving animal–animal or animal–human combat. But in the fourth century, public sports involving animal combat were prohibited, if not entirely ended, by Constantine, the first Christian emperor. After his reign, very few records suggest that animals were being kept for public display, though Justinian, in sixth-century Byzantium, may have revived the tradition of holding public animal-centered spectacles, and there are even records suggesting that the practice of animal combat on a large public scale may have continued into the twelfth century there.[2]

Even in the absence of public display, however, medieval secular rulers continued to keep collections of animals throughout the medieval period for private viewing and for displaying to important visitors at their courts. Exotic species were introduced into Europe through gift exchanges with foreign rulers, through increased trade in luxury items (which animals were considered to be), and through casual collecting when European contact with the Middle East became relatively common, especially, in the later centuries, by means of the Crusades. We know that Charlemagne (742–814) had three menageries including at least one elephant (named Aboul-Abas, a gift from the Caliph of Baghdad); in addition, he had bears, camels, lions, monkeys, and rare birds that lived in the pleasure garden of one of his villas.[3]

In the later Middle Ages, we have reliable evidence of royal menageries in England, France, Italy, the Netherlands, Germany, and Poland. Notable among those in England during this period was that of William the Conqueror, whose menagerie of exotic animals eventually became the core collection of the later, long-enduring Tower of London menagerie. In the early twelfth century, his son, Henry I, housed the animals, which by then included lions, leopards, lynxes, camels, and a porcupine, in pens at Woodstock (Oxfordshire),[4] from which the menagerie was relocated to the Tower of London in 1235 by Henry III. In 1251, the Tower animal collection included some sort of white bear that was allowed to fish in the Thames,[5] and, by 1255, it included an elephant, given to Henry by Louis IX of France. (The elephant lived only two years.) We know, too, that the later Plantagenet royal menageries always contained lions and leopards, the latter animal forming part of the heraldic device of the family.[6]

On the continent as well, major menageries were kept by royalty. Among the Hohenstaufens, both Henry VI (1165–1197) and his son Frederick II (1194–1250), the latter a noted naturalist, kept sizable menageries, Frederick's at his Palermo residence. He also engaged in a recorded exchange of animals, trading a white bear for a giraffe with an Egyptian sultan. Frederick also traveled with his elephants, camels, lions, panthers, and leopards, occasionally displaying them publicly in parades.[7] Italy was the home of a number of impressive collections of lions. For example, the fourteenth-century Visconti court in Milan kept such beasts. Moreover, in late thirteenth-century Florence, leopards and lions were kept, in part to symbolize the city's dominance over its neighbors; the city's lion pit held twenty-four lions that were sometimes pitted against other animals in combat.[8] Rome, too, according to legend, maintained a lion pit at the foot of the Capitol between 1100 and 1414, again displaying the city's dominance, this time at the very center of its administrative power.[9] In France, Louis IX (1214–1270) owned an elephant brought back from the Crusades, as well as lions and a porcupine; following his reign, we have records showing that Philip III, Philip IV, Louis X, Charles IV, Philip VI, and Charles V all had exotic animals at their chateaux—bears, lions, and leopards being the most prominent ones.[10] The latter king, Charles V, added rare birds and marine animals (including a porpoise) to his private menagerie in Paris, erecting elaborate outdoor pens and a pond for the aquatic species.[11]

Even in lesser or more remote European kingdoms, such as those in the Low Countries and in eastern Europe, there were menageries kept by the powerful. In eleventh-century Prague, there were menageries containing lions as emblematic of the royal family's identity.[12] We know, too, that members of the ruling classes in the fourteenth-century Netherlands kept lions, bears, and birds.[13] In addition, the city of Amsterdam owned a civic lion that was the gift of Count William IV.[14] Finally, it is worth mentioning the bear kept on permanent public display in the Swiss city of Berne during the 1330s. This animal was identified as the city's mascot and was kept in a pit under the stairs of the town hall.[15]

It is a scholarly truism that the keeping of menageries by wealthy, largely royal, medieval families was designed to reinforce the symbolic—and actual—distance between such people and those of lower social stations. Indeed, to keep large or exotic species in the Middle Ages meant that one had the money to feed them, the space to house them, and the foreign connections necessary to acquire them in the first place. Moreover, lions, the most common of exotic species to be collected, clearly functioned as emblems of royal power, with the lion being popularly seen as the so-called king of beasts. To have under one's domination a beast that was itself dominant in the animal order surely constituted an exceptional symbolic display of worldly authority, one that was imitated by the Italian city-states in their desire to signal their power to their surrounding communities. But what do we make of the fact that medieval religious institutions also engaged in animal collecting? Throughout the first half of the fourteenth century, from 1316 to 1360, the Avignon popes had menageries attached to their palaces; in 1326, for example, a lion house and a bear house are mentioned in the records, along with references to a camel, peacocks, boars, ostriches, and a number of less exotic beasts, both fur bearing and feathered.[16] John XXII, at great inconvenience and expense, traveled to Rome with a number of wild animals, and Pope Urban V (1362–1370) had a collection of rabbit companions that he brought with him on his travels.[17] To be sure, the late medieval papacy was always attempting to compete with secular rulers in its show of power, and the possession of exotic animals aided it in its efforts. But a few of these accounts suggest that the kinds of animals collected, and the fact that some of them were chosen to be papal travel companions, might make it reasonable to see the animals as pets—a construction we should not immediately dismiss when thinking about any of the animals in wealthy collectors' menageries.[18]

Even monasteries—surely institutions not intentionally involved in overt shows of worldly power—sometimes had menageries. The plan of the ninth-century monastic house of St. Gallen, Switzerland, shows a bear pit and a huge collection of animal pens, noting also the necessary requisitions for keepers, and the nuns at an abbey in Caen kept birds.[19] Most interesting, however, is what we learn in an eleventh-century hagiographical text by Goscelin of Canterbury treating the life of Saint Edith; he notes that as a nun, Edith kept a menagerie of both wild and tame beasts and birds housed in pens outside of her nunnery. Then, in a telling remark, he says that readers should not see this practice as stemming from Edith's royal background or as a sign of any vain curiosity or desire for amusement; rather, he attributes to her the charitable motive of wishing to honor and provide for God's needy creatures.[20] Thus, religious motives for menagerie keeping were certainly voiced in this period, even if these motives may in fact have been invented merely to justify the widespread, perhaps universal, human desire to collect, observe, and, thus, satisfy curiosity about wildlife.

PROCESSIONALS AND CIVIC SPECTACLES

Animals kept in royal or aristocratic menageries were occasionally displayed in public processionals, parades, and civic spectacles with the purpose of reminding onlookers of the social dominance of their keepers or their honorees. Frederick II, whose menagerie was aforementioned, held spectacles at his court that used animals as entertainment. His elephant, for example, accompanied by trumpeters and attendants carrying banners, wore a miniature castle on its back for viewers to admire.[21] When his fiancée, the English princess Isabella, came to Germany for the wedding in 1235, he staged jousting exhibitions with Spanish horses, and, for the same event, he had an exhibition built—illusory of course—of boats rowing on dry land: the boats were dragged by horses concealed under blankets.[22] At the same event, an enormous parade was staged that included camels and dromedaries being led by Saracens, as well as monkeys and leopards guided along by Ethiopian keepers.[23] We should note here that the exotic animals are accompanied by exotic humans, both groups emblematically displaying Frederick's extensive dominion. In an earlier medieval spectacle, described by a twelfth-century monk from Fleury Abbey, Henry I of England paraded through Normandy (which he had just invaded) with a young lion being whipped by an Ethiopian keeper, a leopard sitting atop a horse, a panther yoked to a chariot, and a camel and an ostrich.[24] In this spectacle,

which moved our chronicler immensely, the inclusion of an exotic human dom-
inating an exotic animal offers silent but eloquent testimony to Henry's social
and political authority, for Henry was clearly being implied as the dominator
of them all.[25]

The horse figured prominently in royal public spectacles, because showy,
top-of-the-line horses, caparisoned elegantly in their military gear, went a
long way toward underscoring secular power. In 1265, Charles of Anjou was
welcomed to Rome by horsemen executing elaborate equestrian maneuvers.[26]
When Ulrich von Liechtenstein traveled through Friuli and Carinthia in 1277,
he rode in a procession that included a display of fine riding horses with expensive saddles.[27] And when the city of London staged processions in honor of
Richard II (1377–1399), the planners always included horses. When his future
wife, Anne of Bohemia, visited in 1382, the city presented Richard with a white
steed, decorated in red and gold cloth. As the royal party proceeded through
the streets to Temple Bar, they encountered a mockup of a desert scene, populated by John the Baptist and a variety of exotic beasts.[28]

Animals in medieval spectacles often carried heraldic significance, being
symbolic of aristocratic or civic identity. In 1335, in Lille, there was a procession of costumed knights, each carrying live swans to form a rebus of a local
town's name, "Val aux cygnes."[29] In 1368, at the Milanese court of the Visconti, a wedding feast was held to honor Lionel Duke of Clarence's marriage
to one of the Visconti daughters; during dinner, leopards were brought out
to refer to Lionel's Plantagenet armorial design.[30] And in 1389, the citizens
of Paris welcomed Isabella of Bavaria, about to be wedded to Charles VI, by
creating an enclosed garden that included a live animal tableau, complete with
a stag and rabbits being pursued by greyhounds.[31] This *tableau vivant* was
clearly commemorating the nobility of the couple, since hunting with hounds
was a sport restricted to those with aristocratic credentials. In short, animal
spectacle was part and parcel of noble identity, sometimes being arranged by
civic organizers to honor those who ruled over them and other times by those
who were noble themselves.

EQUESTRIAN WAR GAMES

The development of the tournament, in which mounted knights imitated warfare as a form of sport, has an obscure history. Equestrian games with martial
structures were known in antiquity, of course, but it is not until the medieval period that we find evidence for the thoroughly organized team sport
known as the tournament, in which cavalrymen deployed their units against
one another in a ritualized display of the skills needed in medieval warfare.
As Jusserand astutely describes medieval equestrian sport, "les jeux ressemblaient à la guerre et la guerre ressemblaient aux jeux."[32] Evidence about these

games comes from chronicles, literary texts, manuscript illuminations, and specialized treatises on chivalry—but not all of these sources are equally helpful in conveying information about the rules and conventions of the sport. Northern France, in the late eleventh century, seems to have been the birthplace of the medieval tournament,[33] but the sport reached its central European heyday in the late twelfth century. In Italy, Spain, Sweden, and the eastern European countries, tournaments gained popularity much later.[34] Variations on tournament play, however, continued to be widespread throughout Europe until the late fifteenth century.

Since tournaments involved violence, they often resulted in significant bodily injury to men and their horses, in spite of the use of blunted weapons in later forms of the sport[35] and overt prohibition of intentional injuring of men and beasts. Broken limbs were common; and fatalities, of both men and their horses, are recorded with alarming frequency.[36] Indeed, the object of the tournament was not much different from that of medieval warfare itself: charging with lances, swords, or axes aimed at one's opponent, one attempted to dismount him or otherwise render him unable to fight. Teams were kept in formations by leaders, and prisoners were taken into custody, led into safety zones where they surrendered. Prizes awarded to winners of tournaments sometimes included animals, such as noble lions, bears, falcons, coursers, and greyhounds. But other animals were awarded as well: talking parrots are recorded,[37] as are pigs and fish. Losers often forfeited their armor and their horses to those who had beaten them. A slightly less violent form of the tournament, popular in Germany and perhaps the descendant of earlier Germanic equestrian exercises, involved the use of shields as weapons; called a bohort, this game consisted of a knight trying to push an opponent off his horse by using his shield. Both the bohort and the tournament proper involved highly evolved equestrian skills, for one's horse was usually confined to a very small space and one had to be able to turn it in any direction very quickly. The name "tournament" itself derives from this equestrian turning maneuver, and horses being trained for tournament play were taught to spring rapidly and turn in response to subtle rein, spur, and bit signaling.[38]

The joust, which involved one-on-one combat set up as a spectator sport, evolved from the tournament and was popular among the aristocracy in the later part of this period, from the thirteenth to the fifteenth centuries. Its object, like that of tournaments, was to unhorse one's opponent by the use of a lance—but jousting appears to have had a greater focus on protocol and style.[39] To protect horses from head-on collisions, the tilt was invented during the later years of our period; it consisted of a wooden barrier erected between the paths of the oncoming horses to keep them apart. (See Figure 4.1.) As one late medieval writer, Piers de Massy, rather movingly describes it, the tilt is "in the myddis for to kepe our horses God save and kepe them from harme."[40]

FIGURE 4.1: *A tilt separating knights on horseback* (fifteenth century). British Library, London, MS Cotton Nero D.IX, fol. 32v.

Medieval literary romances feature jousts between mounted knights as major plot motifs, with detailed descriptions of such encounters obviously appealing greatly to their readers and listeners.[41]

The featured animal involved in this related group of martial entertainments was the expensive medieval war horse, called a destrier. These horses were sturdy, broad chested, and bred for endurance rather than speed, yet they were not particularly large by modern standards, possibly only 15–16 hands at their largest.[42] The best warhorses were usually imported into northwestern Europe from Spain,[43] although the stock there may have originally been from North Africa or the Arab world.[44] Italy also provided superior horses.[45] Horse breeding was carried out all over Europe, however, with many large monasteries and royal estates devoting attention to selective development of the animal. The war horse, after all, was viewed as part and parcel of the knight's martial identity; its quality reflected, or contributed to, the knight's own level of social value, and the animal would often be elaborately caparisoned, from shoulder to ankle, in surplices decorated with its owner's heraldic devices.

By the twelfth century, horses in tournaments and jousts were protected by armor and straw-filled cushioning specifically designed to prevent injuries to their heads, necks, and chests. Codes of knightly conduct forbade intentional injury to opponents' horses; it was considered cowardly and dishonorable, both in sport and in actual battle, to focus one's aggression on the animal. In the late Middle English poem *Sir Tryamour,* when the hero accidentally kills his opponent's horse, the opponent says: "Hyt ys grete schame / On a hors to wreke thy grame" (lines 1222–1223). But sources regularly record injury to horses, seeing such occurrences as worthy of comment. Geoffrey de Charny's fourteenth-century treatise, *Questions on Jousting and Tournaments,* muses on what and how soon a knight should be compensated if his horse is slain or wounded during sport.[46] In Ulrich von Liechtenstein's mid-thirteenth-century *Frauendienst,* a literary work that focuses on knightly conduct at tournaments and jousts, horse injury is described as having occurred twice in the course of some 300 jousting encounters, both times with great regret on the part of participants. In literary works (as surely as in life), the bond between a knight and his horse was often so great that the injury or loss of a horse occasioned exceptionally marked grief. In the late Middle English poem, *The Anturs of Arther,* a joust between Gawain and Galeron results in the former's horse, named Gresell, being shamefully beheaded. Gawain, crazed with weeping, laments, "he was the most excellent horse that ever ate fodder" (line 547) and "for grief of a mute beast that thus has died, I mourn" (lines 553–554). Veterinary care for wounded horses was certainly not as professionalized or as systematic as it would become in the early modern period, but Jordanus Ruffus, Frederick II's farrier, wrote a treatise, between 1250 and 1256, on equine medicine that elaborated on the cleansing and treatment of wounds.[47] And Teodorico Borgognoni, in 1267, made available in treatise form a recipe for anesthesia to prevent wounded horses from feeling pain during treatment.[48] Clearly, horses in equestrian games garnered sympathetic responses from their owners and riders, above and beyond their value as forms of social and material capital.

The image of the well-equipped knight on his powerful horse was profoundly affecting in the later Middle Ages. Episodes from romances of the time suggest, for example, that females viewing this figure, even from afar, were inevitably attracted to its suggestion of masculine allure and potency, showing that tournaments, jousts, and the horse that made these activities possible, all played a key role in medieval aristocratic courtship ritual.[49] For the young aristocratic men involved, participation in tournaments and jousts brought personal recognition in their social circles and great material reward if they captured others' horses and armor or succeeded in winning any contest. But the culture at large justified these martial games on the grounds that they provided worthwhile training in preparation for actual military maneuvers. Ecclesiastical criticism of the pride and violence inherent in these games, launched in various papal prohibitions and interdictions between 1130 and 1316, was outweighed by the perceived worth of the military training they provided. In Humbert of Romans's model sermon fashioned for delivery to knights, he denounces those who play war games for sinful reasons, but he also recognizes the possible utility of such games: "if a knight takes part in tournaments in a modest way with a view to making himself better able to fight as a result of such practice, then what he is doing is quite tolerable, because no practical art can be learned without practice" (p. 338). And as great a cleric as Albertus Magnus, writing in the thirteenth century, noted that games on horseback are "useful games" because they contribute to the defense of the land.[50]

Youths who were in training for the tournament, the joust, and the actual military maneuvers that might follow often practiced their equestrian skills and their hand–eye coordination in the common game of quintain. In early depictions of quintain, a post is shown set in the ground to be used as a target for mounted youths riding toward it with lances; as the game became more elaborate, a shield might be hung on the post as a target, or, perhaps, a pivoting wooden representation of an opposing human, which would, if mis-hit, swing around and strike the practicing youth from behind. (See Figure 4.2.) The origins of quintain are obscure, but by the late Middle Ages, it was practiced in every European country. In Spain, it was called *estafermo*, and in Italy, it was sometimes known as *il saracino*, referring to the image of an imagined Saracen enemy being represented as the pivoting target.[51] Matthew Paris and William Fitzstephen say that the game was common in London. Quintain, as practiced by young knights in public places, was a spectator sport very much like jousting. But in the later Middle Ages, quintain was publicly engaged in by the bourgeoisie and mercantile classes, perhaps at times in a kind of comic parody of the noble practitioners of the sport. Thus, it provided those whose social position would never allow them to participate in an actual joust or tournament a chance to engage in equestrian display.[52] By the late Middle Ages, quintain posts were ubiquitous in villages and towns, demonstrating a widespread desire among youths to imitate the equestrian war games of the nobility. The horses used for this game, and for the related game of *bague* (*sortija* in Spain),

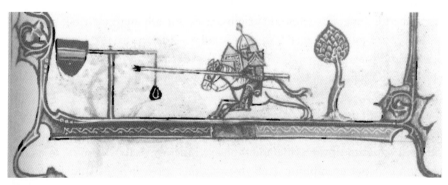

FIGURE 4.2: *Riding at the quintain* (fourteenth century). British Library, London, MS Facs. 237, pl. XIX.

wherein mounted youths aimed their lances at suspended rings, were those deemed to be good sprinters—fast and easily manipulable.[53]

BULLFIGHTING

On the Iberian Peninsula, bulls played a major role in aristocratic martial spectacle. The origin of bullfighting is obscure,[54] but it may have evolved from hunting practices. There are early records of ritualized bullhunting, with lances, in the open countryside,[55] as well as references from the precourtly tenth century to the profession of matador,[56] a figure probably hired to fight a bull on foot before large public, namely, nonaristocratic, gatherings. But in the last decades of the eleventh century and the first half of the twelfth, bullfighting became associated with the noble classes, forming part of the celebratory entertainment for royal marriages and coronations.[57] As in tournaments and jousts, knights would fight the bull on horseback, armed with a lance and sword, and chroniclers suggest that the bullfight was associated with other martial games as well.[58] Unfortunately, chroniclers spend more time describing the trappings of the horses and the array of the knights than detailing the rules of the bullfight itself,[59] but we can assume from the evidence that the bulls were killed, with the focus surely being on the knightly techniques involved in their slaying.[60]

Interestingly, as long as bullfighting was identified as an aristocratic sport whose greatest reward was the honor accrued by displaying bravery, it carried the sanction of the authorities. But in Iberian culture, and perhaps in feudal European culture generally, there was a strong taboo against fighting, or shedding blood, in exchange for monetary reward. Alfonso X promulgated laws in the mid-thirteenth century against matadors (*matatoros*) who were paid to kill bulls in spectacles. The laws decreed that while it was immoral to combat savage animals for money, it was honorable to do so when one was only demonstrating one's valor in the face of such ferocious beasts.[61] In keeping with this cultural taboo against monetary payment for animal combat, it is reasonable to suppose that any medieval Spanish matadors hired specifically to entertain an audience came from humble origins, were socially marginalized, and were considered performers of the lowest rank, lumped together with prostitutes, jugglers, traveling players, and the like.[62] The existence of these hired matadors in records that both precede, and remain continuous with, the courtly forms of bullfighting suggests that bullfighting took place as a public spectacle throughout the Iberian Peninsula in the Middle Ages, beginning well before the courtly versions of the sport. We therefore clearly have two separate, but related, traditions of bullfighting—one popular and one courtly, the latter perhaps developing as a chivalric refinement of the former.

Some scholars have argued that the bull was a powerful symbol of fecundity in Iberian culture.[63] To be sure, many early records note the occurrence of bullfighting spectacles (without the actual killing of the bull) in connection with royal or aristocratic weddings.[64] Whether or not we agree that fecundity is at issue, it seems clear that public confrontations with bulls had something to do with the display of masculinity and perhaps even the ritual channeling of masculine violence into socially acceptable forms. In village life, there were bull-runnings that took place in communal settings; for example, in one event, bulls being led through the streets on the way to the slaughterhouse would be freed, and young men would run with them, dodging their horns. When performed on a wedding day, the male wedding guests would be invited to ritually participate in the running. Sometimes, a rope would be tied to the bulls' horns, and young men would attempt to control the bulls and avoid being wounded in the effort.[65]

The bull's own masculine identity stems not only from its virile physiology and biological sex, but also derives from its service as a stud animal, a role in stark contrast to that of its castrated brethren, the oxen, who were relegated to the ubiquitous and lowly medieval task of plowing the fields. Yet we must not lose sight of the fact that the bull is basically a domestic animal and that therefore whatever ferocity it displays will almost always be provoked by human action. So any cultural analysis of bullfighting must take into account the staged nature of this confrontation between man and beast, an important contributor to its ritual character.[66]

As it did with tournaments and jousts, the organized church made clear its disapproval of bullfighting and bull-running, and clergymen were strictly prohibited from participating in them. And in 1567, Pope Pius V forbad them in all of Christendom. The practice, however, continued apace, and in records about one village, we learn that running with the bulls had become a Pentecost ritual taking place right before the slaughtering of the animal, its meat being served to the poor on the day after the game.[67] In this way, the bull-centered sport was inextricably woven into the religious expression of the community.

HORSE RACING

Horse racing has a continuous history from antiquity through the Middle Ages and beyond. Although there are few records from early medieval Europe about this sport, it seems to have been particularly fancied by the Germanic peoples, showing up in medieval Scandinavian literature and mentioned (negatively) in an Anglo-Saxon prohibition issuing from an eighth-century Mercian Council.[68] Among later medieval royalty, two sons of Henry II (Richard the Lionheart and John) are said to have been patrons of horse racing,[69] as was Richard II,[70] and Froissart tells the story of King Charles VI of France engaging in a cross-country horse race with his brother (37–72). In the late Middle Ages, however, there is much evidence that horse racing was an urban sport, engaged in by citizens of all ranks. In London, the horse and cattle market at Smithfield became a center for horse racing, with youths watching the races, betting on them, and serving as jockeys.[71] In Chester also, festive races were run on Shrove Tuesday;[72] and, all over England, races were held on the day after Christmas.[73] At the French Champagne fairs, where horses were bought and sold, races were ubiquitous.[74]

But the most interesting data comes from thirteenth- and fourteenth-century Italy, where organized horse racing, often downtown in a city's square, became a distinctive feature of urban life. These horse races, called *palios,* first begin to be fully described in urban records of the early fourteenth century, but their origins were surely earlier. Every major Italian commune scheduled *palios* on festival days associated with saints holding local importance to the city. Florence's biggest *palio* was on the feast day of John the Baptist, but races were also held on Saint Barnabas's Day, Saint Onofrio's Day, and Saint Peter's Day.[75] On Saint George's Day, a race was run in Ferrara.[76] Siena opted for the Feast of the Virgin in mid-August, though it, too, had at least three principal *palios* every year.[77] Verona and Pisa also held races on certain saints' days.[78] Though the *palios* were invariably scheduled on religious holidays, it is clear that they were, in essence, events meant to solidify the secular identities and associations of the townspeople, for the races often featured members of various occupational guilds. In Florence, the *Palio de Tintori* on Saint Onofrio's Day was run by the wool dyers, each of whom had a horse, ridden by a boy. The boy jockeys were often dressed in the liveries of their employers.[79] Sometimes, animals served as prizes: oxen, rams, cocks, geese, dogs, horses, hawks, and pigs are all recorded as awards.[80] These public races occasioned much high-spirited fun, but, as with large modern sporting events, fans could sometimes turn violent in their advocacy—and records suggest that rioting in the streets was not infrequent.[81]

Organized racing among the medieval aristocracy and gentry also appears in the later Middle Ages. These social groups, after all, were the ones who could afford to own horses, and even though members of the lower social orders may have been allowed to participate in horse racing as observers or as jockeys, it was not a sport for the poor. In England, there was a fashionable racing season during the Easter and Whitsuntide holidays.[82] In France, we have a cryptic record of horse racing sponsored by the local gentry in twelfth-century Villefranche; poor local villagers, however, seem to have been the ones who actually organized, and served as jockeys in, the races.[83]

Horse racing provided humans with a number of pleasures, gambling being one of them. But for those who actually served as riders, the pleasure would have been exhilaratingly competitive. The sport also affected the breeding of horses; the specialized racing animals, known as coursers, were selectively bred, and highly prized, for their swiftness.

ANIMAL–ANIMAL COMBAT GAMES

To most modern readers, the very idea of spectacles and games involving animals pitted against one another in mortal struggle, often after humans have antagonized them into heightened states of frenzy, seems cruel and unjustifiable. Yet games of this sort survived from antiquity into the modern period, where they flourish today in some communities. In the Middle Ages, the commonest games pitted domestic animals against one another, such as cockfighting and bullbaiting. Bearbaiting, however, involved a wild animal being attacked by domestic ones (dogs). Other, rarer, matches in this category include bull versus lion, ram versus lion, and ass versus lion, all of which are recorded in the late medieval period. There are even observations noting strange wild–wild pairings, such as a late medieval Italian spectacle involving arranged combat between a rhinoceros and an elephant (the elephant was too terrified to fight).[84]

Cockfighting is mentioned in William Fitzstephen's *Description of London* (ca. 1180) as particularly connected with schoolboys, who, on Shrove Tuesday, would bring their fighting cocks to school, where the schoolmasters would oversee the contests and be rewarded by being given the cocks involved.[85] Cockfighting was popular among schoolboys in France as well, a fact we know in part from the synodal interdiction issued in 1260 in Cognac prohibiting it.[86] There are also, however, records mentioning children's Lenten and Carnival cockfights from fourteenth-century France.[87] For a time, cockfighting even became fashionable as an adult sport among the nobility and gentry in England in the early fourteenth century—in spite of formal prohibition.[88] When organized by adults, cockfighting would have almost always been a betting game, and ecclesiastical interdiction of this sport was surely motivated by the desire to prevent gambling rather than by any tenderheartedness toward the animals involved. When sums of money are attached to the physical performance of animals, ways of enhancing the animal's odds of winning a contest are often developed. Although medieval illuminations do not clearly indicate the use of artificial spurs (devices commonly used in later versions of the game), such devices may have been used in the medieval period, at least by adult owners of fighting cocks.[89]

In the early thirteenth century, Alexander Neckam, in his *De laudibus sapientiae divinae*, wrote a vivid account of a medieval cockfight that clearly depicts the excitement created by observing the ferocity of the aroused birds.[90] At the very moments in the poem that might tend to cause modern readers to recoil from the brutality of the sport, namely those moments containing imagery of blood and flying feathers, Neckam grows most enthusiastic. Judging from Neckam's poem, and from two Middle English poems about the bravery of specific fighting cocks,[91] we can surmise that this sport was probably enjoyed in much the same fashion and for the same reasons as the human martial spectacles we have discussed earlier. Spectators carefully followed and analyzed each move of the embattled birds, praising those cocks that seemed to evince the greatest skill in attacking, feinting, and parrying. Cultural justification for the sport, then, would easily have been found in the tacit view that the participating animals were inherently noble and thus members of the fighting classes, who by nature are inclined to battle. Neckam's poem suggests as much, with its use of chivalric military imagery to describe the cocks. Moreover, in one late medieval French account book, we see this idea hinted at in an entry that records money being allotted to buy a royal youth a cock "à faire jouster."[92]

Bearbaiting was another ubiquitous medieval spectator sport. In England, it had been practiced since Anglo-Saxon times and was then specifically connected to royal courts. One record from pre-Conquest Norwich states that the city was required to provide the king with a bear and six dogs to accompany it,[93] and there is a bearbaiting scene in the eleventh-century *Bayeux Tapestry*.[94] The bear would be tethered to a stake, sometimes blinded, and dogs (such as mastiffs or bulldogs) would be let loose upon the restrained animal. (See Figure 4.3.) As in cockfighting, spectators were drawn to the ways in which the bear would defend itself from savage attack, continuing to fight back even when its head and body were covered in blood. Dogs used in this game were also at high risk of injury or death from the bear's teeth and claws, increasing

FIGURE 4.3: *Bearbaiting* (fourteenth century). British Library, London, Add. 42130, fol. 161r.

the likelihood that spectators would witness carnage.[95] Since we have explicit and detailed records from Elizabethan times suggesting that bearbaiting was favored in royal circles, we can probably assume that medieval royalty favored it as well. Richard III, for example, had a bear ward attached to his court; whether or not the bear under his guardianship was there for baiting we cannot know with certainty.[96] Our best English records, however, document bearbaiting as a public spectacle, carried out in bear gardens explicitly built for the purpose in London, where it was a winter sport.[97] Because the bear gardens were located in Southwark, a disreputable part of town that harbored the prostitute trade among other morally questionable forms of pleasure, it might be tempting to see this sport as one designed specifically for men's viewing, but later evidence decisively shows that in royal courts, at any rate, high-ranking women were honored members of the audience.[98] It is likely, too, that even rural villagers would have witnessed informal bearbaitings, for bear wards would often roam the countryside with their animals, and at country fairs and at alehouses they would make their animal available for baiting by dogs locally owned.[99]

Other animals were publicly baited in addition to bears: boars, bulls, badgers, apes, horses, and even asses have all appeared in this role in late medieval or early modern records.[100] Bullbaiting was routinely and informally practiced in late medieval towns before the animal was slaughtered for consumption—it was believed that the animal's meat would thereby be tenderized.[101] The expected outcome of bullbaitings involved the attack dogs being scooped up by the bulls' horns and thrown into the air so that their fall would injure and disable them. A good attack dog, however, would be able to avoid the bull's horns by plunging its teeth firmly into the bull's nose so that it could not be shaken off. The English breed of bulldog was, in fact, selectively bred to have a short snout, a large heavy head, and a projecting lower jaw to better enable such gripping.[102]

There are no extant ecclesiastical interdictions or prohibitions of either bullbaiting or bearbaiting. However, it may have been disparaged in the discourse of popular medieval preaching. In a Franciscan preacher's handbook of the fourteenth century, the author describes the cruelty with which the bears were treated: "we see that on feast-days a bear is ... violently dragged through the villages, tormented with beatings and torn by the dogs."[103] Similarly, there may be some compassion in John Trevisa's description of the bear, an animal who "is ymade blynde with a bright basyne and ybounde with cheynes ... and ytamed with betynge ... and goth therefore al day aboute the stake to the whiche he is strongeliche ytyed."[104]

Finally, in the Scandinavian countries, especially Iceland, horse fighting was a major public spectacle. As the saga literature represents the sport, young men's stallions would be pitted against each other in a kind of symbolic display of their owners' virility—and hostility; in fact, horse-fighting scenes usually predict or advance the feuds described in these texts.[105]

VILLAGE ANIMAL GAMES

In a number of organized sports, people in towns and villages all over Europe employed domestic animals as targets of aggression. One of these, often paired with cockfighting as part of Shrove Tuesday festivities, was "cock-stele" or "throwing at the cock," a boys' game that involved propping up, or burying up to its neck, a cock or a hen at which boys threw sticks.[106] Sometimes the animal was tied to a stake to serve as a moving target.[107] The game was over when the bird was dead. In France and Spain, there were other violent social practices employing poultry. One game, referred to in France as *l'arrachement du cou de l'oie*, had adolescent youths, in competition, attempting to pull off the necks of geese to present to their girlfriends as tokens of their esteem. Geese and cocks were also hung by their feet on cords stretched between two elevated platforms, with youths, sometimes on horseback, attempting to decapitate them with sticks in a vulgar imitation of quintain.[108] The action of killing poultry by focusing on their necks might have found some moral and logical sanction among the peasantry, since poultry were routinely killed for the stewpot by wringing the birds' necks or by swift decapitation. Perhaps these games thus found their justification in peasants' minds in the already routinized slaughter of the animals in everyday life. Likewise, there was a pig-slaughtering game in France, *getter au cochon*, in which four players were blindfolded, armed with sticks, and sent into an enclosure to beat a sow to death.[109] This game, too, was perhaps justified by the routine winter slaughter of domestic swine for consumption. Other similar French boys' games involved the butchering of sheep or cows, the flesh of which was subsequently consumed.[110] Certainly, among boys' rural diversions there are always those that involve animals, often as unfortunate victims. Keith Thomas records, for the early modern period, a number of activities engaged in by rural English boys, including poking birds' eyes out, cutting off pigs' tails as trophies, inflating live frogs by blowing into them with straws, hunting and killing squirrels, robbing birds' nests of their eggs, and so forth.[111] Some of these activities may have taken place in the course of securing food to supplement the sparse peasant diet. Nonetheless, it is important to note that casual infliction of pain and suffering on these animals was clearly considered within the bounds of normalcy. We can conclude that, in the medieval period, common wild animals found around rural habitations did not form part of the moral community of the humans living near them, a fact that we perhaps too readily think distinguishes medieval and early modern culture from our own.

A few other animal-centered games in the medieval period should be mentioned. One, recorded in France and Germany, involved town confraternities of archers who would hold an annual competition, *tir à l'oiseau* (Auvergne), or *jeu de l'oiseau* (Bourbon), both variants of a game generally called *jeu du papegault* or *jeu du perroquet*. This game involved using crossbows to shoot at either a live bird or at a painted wooden representation of a bird, mounted high on a platform.[112] Sponsored by rank-conscious and very hierarchical men's brotherhoods, this game was sometimes played on horseback and may well have been an imitation of the athletic martial games of the nobility, but employing the distinctly nonnoble weapon, the bow.[113] In Germany, in the year 1400, animal prizes—an ox and a goat—are recorded for this game.[114] Likewise, in village wrestling matches, animal prizes were common, especially rams, as Chaucer reminds us in his portrait of the Miller: "At wrastlynge he wolde have alwey the ram" (line 548).

Turning to the role of representations of animals, rather than animals themselves, in children's games, we can note the medieval French game, *queue au loup*, an imitation of pastoral life in which one player was identified as the shepherd and the others as wolves who would try to invade the shepherd's space to capture imaginary sheep.[115] But we must also consider the widespread use of hobbyhorses in late medieval and early modern Europe. From their appearance in medieval manuscript and early book illustrations, we can deduce that these toys could range from being simple sticks to being more complexly constructed contraptions with heads, necks, and manes. They testify, of course, to the importance of the horse in medieval culture, as well as to children's chivalric fantasies surrounding the figure of the knight.[116]

PERFORMING ANIMALS

There exists a continuous record of performing animals from antiquity through the Middle Ages, though surviving accounts of such entertainments are often terse, sometimes being nothing more than financial entries recording payments made to various minstrels or *joculatores* traveling with their trained beasts. Dogs, asses, apes, bears, horses, and monkeys traversed medieval Europe with their trainers, headed for the courts of royalty and the halls of the wealthy—any place where gathered crowds of privileged spectators might be willing to watch, and reward, the entertainment. Some of the entertainers merely exhibited their beasts (usually bears or apes, but also hares, horses, dogs, camels, and, rarely, lions).[117] But virtually all of the acts that leave traces of their content involve animals performing human behaviors, leading us to conclude that medieval observers found the breaching of the traditional animal–human divide to be the most entertaining form of animal entertainment. Easiest to imagine are the dancing animals, such as bears, dogs, and horses; visual evidence of their antics in the margins of medieval manuscripts show them with their trainers, sometimes even beating on small drums to accompany their

FIGURE 4.4: *Performing horse* (fourteenth century). The Bodleian Library, University of Oxford, MS Bodl. 264, fol. 96v.

own moves.[118] (See Figure 4.4.) Evidence of a trained bear, possibly playing dead, survives from the early Middle Ages, for in a tenth-century Psalter, a bear on a leash is pictured curled up in a sleeping position, with its trainer holding a switch in his hand.[119] In *Lippiflorium*, a twelfth-century Latin poem on the life of Bernhard of Lippe, we hear of a performer with a dog and a horse, both of which would imitate human actions on command.[120] From medieval Scandinavia, we have evidence that Harald Fairhair (late ninth to early tenth century) employed an entertainer with a trained dog: "he makes the king laugh," notes the thirteenth-century source.[121]

More complex animal imitations of human behavior are described as well. Alexander Neckam, in *De naturis rerum*, tells of jesters with small dancing apes that also rode astride dogs, imitating mounted knights in a tournament.[122] In a fourteenth-century manuscript, a dancing rooster is shown on stilts,[123] and apes could be taught to juggle, tumble, and push carts.[124] In apparent defiance of the fact of animal speechlessness, one early twelfth-century English manuscript depicts a muzzled bear being forcibly taught the alphabet by its trainer; the bear manages to voice an *A* in the depiction.[125] (See Figure 4.5.) There also seems to have been a traditional animal act featuring a weeping dog, references to which can be found in the twelfth-century German poem *Ruodlieb* and in the Middle English *Dame Sirith*.[126] Certainly bears were trained to carry out mock attacks on human actors, who would then wrestle with them in a fabricated drama of human victory over ferocious beasts.[127] In the *Acta sanctorum*, in the Life of Saint Poppo, we learn of a famous eleventh-century *ludus* that

FIGURE 4.5: *Performing bear* (twelfth century). Trinity College Cambridge, MS O.4.7, fol. 75r. © The Master and Fellows of Trinity College Cambridge.

included bears and a male actor with honey smeared on his exposed genitalia. The unfortunate actor ended up needing Poppo's saintly intervention.[128]

Traveling animal acts seem to have attracted professional performers willing to traverse long distances with their animals, seeking reward in the most auspicious social surroundings. In 1312, at Canterbury, the king was entertained by John de Colon, a Lombard minstrel, who had with him some performing snakes.[129] Many animals themselves traveled great distances before becoming participants in their trainers' acts. Although most performing animals in medieval Europe were common animals, such as horses and dogs, the fact that bears, monkeys, apes, and snakes were among these performers suggests that there was professional commerce in animals between central Europe and nations far removed from it, commerce separate and apart from the acquisition of exotic animals by the aristocracy for menageries. In the case of apes, Janson notes that the small Barbary ape of North Africa was the one most commonly imported and trained.[130] Bears probably came from Scandinavia,[131] their itinerant leaders, *ursinarii*, being alluded to frequently in medieval Latin documents.[132]

FIGURE 4.6: *Mummers wearing animal masks* (fourteenth century), The Bodleian Library, University of Oxford, MS Bodley 264, fol. 21v.

Although animals were commonly trained to imitate humans, it is also the case that human performers sometimes entertained crowds with their imitations of animals, another example of the attempt to breach the traditional animal–human divide. In medieval Provençal, textbooks for *joglars* urged prospective entertainers to learn the art of imitating birds.[133] One jongleur is mentioned who could counterfeit a cat and another an ass, including its distinctive bray.[134] In ca. 1300, the Bishop of Salisbury recorded actors using masks and costumes to impersonate dogs, birds, asses, and monkeys,[135] a practice vividly illustrated in a famous fourteenth-century French manuscript decorated with images of people in animal guises, specifically with stag, goat, ass, bull, and cock masks.[136] (See Figure 4.6.)

MASKS AND MUMMINGS

Human impersonation of animals was an extremely common medieval social practice, its importance extending beyond its mere entertainment value and reaching deep into medieval structures of popular belief. Since antiquity, animal impersonations had been ritualized as part of the Kalends of January celebrations, a time for rural communities to prepare for the upcoming agricultural season. Century after century, ecclesiastical prohibitions of the animal disguises commonly adopted during January festivities indicate exactly how widespread this practice was—and how enduring. Saint Augustine (fourth century) inveighs against people dressing up like horses or stags; Caesarius of Arles (late fifth century) warns his countrymen to stop the practice of putting on the heads of beasts; Isidore of Seville (seventh century) berates the Spanish rural population for their January adoption of the identities of beasts, cattle, and bull calves; Aldhelm of Malmesbury (seventh century) laments the practice among the West Saxons; Regino of Prüm (tenth century) warns his parishioners that they are behaving like pagans, going about in the guises of stags or calves; and Burchard of Worms (eleventh century) assigns 30 days' penance to those who put on the disguise of a stag or calf.[137] The reason for such vigorous ecclesiastical disapproval of these disguisings certainly had to do with their pagan origins, either in classical antiquity or in the local religions of Germanic and Celtic Europe. Christian interdiction, however, did not stop the practice, in part because the medieval folk calendar featured numerous annual festivals reflecting the closeness of the rural populace to the rhythms of the natural world, its animals included. Clearly, animals formed a fundamental part of medieval human consciousness.

Medieval folk practices involving animals and animal disguises sometimes hint at (or actually perform) the ancient rite of animal sacrifice. Chambers records Devonshire and Oxfordshire May Day ritual slayings of rams and lambs and the display of the heads and hides of dead horses and cattle, sometimes as parts of costuming for festival participants.[138] In Spain, France, and Germany (perhaps in England as well), the hobbyhorse often featured in village festivals, the adult version of this toy actually being a horse disguise that served, at least in some scholars' views, as a symbol of a sacrificial beast.[139] From the north and the east Midlands of England, there survives evidence of ritual dramas that took place on Plough Monday (the Monday after Twelfth Night); in these ritual dramas, local lads would impersonate the yoked oxen and would drag the plow, to be ritually blessed, through the streets of the village.[140] In an extant Scots version of a text of a performance from 1500, the killing of the old plow ox is mimed, and the finding of the new plow ox is celebrated.[141] Although the lost details of many medieval village festivals have been reconstructed by overzealous and overly imaginative nineteenth-century enthusiasts, enough indisputable evidence remains to convince us of the importance of animals in medieval village festival life. Their crucial role in agricultural success made them participants, both literally and symbolically, in the ritualized hopes and fears of the agricultural community.

The carnivalesque celebrations that took place in rural settings throughout the Kalends of January and that were so roundly criticized by ecclesiastical prohibition eventually showed up even in larger towns and cities, folded into New Years' celebrations involving the bourgeoisie and the lower clergy, celebrations that can be traced from the twelfth through the sixteenth centuries. These civic celebrations involving animals, namely the Feast of Fools or the Feast of the

Ass, took place primarily in France but have been recorded in both Flanders and Prague.[142] They seem to have had carnival dimensions. One such festival, in Beauvais, involved bringing a live ass into church; after a solemn Mass was conducted, the ass's bray was imitated, with parishioners joining in.[143]

Performers in animal disguises also entertained royalty in entirely secular settings. Froissart reports that at the 1389 coronation of Isabel of Bavaria, the wife of Charles VI of France, mummers dressed as a bear and a unicorn brought her gifts.[144] In 1384, the court of Edward I commissioned 53 masks to be made in the form of lions' heads, elephants' heads, and men's heads with bats' wings.[145] Boccaccio's *Decameron* depicts a secular festival at Saint Mark's (Venice) wherein a man dressed as a bear is displayed.[146]

Finally, it is worth noting the ways in which live animals may have been employed to play various roles in medieval religious drama. In 1223, Saint Francis is supposed to have staged a nativity scene using a live ox and ass to represent the animals present at Christ's birth. This form of Franciscan commemoration seems to have been theologically problematic, however, for Bonaventure's account of it takes precautions to suggest that papal approval had been secured beforehand.[147] But in later religious drama of the fourteenth through sixteenth centuries, live animals had become ecclesiastically sanctioned cast members of religious cycle plays, with locally available animals such as oxen, asses, doves, ravens, and horses almost certainly routinely featured.[148] Interestingly, in several European cycle dramas focusing on the torturing of Jesus before his crucifixion, both the dialogue and the action hauntingly suggest that he is to be briefly envisaged as an animal victim of gaming torturers. Led onto stage by a leash and spoken to as a recalcitrant beast, he is struck with sticks while the torturers mock him using terms drawn from children's games.[149] This animalization of Christ serves as a ghostly but powerful reminder of the centrality of the animal body in the sporting life of medieval Europeans, and it may also laconically register some horror at the cruelty of the accompanying torture.

CONCLUSION

Between 1000 and 1400, medieval people were frequently exposed to animals playing the parts of entertainers, engaging in public combat, or serving as displays of their owners' status. In all cases, the animals were objects of the human gaze in a complex drama underscoring medieval conceptions of identity and medieval beliefs about the fixities of social class. Many of these animals, especially those extracted from their native habitats and those pitted in combat against humans or other animals, clearly suffered while taking part in these social games and displays, with their physical needs ignored and thus their life spans shortened. Yet, even in this age of the cruel domination of animals by humanity, there are hints here and there of sympathy for these beasts. I have tried to include some of the compassionate, and thus perhaps dissenting, voices in the medieval period, voices that work against our having any overly monolithic view of the cultural significance of animals in the medieval world.

CHAPTER FIVE

Like a Book Written by God's Finger

Animals Showing the Path toward God

PIETER BEULLENS

The inclusion of a chapter dealing with science in *A Cultural History of Animals in the Medieval Age* is less evident than it seems at first sight. It implies that a science of animals existed as such between 1000 and 1400, a period that only partially covers what is generally known as the medieval age. Yet, even for this relatively short space in time it is virtually impossible to produce an overall view of approaches toward zoology without omitting interesting but less widely spread scientific attitudes regarding animal life. Therefore, the focus herein is on western Europe, thus ignoring most of the zoological research in the Byzantine empire and the Arabic world.

Measured by modern days' standards, the medieval approach to animals can hardly be called scientific. In our view, the validity of scientific research is first of all based on the systematic collection of facts on individual animals and single animal species through observation and experiment. The repetition of these events subsequently leads to the development of generally applicable theories and finally the establishment of fixed taxonomic relations between species.

It would be unfair to anachronistically judge medieval efforts in the field of zoology by these principles. The concepts on which they are based gradually developed over a longer period in the last centuries. Accordingly, the definition of scientific activity itself will have to be broadened to match the zoological interest of the period and to avoid the feeling of superiority based on our lack of understanding in the approach of the subject. The following passage, which discusses medieval moralistic interpretations of animal behavior, provides an enlightening example of this patronizing attitude: "Les balivernes que l'on y rencontre montrent bien la crédulité de ceux qui les écrivaient, les lisaient ou les propageaient. (…) Nous n'insisterons pas sur toute cette littérature qui relève davantage du folklore que de la Science." (The twaddle that one meets there nicely reveals the gullibility of those that wrote them, read them, or spread them. […] We will not dwell on this body of literature, which reveals more about folklore than about science.)[1]

Obviously, it was practically impossible for medieval researchers to compile the same amount of observations that zoologists in later periods brought together, as they did not have the leisure to collect them nor the means of transport to travel to distant regions. Nor did they want to: others had done better before them, and there was no need to question their authority. And even if they had doubts about the accuracy of the information, the matter was considered too futile to pursue it. It was simply inconceivable that a zoological subject matter could deserve that much interest as to promote it to a lifetime fulfilment.

Zoological knowledge was not pursued as an aim in itself. Knowledge of the animal world was seen as part of a more important goal. The better understanding of the animal world was valued as a means toward a deeper insight into the divine plan governing the sensitive world, God's creation. As a consequence of this point of view, no medieval author can exclusively be labeled a zoologist. Those writers who dealt with zoological topics did so within the framework of larger projects, either philosophical or theological, or even as part of medical studies. And when they studied animal life forms, they were also aware that all creatures are pointing toward God's existence, or, as it is written in the Gospel: "Invisibilia enim ipsius a creatura mundi per ea quae facta sunt, intellecta conspiciuntur" (Ever since the creation of the world, his invisible attributes of eternal power and divinity have been able to be understood and perceived in what he has made.).[2]

The awareness that God had created the world not only as a sign of his power, but also as a gift to humankind, was formulated in the first half of the twelfth century by Honorius of Autun (Honorius Augustodunensis) in his *Elucidarium* in a section entitled *De animalibus ad hominis bonum conditis* (About the animals that were preserved for the benefit of man):

The ants or the spiders, or similar beings that apply themselves to their tasks, are created for the purpose that we take them as examples for our study and our pious labour. Thus for him who contemplates it, God's

entire creation is a great delight, since in some creatures beauty can be
found, as in flowers; in others medicine, as in herbs; in others food, as in
crops; in others a meaning, as in worms and birds. Therefore, all things
are useful and created for man.[3]

Honorius's conclusion obviously refers to the words of God following the creation of man. God's mission to man included the liberty to make use of all
creatures of the world.

God blessed them, saying: Be fertile and multiply; fill the earth and sub-
due it. Have dominion over the fish of the sea, the birds of the air, and all
the living things that move on the earth.[4]

Further proof for these claims could be gained from Paul's first letter to the
Corinthians: "Numquid de bobus cura est Deo? An propter nos utique dicit?
Nam propter nos scripta sunt." (Is God concerned about oxen, or is he not re-
ally speaking for our sake? It was written for our sake.)[5]

Obviously, most Christian writers stressed the clear-cut line dividing beasts
from man. The latter was commissioned by God to rule creation and the animals living in it. Although scholastic literature did not shrink from questions
that explored the limits of the analogy between animals and man, such as
whether animals would resurrect or whether they were allowed to eat normally
during Lent, features that distinguish man from other living beings as a rational
being rather than resemblances with them were emphasized. No wonder, then,
that some of Aristotle's doctrines were incorporated without great problems
into Christian thought. His tripartition of the soul into a vegetative part (the
only part present in plants and similar life forms), a sensitive part (the sense
faculties shared by animals and man), and a rational part (the soul, which was
only found in man) became known in the Western world when the *De anima*
was translated for the first time from Greek into Latin by James of Venice in the
twelfth century. In the following century, the idea of the *scala naturae*, the gradual rise in complexity within the natural world, from plants to animals, with
intermediary life forms that are sometimes difficult to attribute to either class,
entered the Latin world by means of two different translations of *De historia
animalium*.[6] These sentences ended up as the most frequently quoted passage
from this enormous work in scholastic literature, along with another (apocryphal) sentence stating that man is the most noble and highest being (added by
the Latin translator Michael Scotus or by the author of his Arabic model).[7]

It is significant that the question of man's definition is seldom explicitly
addressed in medieval literature. Since God had made man the ruler of the
world and its creatures, there was no continuous line from the other life forms
to humankind, as we have grown accustomed to since the introduction of the

theory of evolution. It is not surprising, then, that even in the rare cases where a definition of man is proposed, there is no attempt to single out the features that distinguish him from the animals.

Since animals are on an incomparably lower level than humans, there seems to be no compelling reason to study zoology, unless it can lead to a better understanding of God's plan with the world. It may well be that the medieval writers interpreted Saint Augustine's words in that way, although in the same passage the church father warned his readers against the vain pursuit of secular knowledge out of mere curiosity.

> An ignorance of things makes figurative expressions obscure when we are ignorant of the natures of animals, or stones, or plants, or other things which are often used in the Scriptures for purposes of constructing similitudes. Thus the well-known fact that a serpent exposes its whole body in order to protect its head from those attacking it illustrates the sense of the Lord's admonition that we be wise like serpents. That is, for the sake of our head, which is Christ, we should offer our bodies to persecutors lest the Christian faith be in a manner killed in us, and in an effort to save our bodies we deny God. It is also said that the serpent, having forced its way through narrow openings, sheds its skin and renews its vigor. How well this conforms to our imitation of the wisdom of the serpent when we shed the "old man," as the Apostle says, and put on the "new"; and we shed it in narrow places, for the Lord directs us, "Enter ye in at the narrow gate." Just as a knowledge of the nature of serpents illuminates the many similitudes which Scripture frequently makes with that animal, an ignorance of many other animals which are also used for comparisons is a great impediment to understanding.[8]

The treatment of the subject as Augustine recommended it in late antiquity may find some points of comparison with the medieval Biblical exegesis, where the literal sense of the word only formed one part of its meaning, carrying and sometimes even hiding the allegorical and moral aspects of the message, as Thomas Aquinas learned in his *Summa theologica*:

> That God is the author of holy Scripture should be acknowledged, and he has the power, not only of adapting words to convey meanings (which man also can do), but also of adapting things themselves. In every branch of knowledge words have meaning, but what is special here is that the things meant by the words also themselves mean something.[9]

As the approach in animal studies did not necessarily start from correct and factual information, but rather asked for data that was fit for interpretation and allegory, it entails that students of the medieval science of animals mainly worked from literary sources and did not build on their own experience. Thus, the search for similitudes was the predominant characteristic of zoological research as it was carried out for most of the Middle Ages.

SIMILITUDO

Physiologus

The most widely consulted tool for knowledge of the animal world in the Middle Ages was known under the name of *Physiologus*. The text probably originated in the early Christian era in Egypt, but it was so often translated, revised, and abbreviated from late antiquity onward to the fifteenth century that the text has to be considered as a genuine medieval product.[10] The original Greek text combined zoological facts and fictions with Christian moralizations and allegories. The question is still open to debate whether a single author wrote the full text or different writers independently conceived the nearly fifty zoological sections and added the moralizing comments in subsequent stages. (See Figure 5.1.) The various attributions in the manuscripts, to King Salomo, Saint Basil, and Saint John Chrysostomus, among others, are definitely apocryphal. The work was known as *Physiologus* since many of its sections begin with the sentence "The *physiologus* (naturalist) says. ..." Already in late antiquity a Coptic version was made, which is only fragmentarily extant. It was also translated into Ethiopic, Armenian, Syriac, and Arabic. The earliest Latin translation of the *Physiologus* probably dates back to late antiquity as well, since it contains several verses from the *Vetus Latina*, the Latin Bible translation that was current until the fifth century, when it was gradually superseded by Saint Jerome's *Vulgata*. Admittedly, though, no Latin manuscripts prior to the eighth century are preserved.[11]

More importantly, the text proved extremely susceptible to changes and revisions. Three different Greek versions were completed before the end of the thirteenth century.[12] In the Latin West, many more adaptations were composed, both in prose and in verse, some of which only survive in single manuscripts. Others developed into standard school texts and were widely spread. The text was also translated into numerous vernacular languages. Most of the information about animal behavior in the *Physiologus* is equally found in other ancient sources. Aristotle, Pliny, Plutarch, and Aelian provide for the majority of the parallels, though it is not always possible to distinguish between source and influence. The work's adjustments of the subject matter in order to make it suitable for allegorical interpretations have no parallel in ancient literature.

tursima &dum uider & uirginem statim uenit man
suetus &insinuerur se conlocat. Et dum calefia siceu
portat festinans indomoreges. Nam nullus eum
uenctor adphendere uale Ja&saluator noster e
dequoppheta dix. Erexit cornu salutis nobis indo
mo dauid. Dumenim insctm uideretur null i reges
nulliq. potestaer maligne ualuerunt nocere eum.
cum uerbum caro factu e &habitauit innobis.

OECERAO   Physiolocus dicit quia
inimicus e draconis &psequitur occidere eu uult.
Dum fugerit draco inteeum &absconderit se in
scissuris uelocit cer uus uadit adfontem &impla
uisceratua aqua multa &uenienf uomens posteu.
Turbatur draco abaqua exit &absorb & eu cer uus.
Itaque dns ihs xps e.draconem magnum diabolum

FIGURE 5.1: *Stag. Physiologus*, Burgerbibliothek Bern, MS 318, fol. 17r.

Bestiaries

Alterations within the *Physiologus*'s content and composition were sometimes so far reaching that the results could no longer be considered as revisions but rather constituted new works on their own strength. Although their basic material was drawn from the *Physiologus*, they incorporated information from other sources as well. These reworkings are commonly known under the general denomination of *bestiary*, a type of text that started to surface from the twelfth century onward. Its influence cannot be overestimated. Within the field of literature alone it stretched to the chivalric love prose in the form of Richard de Fournival's thirteenth-century *Li bestiaire d'amour*, in which a knight tries to convince his loved one that they are meant for each other by conveniently interpreting instances of animal behavior. Christian moralizing was aptly changed into counseling for desperate lovers.

Several attempts have been made to classify the various types of bestiaries available in the Latin manuscripts into families. The earliest classification was made by James in 1928.[13] He divided the manuscripts that he had been able to catalog into four different families. McCulloch refined the distribution into families by defining subfamilies within them.[14] Though this classification system is not undisputed, it remains the most generally accepted view regarding the relations between the different stages in the development of the bestiary.[15]

According to this classification, each manuscript family is characterized by its own rearrangement and ordering of the original *Physiologus* chapters and by the sources from which additional chapters were incorporated. The first family excerpted Isidore of Seville's encyclopedia *Etymologiae* (seventh century AD). His work was based on Latin authors from antiquity who wrote about animal history, in particular the encyclopedia of Pliny the Elder and Solinus's travel guide, which displays a special interest in marvelous creatures and places. Isidore's focus on the etymology of animal names is reflected in the newly added sections of this family's manuscripts. In the second manuscript group more information that came directly from Isidore's sources and from Hrabanus Maurus (ninth century AD) was included. The smaller third and fourth families expanded the work even further, incorporating details about fabulous humans and peoples. In general, they create new sections while they rely on the same sources as the others.

Not just the text of the bestiary varies according to the family to which it belongs and the sources that were used. The illustrations, which in many instances raise the manuscripts to the status of lavish works of art, originate from very diverse backgrounds as well. Many of them go back to antiquity, when manuscripts of the *Physiologus* with illustrations must already have circulated. Others were based on the illustrated copies of the Book of Creation or its commentaries, while images from ancient zoological and geographical works also certainly influenced their illustrations.

The *Physiologus* and the bestiaries had a huge impact on literature and iconography, in particular on heraldic emblems. The stories about the pelican who kills its young and opens its breast after three days to revive them or about the unicorn captured by a virgin were widely known and represented in iconography after having been turned into common knowledge under the influence of the images in bestiary manuscripts. This fact does not mean, however, that people really believed that those reports were accurate. Isidore of Seville already mentioned both stories with a reference to other anonymous sources, thus expressing his doubts about the veracity of the information.[16] What really counted was the similitude, the suitability of the subject matter to illustrate theological or moral learning. As the target audience of bestiaries was mostly illiterate, they mainly conveyed their message by means of their illustrations. For those who could read, but knew little or no Latin, many versions in vernacular languages were made, both in prose and in verse, most of them in French or English, although examples in nearly all European languages are documented, including Icelandic, Welsh, and Provençal.

The latest examples of lavishly illustrated bestiaries date from the early fourteenth century. It may well be that new forms of encyclopedic knowledge transfer, which included the new scientific insights gained through the works of Aristotle, reduced the interest in bestiaries, and eventually totally eclipsed them.

Aviarium

The huge popularity of bestiaries prompted the composition of similar works with a more limited scope and interest, like the *Aviarium,* which exclusively deals with birds in an allegorical way. Hugh of Fouilloy, a canon of the order of Saint Augustine, who lived near Amiens, wrote it around 1130–1140. The popularity of the book can be measured from the 125 manuscript copies that were preserved, as well as a French rhymed and a Portuguese prose translation. Moreover, it influenced several bestiary manuscripts of the first family, including the famous Aberdeen and Ashmole bestiaries.[17]

The work contains two separate sections. The first opens with a long meditation on the allegorical meanings of the dove as they are found in the scriptures. (See Figure 5.2.) After short paragraphs on each of the four winds, the writer turns to the most exquisite hunting bird, the hawk, and its features. Then follows the treatment of two birds that form the hawk's prey, the turtledove and the sparrow. In the second section, twenty-three birds and their characteristics are discussed in a catalog consisting of the same number of chapters. They draw mostly on information found in the works of Isidore of Seville and Hrabanus Maurus. Hugh directs the allegories to life in the monasteries. The intended audiences were the lay brothers, who had not yet received the required formation before taking on the monastic life. His book was conceived from the beginning as an illustrated learning tool, in which text and image were combined to facilitate memory: "For what Scripture means to the teachers, the picture means to simple folk."[18] On some pages the text was ordered in the form of a diagram around the illustration to make the general outline of the content readily visible.

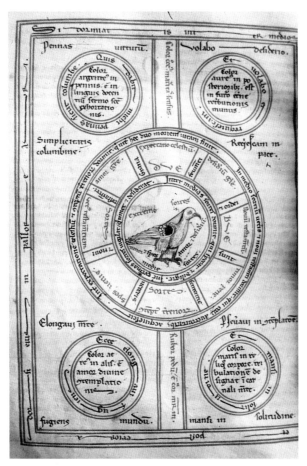

FIGURE 5.2: *Dove diagram*. Hugh of Fouilloy, *Aviarium*
(thirteenth century), Stift Klosterneuburg, MS 929, fol. 126v.

As can be assumed on the basis of the work's purpose, a great number of
extant manuscript copies originate from monastic circles, mainly Cistercian and
Benedictine, and to a lesser degree from Dominican or Franciscan friars.[19] It is
argued that the recently founded friar orders focused their scholarly attention
on philosophy and science, while the older orders held on to more traditional
approaches toward theology. As a result, the Dominicans seem to have been the
first to absorb sources that became newly available in the thirteenth century.[20]

AUCTORITAS

Aristotle Translated

The thirteenth-century Dominican writer Thomas of Cantimpré opens the prologue to his encyclopedic work *De natura rerum* by listing the written sources
he used.

So these are the writers who illustrate the following work. First of all there is Aristotle. He took pride of place above all others not only in this field, but also in all fields that touch upon philosophical research. Pliny comes second. He also is venerable for his Antiquity and his authority, and he shone as a prolific writer amongst the authors who treat these subjects. We put Solinus in third place. He is very admirable for his eloquence in the book he published about the wonders of the world. As an industrious researcher he included numerous details about the nature of things into the work. Fourth is the blessed bishop Ambrose of Milan. He distinguishes many features regarding beasts and birds in the book that is called *Exameron*. He certainly followed on all points, by his style of writing as well as by the order, Basil the Great in his book that he published in the Greek language, equally under the title *Exameron*. We also deemed some of his opinions worthy of inclusion into our work at the right places, which the blessed Ambrosius certainly did not include for the sake of brevity. The fifth is bishop Isidore, who in his book *Etymologies* covers a wide field and is very useful.[21]

It does not come as a surprise that Cantimpré refers to the vast richness of the zoological work by the elder Pliny's work, an author who enjoyed a relatively large popularity during the Middle Ages.[22] Solinus, the third-century author of a work about remarkable phenomena, and the commentaries on the six days of creation by the church fathers Ambrose and Basil, were also traditional sources of zoological knowledge used by the compilers of the bestiaries. What is new, however, is that pride of place is taken by Aristotle's recently discovered zoology.

Aristotle was already an authority in the Latin world long before the thirteenth century. He was most often simply referred to as *philosophus,* the philosopher beyond competition. While very few people were able to read his works in the original Greek, Latin translations gradually conquered the intellectual world of the West. Aristotle's logical works, translated and commented upon by Boethius in late antiquity, formed the standard introduction to the curriculum of advanced studies, and most of his treatises on natural philosophy and ethics had been translated in the previous century from Arabic intermediaries or directly from the Greek original by scholars such as Gerard of Cremona, James of Venice, and Burgundio of Pisa.[23]

Cantimpré gained access to the philosopher's zoological books through a Latin translation that had recently become available. In the early decades of the thirteenth century, Michael Scotus had translated Aristotle's three major treatises on zoology into Latin from an Arabic version, in which *De historia animalium* (History of animals, ten books), *De partibus animalium* (Parts of animals, four books) and *De generatione animalium* (Generation of animals, five books) were molded into a unity of nineteen books.[24] At that time Scotus worked in Toledo, where interaction among Christian, Jewish, and Arabic scholars made science flourish. His work attracted the attention of Frederick II of Hohenstaufen, who invited him to his court in southern Italy. There in around 1230, Scotus translated what looks like an extensive compendium of the commentary on the nineteen books of Aristotle's zoology by the Arabic philosopher Avicenna (Ibn Sinā), which became known to the Latin Middle Ages under the name *Abbreviatio Avicenne*.

Almost half a century later, in around 1260, the Dominican friar William of Moerbeke, who eventually became the Latin archbishop of Corinth, translated the same treatises as in Scotus's version, but this time directly from the Greek.[25] His efforts were part of a larger project to correct the existing Greek–Latin translations of Aristotle's works and to make new ones for those that had not yet been directly translated from Greek into Latin. Besides this, Moerbeke translated a number of Greek commentaries on the works of Aristotle, as well as several other texts with philosophical or scientific contents. In the process he enriched the zoological corpus with two shorter treatises, *De motu animalium* (Movement of animals) and *De progressu animalium* (Locomotion of animals), which were previously unknown from other—Arabic—intermediaries.[26] He thus expanded it to twenty-one books in all, a formidable body of transmitted knowledge, though still less than half of the fifty books on animals that Pliny credited Aristotle with, as Roger Bacon testified, not without regret: "Quinquaginta etiam libros fecit de animalibus praeclaros, ut Plinius dicit octavo Naturalium et vidi in Graeco; sed Latini non habent nisi decem novem libellos miseros imperfectos" ([Aristotle] also composed fifty famous books on animals, as Pliny says in the eighth book of the *Natural History* and as I saw in Greek; yet the Latins merely have nineteen miserable and imperfect books.).[27]

Bacon's commentary on *De animalibus* unfortunately no longer survives, but his statement that he saw the books in Greek must be doubted. The fact that he only saw nineteen books—apparently in Scotus's translation—is more significant. While Moerbeke's other translations often eclipsed the older versions, in the case of the zoological works Moerbeke's translation did not completely replace Scotus's: it is preserved in about forty manuscripts, while Scotus's is found in approximately sixty. Yet, the former is obviously more complete and closer to the Greek text. It is possible that the rigidity of Moerbeke's translation method, which consistently renders every syntactical nuance of the Greek original, and introduces numerous nearly incomprehensible words transcribed from the Greek, was defeated by the greater fluency of Scotus and his Arabic intermediary, although that equally contained plenty of barbarisms.

As for the two smaller treatises, Moerbeke's versions yield over one hundred copies each. The reason for their greater popularity must lie in the fact that they were often combined with other shorter Aristotelian texts known

FIGURE 5.3: *Human and animal parts.* Moerbeke's translation of Aristotle, *De partibus animalium*, Merton College, Oxford, MS 271, fol. 100v. © The Warden and Fellows of Merton College Oxford

under the common denominator of *Parva naturalia*. Finally, two anonymous Greek–Latin translations, one of *De partibus animalium*, the other of *De motu animalium*, were not widely spread: the former is extant in a *codex unicus*, while the latter was indirectly preserved in the form of quotations incorporated within the commentary on the treatise by Albert the Great.[28] (See Figure 5.3.)

Aristotle and Zoology

The newly acquired access to Aristotle's zoology opened possibilities for a wholly innovative approach to the science of animals. Following Pliny's zoological work, animals and their characteristics were traditionally treated according to their species. Chapters in zoological works were often arranged along with the larger animal classes, usually consisting of the four-footed animals (*quadrupedia*), birds (*aves*), aquatic animals (*aquatilia*, which not only included fish, but also water reptiles and even water-dwelling mammals or birds), snakes (*serpentes* or *reptilia*), and vermin (*vermes*), an ill-defined collection of insects, worms, and other small animals. Aristotle's works, however, provided studies of general themes such as animal parts or procreation cutting through all species and observing and analyzing analogies and differences between them. His taxonomy divided the animal kingdom between blooded and bloodless animals. Within each group, further divisions were made into large classes: blooded animals included four-footed life-bearing animals (more or less coinciding with the modern class of mammals), birds, fish (including the cetaceans, although he was quite aware that they formed a group with different characteristics, being live-bearing and lactating their young), and four-footed egg-bearing animals and snakes. The division of the bloodless animals, which were all indistinctly treated as *vermes* in the traditional medieval taxonomy, posed serious problems to the medieval mind. Aristotle distinguished between the soft-bodied or cephalopods, the soft-shelled or *crustacea,* the hard-shelled or *testacea,* and the incised or insects. Yet, it would be anachronistic to credit Aristotle with the development of a hierarchical classification of the Linnaean kind. Nor did he intend to develop one. Aristotle deliberately changed the contents of his groups and classes whenever he judged it fitting, in order to provide a better understanding of the differences and analogies between them. The kind of systematization that the taxonomists of the eighteenth century were so fond of is totally absent from the philosopher's works.

In any case, as one considers the relatively low number of extant manuscripts of both Latin versions, it must be concluded that Aristotle's zoology never enjoyed the same interest as other sections of his output. Yet, several universities, notably those of Paris and Oxford, put his works on animals on the curriculum of the advanced students from the mid-thirteenth century onward. Probably, the production costs of the large manuscripts that could contain these lengthy works may have prevented them from being copied on a really massive scale.

Aristotle Summarized

The size of Aristotle's zoological works may also partly explain the fact that the content of the works was soon spread in different, more condensed, forms. Instead of copying the entire text, summaries and anthologies started to circulate. In addition to their more economical sizes, these types of summaries offered the advantage that they grouped all relevant quotations concerning a specific topic or animal species under one entry. Thus, there was no longer any need for the cumbersome excerpting of massive volumes in search of information spread throughout the work. The desire for an editorial intervention in that direction was no innovation of the Middle Ages, though. Already by the second century BC, Aristophanes of Byzantium had condensed the Aristotelian zoology in an *Epitome,* or summary.[29] He explicitly stated that his aim was to make the work easier to handle, as information no longer had to be gathered from different chapters and books of the work. Moreover, since the rise of paradoxographical literature in the Hellenistic period, interests had shifted toward animal behavior and ethology, with a particular taste for the marvelous, rather than for further causal explanation. Unfortunately, the exact content of the *Epitome,* as well as its immediate sources, cannot be traced without great difficulty, as only the first two books of the work are extant in the truncated and revised form it received in the tenth century during the reign of the Byzantine emperor Constantine VII Porphyrogennetos.

Some manuscripts of both Scotus and Moerbeke's translations still contain traces of the preparatory activity in view of abridgement. Their margins display catchwords referring to the content of the passages, as if a reader had used the book for the preparation of a personal filing card system.[30] As a result of this practice, the users of abbreviated versions of various kinds ran the risk of losing sight of the overall structure of Aristotle's works. Although a complete survey of the various abbreviated forms in which Aristotle's zoology circulated is indispensable for the correct understanding of its reception in the Latin Middle Ages, an exhaustive study has not yet been made. The inventory of manuscript witnesses and the study of some cases in point have so far yielded interesting results.[31] In their most condensed form, Aristotle's books on animals were reduced to glossaries, in which catchwords in alphabetical order introduced noteworthy quotations from the philosopher's work. Several manuscripts from the fourteenth and fifteenth centuries are reported, but a comprehensive study of the literary genre is still lacking.

The most influential and widely spread condensed form in which Aristotle's thought was conveyed was the compilation known as *Auctoritates Aristotelis* or *Parvi Flores,* recently attributed to Johannes de Fonte.[32] Several hundreds of manuscripts and some forty early-printed editions of the anthology have been listed. It contains quotations from many works of Aristotle and some other philosophers, including Moerbeke's *De motu animalium,* and the other zoological works in Scotus's translation. The entries are grouped under the titles of the separate works.

Another anthology with specific interest to the books on animals bears the title *Auctoritates extracte de libro Aristotilis de naturis animalium* in some of the ten manuscripts that have preserved it.[33] The anonymous compiler arranged the excerpts thematically according to a clear plan, starting with the general statements such as the influence of the sun and the moon on the inferior bodies, then proceeding to the parts and humids in the living beings, and their acts, finally separately surveying animal species according to the larger divisions, namely, land-dwelling animals (starting with man), birds, fish (including dolphins and frogs), and insects (including spiders).

The content of Aristotle's work was condensed into full prose summaries as well. It seems that at least two different abstracts circulated. Three English manuscripts preserve fragments of an incomplete compendium from the end of the thirteenth century, while several later manuscripts of German origin still await positive identification of their precise contents. Finally, a more surprising use of Aristotelian knowledge turned up in three English manuscripts from the fourteenth century.[34] They contain an anonymous compilation of the nineteen books on animals enriched with allegorical commentaries. Zoological facts are excerpted and then put to parenetical use, with explicit reference to specific groups within the society of the secular and the religious.

The abbreviated forms under which Aristotle's biology circulated allow for two concluding observations. A first observation, which is somewhat difficult to substantiate, is that most of these collections originated within the mendicant orders of Franciscan and Dominican friars. As the last example shows, they were at pains to bring the knowledge of the ancient authorities in accord with Christian doctrine. Yet, while other clerics preferred to use traditional material available from the bestiaries, the newly founded orders explored the more recently acquired knowledge from Aristotle's writings, which for some reeked of heresy. As a second remark, it is interesting to notice that all compilations were based on Scotus's translation from the Arabic; only one manuscript preserves an anthology from Moerbeke's translations.[35] This is all the more surprising if one considers the fact that Moerbeke was a Dominican friar himself and most certainly worked under orders from his superiors.

Aristotle Commented

As for the academic level, it was mainly but not exclusively dominated by Scotus's translation. The truncated commentary by Peter Gallego, confessor of King Alfonso X the Sage, preserved in a *codex unicus*, takes a somewhat separate position, as its author claims that he read the books on animals in Arabic and Latin, and that he translated a summary that he subsequently commented on and glossed. It was recently established that his translation is actually a reordered summary of Scotus's version.[36] Another commentary in the form of *quaestiones* was the subject of a recent scholarly discussion. It was thought that Petrus Hispanus, who was identified as the later Pope John XXI, wrote two successive versions of his commentary on *De animalibus*. However, in the last decade it has been confirmed that two different authors were at work and that neither of them were identified with the eventual pontiff. Whoever were the authors of these commentaries, they afford an interesting view of the endeavors of mid-thirteenth-century scholars to bring the new Aristotelian science into accordance with ancient medical learning, most of which was transmitted through the writings of Arabic authors.[37]

Gerard of Breuil wrote the only commentary on the three major treatises that takes Moerbeke's translation as its starting point late in the thirteenth century.[38] There are very few biographical details available about him. Gerard proceeds along a very strict method. He first divides and paraphrases the text and focuses in the process on the difficulties that the translation of Moerbeke brings about by comparing it with the corresponding passage in Scotus's version. Finally, he formulates a number of questions, mainly concerning medicine and human embryology. His method is typical of scholasticism, without great originality. As for the knowledge of the animal world, Gerard disappointingly offers little progress, as the following example tellingly shows. When confronted with a passage where Aristotle quotes several fish species, Gerard leaves the paragraph uncommented on, adding the following: "Et illa pars habet tot partes quot sunt modi piscium in quibus inducit ibi et patent omnia nisi quantum barbaries nominum impedit." (And that passage has as many parts as there are types of fish that he considers, and everything is understandable insofar as the strangeness of the names does not impede it.).[39] Yet, Gerard's commentary was the most successful in its kind, as some ten manuscript copies of it survive— yet, his modest success leaves him a respectful distance from Albert the Great, whose works on *De animalibus* will be dealt with subsequently.

Encyclopedias

The availability of the Aristotle translations in the thirteenth century also seems to have sparked the rise of a new literary genre, the natural encyclopedia. Key figures were Bartholomaeus Anglicus (*De proprietatibus rerum*), Vincent of Beauvais (*Speculum universale*), and Thomas of Cantimpré (*De natura rerum*). Not surprisingly, the three of them belonged to the friar orders: the first was a Franciscan, and the latter two were Dominicans. Their working methods are comparable: they claim that their work was begun at the request of their brethren, and that it resulted from team effort. The ultimate objective of their work was to facilitate the preparation of sermons. The idea was that a better knowledge of the natural world directly leads to the understanding of the divine grace, as Vincent metaphorically formulated it: "Mundus iste sensibilis, quasi quidam liber est scriptus digito Dei" (This sensible world is like a book, written by the finger of God.).[40]

Of these three enterprises, Vincent's was the most encompassing. Starting with the *Speculum naturale* about the natural world, he and his team later added the *Speculum doctrinale*, a student's guide to scholastic knowledge, and the *Speculum historiale*, a world history. With the posthumously finished part on ethics (*Speculum morale*) it formed the formidable *Speculum universale* or *Speculum maius*. Interestingly, the three compilers quite deliberately order their material on natural history in different ways and thus implicitly reveal their view of the organization in the universe. Vincent follows the sequence of the six days of creation, ending with the animal world and man. Bartholomaeus respects the hierarchy by starting with God and the angels and then gradually reaches man and finally the animals and plants. Thomas starts with man, his anatomy and his immortal soul. Perhaps he remembered Aristotle correctly, who says that scientific research should start from what is best known and closest. After the treatment of the monstrous men of the Orient, Thomas progresses with animals according to their traditional classes, then plants and the inanimate materials.[41]

Thomas's composition in particular shows a great preoccupation with improving his work and keeping it up to date. During his lifetime, a revision was produced, and some manuscripts demonstrate that he was continually adding, correcting, or withdrawing material. More than two hundred manuscripts preserve the text, either in the versions Thomas prepared himself, or in two other, posthumous redactions. Albert the Great largely relied on Thomas for the compilation of the last part of his work *De animalibus*.[42] The encyclopedias were also spread through various vernacular translations. At the end of the thirteenth century, Jacob van Maerlant made a Middle Dutch rhymed adaptation of long sections from Thomas's encyclopedia and of parts of Vincent's historical outline.[43] (See Figure 5.4.) In the fourteenth century, Konrad von Megenberg translated Thomas into German, while Jean Corbichon made Barthomaeus's compilation available in French.

Thomas of Cantimpré also produced a treatise on the life of bees, which can more or less be seen as an offshoot of his encyclopedic work. The *Bonum universale de apibus* is a moralistic and didactic work, which illustrates the life in a monastic community through comparison with the beehive. Thomas's main source of zoological information is Pliny, but he often explicitly refers to his own encyclopedia. He also shows good knowledge of Seneca's moral letters. The use of a zoological simile as a guide to the monastic life strongly calls to mind Hugh of Fouilloy's *Aviarium*. It may well be that the use of classical sources as opposed to the traditional bestiary lore provided the Dominican counterpart for this work. Its spread in over one hundred manuscripts and several vernacular translations confirms the attraction it exerted.[44]

Preaching Tools

By the end of the thirteenth century, Aristotle's zoology was fully absorbed into the teaching at universities and in religious orders. Its use within biblical commentaries and moralizations had become generally accepted. The works of the Dominican theologian Thomas Waleys (first half of the fourteenth century) display his knowledge of Aristotle's *De animalibus* and the commentaries of Avicenna and Albert the Great on almost every page.[45] An interesting sample of

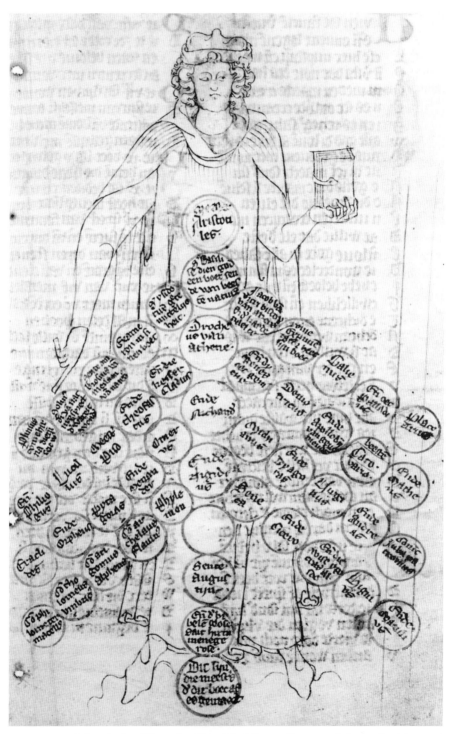

FIGURE 5.4: *Aristotle (or Albert the Great) holding a diagram of the authorities used by Thomas of Cantimpré.* Maerlant, *Der naturen bloeme.* Koninklijke Bibliotheek van België, Brussels, MS 19.546, fol. 2r. © Royal Library of Belgium.

how zoological knowledge was assimilated by students is found in a student's notebook, which until recently had remained unnoticed.[46] The poor quality of the parchment, crammed with tiny handwriting, shows that the owner had little financial means. The small volume contains reading notes: it is obvious that a student, possibly an English Dominican, had taken down those passages that seemed useful to him. Some entries were filed under subject headings, while other items were presented in the form of diagrams to distinguish various approaches to the same subject. For the sake of convenience, the scribe had introduced an elaborate internal reference system in the margins and between the columns. The manuscript also contains sample sermons developing themes such as penitence, preachers, or silence.

This type of quarry book remained in use for several centuries. A similar collection of sample sermons is extant under the heading *Proprietates rerum naturalium adaptate sermonibus de tempore per totius anni circulum* (The properties of things of nature adapted to sermons following the time of the whole year's cycle). The sermons in this collection are arranged in the chronological order of the feasts of the liturgical calendar for which they were to be used.[47]

EXPERIENTIA

The preceding sections may somewhat misleadingly suggest that zoology in the Middle Ages equaled philology and that the authority of ancient sources had a greater weight than experience gained from observation. There are, however, several examples of a real sense of empirical exploration. It seems that Frederick II of Hohenstaufen (1194–1250), an educated monarch, and his court displayed particular interest in what can be called practical zoology.

Frederick of Hohenstaufen

In the mid-thirteenth century, southern Italy and Sicily were the point where Latin, Greek, and Arabic cultures met. Frederick had a keen eye for scientific talent, and he attracted scientists and translators, such as Michael Scotus, to his court. Frederick certainly studied Aristotle's writings in detail, but when he finally decided to have his experience of falconry taken down in the form of the book *De arte venandi cum avibus* (The art of falconry), he emphatically distanced himself from Aristotle's mistakes, which were apparently caused by his lack of practical experience in the field.

> In our writing we followed Aristotle where it was appropriate. For on many points, as we learned by experience, and in particular on the characteristics of certain birds, he appears to be inconsistent with the facts. Therefore, we do not follow the prince of the philosophers on all points, as he seldom or

never was engaged in falconry, while we always loved it and were engaged
in it. Yet, on many points that he cites in his book *On Animals* he reports
that others have reported so, although he may not have seen it himself, nor
had his informers seen it. For firm reliability is not produced by hearsay.[48]

On the basis of this statement, it cannot come as a surprise that Frederick
entertained an impressive menagerie in his palace.

A similar ambiguous relation between ancient authority and applied knowledge can be observed in the field of hippiatry, as it is witnessed at the Sicilian
court. Shortly after Frederick's death, the head of the imperial stables, Jordanus
Rufus, published a work about the breeding and curing of horses. The treatise shows, as his master would have wanted, that is was based on hard-won
experience. Jordanus displayed a modern-looking approach to horse diseases:
he observed the symptoms, then looked for their causes, and finally applied the
appropriate remedies. The work's influence can be gathered from the twenty-six
Latin manuscripts that are still extant. In addition, translations were made in
six vernacular languages. In the end, it proved to be the precursor to a long list
of similar works on the same topic.[49]

Yet, ancient knowledge was not abandoned. As a counterweight, or so it
seems, Bartholomew of Messina, who translated several medical and pseudo-
Aristotelian texts at the court of the Sicilian King Manfred (1258–1266), made
a Latin version of the Byzantine *Mulomedicina* by Hierocles. The extraordinary blend at the Sicilian court of experimental research on the one hand and
thorough knowledge of ancient learning on the other may ultimately derive
from the practice at the medical school of Salerno. Frederick had been a student at that university. He may have had access to a remarkable text that was
probably written in the second half of the previous century by Copho the Salernitan. In the opening lines of the so-called *Anatomia porci* (Anatomy of a pig),
the author suggests that the unknown interior of man can be effectively studied
by dissecting a pig. (See Figure 5.5.)

> Since the composition of the interior members of the human body was
> generally unknown, the ancient physicians, and Galen most of all, resolved
> to expose the positions of the internal organs by dissecting animals. Al-
> though among the animals certain ones, such as the monkeys, appear to
> resemble us externally, and others such as the pig, internally, the internal
> structure of none appears to be more like ours than is that of the pig, and
> therefore we shall conduct an anatomy upon this animal.[50]

Although the text at least partially relies on ancient written sources, and although the question as to whether it describes a genuine dissection is still
open to debate, it is noteworthy that it evokes the possibility to gain scientific

FIGURE 5.5: *Anatomia porci*. K. Sudhoff, "Die erste Tieranatomie von Salerno und ein neuer salernitanischer Anatomietext," *Archiv für Geschichte der Mathematik, der Naturwissenschaften und der Technik* 10 (1927): 152.

knowledge through empirical research. Moreover, it also implies the relative analogy between man and brutes. Arguably no other medieval scholar showed a similar open-mindedness and scientific curiosity before Albert the Great in the thirteenth century.

Albert the Great

There is a tenuous link that connects Frederick II with Albert the Great (ca. 1200–1280). During a visit to Germany, the emperor displayed a giraffe from his menagerie, and Albert reports this feat, although it is not clear whether he personally saw the animal.[51] The detail is significant: Albert combined an enormous erudition with a sense of scientific curiosity. Reason and experiment should collaborate, he wrote, but only the investigation of facts can provide certitude: "Experimentum enim solum certificat in talibus" (For experiment is the only safe guide in such investigations.).[52]

Albert was born as the son of a Swabian count. He studied at the University of Padua, where he joined the Dominicans. This proved to be a decisive step in his life, which he entirely devoted to study and teaching in the service of his order. It is not untypical that, when the Pope appointed him as bishop of Ratisbon in 1260, he only resided there for two years in order to find a suitable successor and then resigned in order to pursue his scholarly activities. He was probably the most versatile and prolific scholar of his age and therefore received the epithet of *Doctor Universalis*. When Albert was sent to Paris at the start of his academic career, Aristotle had come into disrepute and ecclesiastical authorities had issued several bans on the teaching of his works on natural philosophy. Although the effect of these bans seems to have been minimal, the suspicion surrounding the acceptability of the philosopher's thoughts remained. It appears to bear a strong link with the fact that most commentaries on Aristotle's works had been translated from the Arabic and often conflicted with Christian faith. At that point Albert played a decisive role in the development of his newly founded order's study program. His main goal was to reconcile Christian revelation and ancient science. He therefore thoroughly studied theology and philosophy. His enormous learning and productiveness resulted in commentaries on virtually every book of the Bible and all works by Aristotle, including some spurious treatises that were then thought to be original works by the philosopher.

In Albert's view, nature as a whole presents a continuous line from God to the sensible world. Each part of it is worth studying, and Albert constructed the order of his commentaries according to the level of eternity. The first and highest subject of study is God, and theology is thus equated with the Aristotelian metaphysics as the study of the first principle. Then comes mathematics, as it investigates the invariable relations between numbers. The third level is constituted by the sensible world, starting with the regular movements of the celestial bodies, continuing with earthly mobiles and their local movements and their evolution in time. On the lowest level, Albert investigated the nature of stones and minerals, as well as the earthly bodies with a soul, divided into plants and animals.

There are two different written reports of Albert's intellectual activity concerning Aristotle's books on animals, both of which are difficult to date. A series of questions Albert taught at the Dominican *studium* of Cologne were compiled by a certain Conrad of Austria as a set of student's notes. They are preserved under the title *Quaestiones super de animalibus*.[53] More importantly, Albert wrote a monumental commentary on Scotus's translation of the nineteen books of Aristotle's zoology, which he conceived as the final piece of his treatment of Aristotle's natural philosophy. As the autograph of the commentary is still extant, though in a somewhat damaged condition, it offers a privileged view of Albert's working process and the revisions he gradually introduced into the text, including a completely new preface to the work. In general, his working method consisted of the combination of quotations or paraphrases from Scotus's translation with his own explanations and interpretations.[54]

Albert certainly preserved a healthy amount of critical sense vis-à-vis the bulk of Aristotle's works and he avoided slavishly defending every word or resolving each seeming contradiction. As he stated in the first chapters of the commentary on another Aristotelian treatise, the philosopher had not reached divine status and therefore was not to be considered infallible: "However, someone could say that we have not understood Aristotle and therefore do not approve of his words, or that we may disagree with him on the basis of a certain knowledge with respect to his person and not with respect to the truth of the subject. And to him we say that he who believes that Aristotle was a god, must believe that he never made a mistake. However, if he believes that he is a man, then he could without any doubt make a mistake, just as we can."[55]

Albert significantly added to the zoological material provided by Aristotle. In particular, he was aware of the fact that the Mediterranean fauna illustrated by the philosopher differed substantially from the animals he observed in Germany and the Low Countries. He described a considerable number of animals from northern areas of Europe, including the now-extinct aurochs or the previously unknown white (polar) bear. His interest seems to have been focused on ornithology, particularly on birds linked with falconry, with which he had practice as a young man. He also shows a good knowledge of local fish species.[56]

Considering this broad field of interest, it is not surprising that Albert's knowledge of Latin vocabulary sometimes proved to be insufficient. In those cases when he did not know the correct Latin terminology or thought that there was not yet a name available, he chose to use the vernacular word, occasionally in a latinized form. As a result of this method, which was previously adopted by the German nun Hildegard of Bingen (1098–1176) in her work on dietetics, Albert's work provides important information on Middle German animal names.

Apart from his own experience, Albert incorporated the expertise of hunters, fishermen, and whalers in his commentary. He even conducted experiments, though in a very rudimentary form, in particular to seek for corroboration or falsification of traditional views or popular beliefs. His dissection of a mole in search of its missing eyes has somewhat undeservedly gained the status of a classical experiment. Albert concluded that Aristotle had made a mistake in claiming that the mole's eyes cannot be easily distinguished through its fur. He himself had observed that there are no openings where the eyes should be positioned, and he found no internal sensory organ when he made an incision. It is now generally accepted that Aristotle was closer to the truth than Albert. In another experiment, Albert examined the claim that salamanders by their humid complexion are able to live in fire. As he had no salamanders to hand, Albert conducted the experiment by means of spiders. He saw that a first spider remained for a while unharmed by the fire in which it was dropped, while another quenched the flame of a small lamp. It is clear from these examples that Albert's sense of experiment contains interesting initiatives but comes nowhere near the modern concept of investigational science.[57]

An important point of evidence showing that Albert conformed his work to the traditional concept in medieval zoology can be drawn from the composition of the complete work *De animalibus*. It not only contains the commentary on the nineteen books of Aristotelian zoology: after two books on isolated subjects, which initially formed separate treatises on their own, five other books follow. They treat the animal species according to the conventional larger classes of the bestiary tradition. Man and the walking animals (*gressibilia*) are dealt with in book 22, the topics of the remaining books are the flying (*volatilia*), swimming (*natatilia*), and crawling animals (*serpentia*), while the final section is being reserved for vermin (*vermes*). Albert's source by and large for these books is the encyclopedia by his fellow Dominican Thomas of Cantimpré. It is quite puzzling to see that in this part of the work he seems to abandon his original Aristotelian stance, and returns to the traditional medieval approach of zoology, including its taste for the fabulous and mythological. Even more surprising is the fact that Albert, while compiling excerpts from Thomas's work, seems to lose his critical judgment and simply repeats stories that he had previously condemned as untrustworthy. In some instances, information on the same animal is ranged under two or three different headings, as in the case of the giraffe, which alternately is called *anabula, oraflus,* or *camelopardulus.* Even more surprisingly, Albert seems to have accepted the existence of animals that ultimately found their origin in incorrect transcriptions or translations from the Arabic. In his works, as in many other commentaries and anthologies based on Scotus's version, the animal called *koki* is discussed at length. Obviously, the meaningless word entered the Latin language due to a clumsy Arabic transcription of its Greek name. To make matters worse, Albert uncritically copied the entry about the fish called *trebius niger* or black trebius from Cantimpré's encyclopedia. Unfortunately, in that case as in others, Thomas misinterpreted his source. In fact, Pliny refers to the author Trebius Niger, from whom he had drawn ichthyologic information. Similarly, other imaginary creatures entered the zoological universe of the encyclopedists and Albert alike.[58]

Although Albert's double-faced attitude toward the zoological material available to him may trouble the modern mind, he himself probably noticed no ambiguity in it. On the contrary, the two-sided approach demonstrates that a similar subject matter could function in different contexts: on the one hand in a new, philosophical and Aristotelian discourse, on the other in the traditional moralizing framework of religious literature. Albert, as a theologian and a philosopher, considerately brought both sides of the same zoological coin together.

CONCLUSION

The medieval science of animals hardly allows for a comparison with its modern counterpart. It rather reflects the medieval mind, which conceived truth as a hierarchical and multilayered notion. Different approaches do not necessarily cause contradictions; on the contrary, in some cases they may lead to a better understanding of a higher reality. What matters, then, is not the degree of reliability of the report, but its suitability to illustrate the ethical or moralistic truth that forms the ultimate objective of the author.

Even if medieval zoology is radically different from the modern science, the attitude toward animals in the later Middle Ages contrasted with the general lack of interest in the subject during the preceding centuries. Mendicant orders, following the tracks of Francis of Assisi and his legendary love for animals, opened the possibility to consider zoology as a potential study topic, albeit as an auxiliary discipline to be used in moderation by the theologian. From that point of view, Albert the Great's work, which was the first treatise on the subject for more than a millennium that had a considerable readership, forms a landmark in the history of zoology.

CHAPTER SIX

Animals and Anthropology in Medieval Philosophy

PIETER DE LEEMANS AND MATTHEW KLEMM

If, however, there is anyone who holds that the study of animals is an unworthy pursuit, he ought to go further and hold the same opinion about the study of himself.

—Aristotle, *De part. an.* 645a27[1]

For medieval philosophers, the ultimate purpose in the investigation of animals was not to speculate about the beasts for their own sake, but to better understand human nature. With this general purpose in mind, philosophical thought about animals and their rapport with humans was informed by two sensibilities. The first of these sharply distinguished between humans, created in God's image, and other animals. On this view, humans alone were said to possess the reason and will necessary to transcend the natural world. Through reason, we form thoughts completely abstracted from our physical sensations. By will, humans are moral free agents who can act in opposition to natural inclinations. At the same time, natural philosophers considered humans to be part of the animal world. We share significant parts of our souls with animals; our bodies have the same physiology and thus are subject to the same kinds of passions.

These two sensibilities were neither mutually exclusive nor restricted to philosophy. Rather they reflect broader medieval mentalities about the place of humans in nature, often uneasily coexisting in the same author. These ways of thinking are still recognizable in our own ambivalent relationship to other animals today. In the Middle Ages, they are concisely captured in the standard definition of man as a rational animal—"Homo est animal rationale mortale"—at once naming our status as animals and our distinctive characteristic of reason. Most medieval philosophers dwelled on the latter, transcendent, part of humanity; others on our underlying animality. However anthropocentric thought about animals may have been, when philosophers turned their attention to man's natural and organic characteristics, it was impossible to ignore the essentially zoological foundation of human nature. In this way, consideration of animals reinvigorated medieval anthropological ideas and ultimately contributed to new conceptions of the human relationship to the natural world that emerged during this period. Although not its primary purpose, such study also resulted in a more just account of the animals themselves. As inherited from both Christian and pagan sources, animals corresponded to an inherently irrational part of the human soul. As such, the most comprehensive accounts of animals originated with those philosophers who regarded this irrational aspect of human psychology as critical for understanding human nature as a whole. For them, people may have reason, but it is far from sufficient to explain human nature. Perception, emotion, habit, instinct, imagination, and cognition—characteristics we more or less share with animals—were more realistic categories by which to understand the way we actually live our lives on a day-to-day basis. This was not a total rejection of a rational basis for our behavior, but a proposal that the kind of capacities we share with animals offer another perspective. For students of natural philosophy, some of these psychological categories existed in a purer form in animals as their defining characteristics; others occupy the borders between humans and animals. Philosophers found room for these issues concerning continuity and discontinuity, similarity and difference, between the animal organism and the human organism in the psychology of Aristotle.

This is not to say that other types of thinkers paid no attention to animals. Animals were frequently put to use in biblical exegesis and analogy. Scholars moralized the habits of lions, ants, or bees as ideals of bravery, prudence, and wisdom, respectively. Augustine, in his *De doctrina Christiana,* noted such moral uses in the Bible when he exhorted Christians to the study of animals. This was echoed most prominently in illustrated bestiaries, which idealized the characters of animals, simplifying their complexities to ascribe deeper allegorical meaning. Where meaning and rationality is located in animal behavior, it is sign of an external rationality. Moral meanings derive not from the animal's own willed conduct but from the purpose of God acting through nature and from the ability of humans to recognize God's purpose. In this sense, it was not the animal as agent of its own behavior that was the focus, but the animal as a blank slate for human meanings. While this is not to say that these meanings did not require careful observation and interpretation of animal conduct in some cases, many of the actions attributed to animals are either completely invented or notable solely for the purpose of obliging a predetermined exegetical plan.

Beavers are a good example of this. Beavers were hunted for their testicles, which were useful for medicine. For this reason, whenever they realized that they could not escape capture, they were said to gnaw off their own testicles and throw them back at the hunter, thus saving their own life. (See Figure 6.1.) For moralists, this behavior signified that we must cut out sin (conveniently represented by testicles) from our lives in order to save our souls.[2] It is unlikely that anyone actually witnessed this behavior from a beaver.

Those thinkers who emphasized human transcendence did not neglect animals, but certainly had less interest in careful study of them. For philosophers and theologians who concerned themselves with reason, will, and immortality, the study of animals did not play a very significant role.

Like all medieval learning, the study of animals was largely based on reading and commenting on authoritative texts, rather than on observation or experiment (luckily for the animals). Observation had its place, which might be expected considering the ubiquity of animals in medieval life, but a small one. Many of the particular examples of animal behavior that would otherwise suggest direct observation, such as a sheep's reaction to the sight of a wolf, are repeated by numerous authors without alteration. This repetition is a product of the scholastic milieus from which almost all medieval philosophical texts originated.[3] The medieval curriculum was composed of a limited number of canonical texts and their commentaries, to which scholars repeatedly turned. Moreover, much of medieval philosophy was abstract by nature and privileged universal knowledge over particular examples. Scholars recognized the traditional division of philosophy into theoretical and practical branches, but the theoretical branch was more highly regarded. The goal of theory was to discover universal and eternal truths, that is, scientific knowledge. But unlike our modern notion of science, in which the collection of empirical evidence is generally regarded as a vital part of the process, medieval *scientia* was syllogistically discovered. The texts that we regard as philosophical sought to understand natural principles and then to explain nature in terms of known principles. Because of this definition of science, it is almost impossible to separate science from philosophy in the Middle Ages.

The texts we consider here were written at cathedral schools at the beginning of our period, and then at the universities after circa 1200. Medieval philosophy had its origins in the monastic schools, where logic was applied to religious beliefs, but animals figured hardly at all in these concerns. At the schools, there was not a distinct faculty of philosophy. The faculty of the arts included the study of *trivium, quadrivium,* and philosophy—especially Aristotle. Theology, medicine, and law required the previous study of the arts. Work devoted

FIGURE 6.1: *Beaver*, Bestiary (around 1200), University Library Aberdeen, MS 24, fol. 11r.
© University of Aberdeen.

primarily to animals made up only a small portion of philosophical texts. The
impact of centers of translation also deserves to be mentioned here.[4] Because
medieval philosophy was so dependent on authoritative texts, new translations
had a profound effect on doctrine. From Toledo, southern Italy, and Sicily, the

texts translated from the Arabic and Greek were often rapidly incorporated into the Latin curricula at schools. The most revolutionary developments for the study of animals would not have been possible without the translation of Aristotle's complete zoological corpus and the steady stream of biological, medical, and generally naturalistic works produced by translators.

We divide this chapter into four sections. In the first, we summarize in a general way the psychological framework that made the study of animals fruitful for medieval philosophers. Here we give an overview of all living creatures and identify those parts of the soul that were particularly pertinent for speculation about animals. We follow this with some remarks on the sources and the nature of the study of animals in the twelfth century, prior to the appropriation of the Aristotelian corpus. This corpus significantly altered the way scholars studied animals; thus, in the third part of this chapter we examine this thirteenth-century appropriation in some depth. We conclude with some observations about the use (or neglect) of animals in the thought of the later Middle Ages.

ANIMALS AND THE ORGANIC SOUL

Diversity of philosophical opinion about animals was accommodated within an inclusive framework of the embodied soul.[5] In distinction from the modern tendency to confine soul to strictly human characteristics, the medieval notion of soul was intertwined with all life. Soul was considered to be the first principle of each living creature. The completely developed soul was also regarded as a continuum of all the capacities possible for the entire range of living things. According to the broadly Aristotelian conception of soul that came to dominate during this period, the soul had three main divisions: the vegetative, sensitive, and rational parts. Of these three parts, plants possess the vegetative, animals both the vegetative and the sensitive, and humans possess all three. The parts correspond to three general categories that characterized the activities of living creatures: each creature lives by means of its vegetative soul, perceives and moves with its sensitive soul, and thinks with the rational part of the soul. Every problem of psychological investigation could be more or less precisely located on this continuum, where it could then be connected to a web of interrelated issues. Even those distinctively abstruse medieval discussions about angels and so-called separated intelligences can be included within this ambit from a certain perspective: they are entities endowed with a rational part of the soul, but no other. For issues about animals and their relevance to human nature, this psychological framework was sufficiently supple to allow the extremes of philosophical opinion.

On the one hand, this idea of a hierarchically organized soul did not preclude traditional formulations handed down from the monastic schools about the superiority of humankind among God's creatures. As the Venerable Bede

(d. 735), one of the more influential representatives of this thought, opined in his commentary on Genesis, the fact that God gave Adam the responsibility to name the animals showed the precise character of Adam's superiority, manifest in his rational capacities. Adam's abilities to *distinguish* and *discern* the essential nature of the animals were rational functions available to humans alone.[6] Such functions could easily be inserted into the Aristotelian psychological continuum; this flexibility certainly helped its acceptance.

On the other hand, close examination of creatures exposed more nuanced distinctions in the threefold soul. As Aristotle had written in the *History of Animals:* "Nature proceeds from the inanimate to the animals by such small steps that, because of the continuity we fail to see to which side the boundary and the middle between them belongs."[7] This gradualism is also readily apparent on the border between animals and humans. In books 8 and 9 of the *History of Animals,* Aristotle speaks of animals as possessing traits akin to gentleness, intelligence, confidence, and virtue. These traits should be more developed in humans, but at least in some of his zoological works, the distinction between human and animal behavior is presented as a question of more or less, rather than a radical difference in kind. Animals are like children in whom we are able to see the seeds of future characteristics.

For the precise enumeration of the differences between humans and animals, the sensitive part of the soul was pivotal. If the Aristotelian conception of the

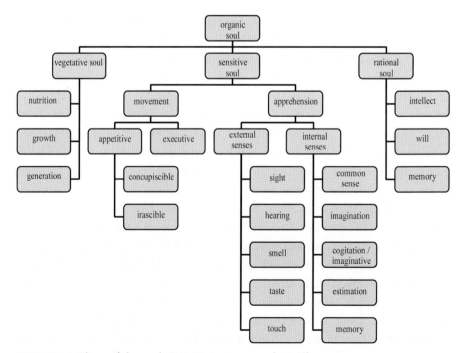

FIGURE 6.2: Chart of the soul. © P. De Leemans and M. Klemm

soul denied reason to the animals, it also endowed them (and therefore us) with robust sensitive capacities. (See Figure 6.2.) These capacities provided animals with the means to behave in ways that parallel operations in humans. The competence of the sensitive soul was apparent in the fact that advanced animals were able to perform fairly complex operations with the sensitive powers alone. The sufficiency of sensitive powers in animals pointed to a similar critical role in humans. Of critical anthropological interest to medieval thinkers, the means to a philosophical explanation of the mysterious union of the immortal soul and the corruptible body was to be found in the sensitive part. Sensation also supplied the intellect with phantasms derived from sense perceptions, providing the means for abstract thought. Finally, our motive functions belong to the sensitive soul, linking sensation to the orders of the rational will. Before this conception of the soul came to be the dominant framework in which animals were understood in the thirteenth century, there were a number of twelfth-century developments.

TWELFTH CENTURY

The reawakening of intellectual interests in Europe known as the twelfth-century renaissance has been well documented.[8] This period witnessed the application of rational habits of thought to many aspects of culture, including law, government, religious doctrine, and of course, philosophy, the area most wholly defined by the use of reason. The place of animals in philosophy is limited in this era before the translation of Aristotelian zoology or biology (even if animals had played a major role in the social changes that had provided the preconditions for intellectual vitality).[9] Yet the naturalism that emerged in the twelfth century established the intellectual structure that would allow animals to have a greater role in the following century. There are two contexts that were notable in this regard. The first of these was the naturalistic and syncretistic cosmology sometimes associated with the cathedral school at Chartres, but ranging much farther afield.[10] For many Chartrians, particular knowledge of the natural world took on a new light when it was united to a Neoplatonic contemplative habit that sought to understand underlying causes and deeper truths in the most mundane objects. Another context that would provide inspiration for the study of animals was the burgeoning study of medicine, centered especially at the school of Salerno in southern Italy.[11] Here animals occasionally found a practical place in the study of human anatomy and physiology. By contrast, in the thought of the most famous philosophers of this time, such as Peter Abelard (d. 1142) and Anselm of Canterbury (d. 1109), animals hardly figure. For these and other thinkers, historians celebrate their ambitious use of logic and its application to the most central Christian beliefs, leaving little room for animals.

The best source of basic information about animals in the twelfth century was the encyclopedic tradition. The most popular included Pliny's *Historia naturalis,* Solinus's *Collectanea rerum memorabilium* (derived from Pliny), and the *Etymologies* of Isidore of Seville (d. 636). These encyclopedias contained numerous facts and fiction about animals (among many other topics), but cannot themselves be counted as philosophy. However they provided useful information for more philosophical approaches to animals. Albertus Magnus (d. 1280) certainly made heavy use of all three of these encyclopedias in his later work. Isidore's descriptions of animals, comprising all of book 12 of his work, found particularly wide circulation. Encyclopedias would continue to be a living tradition, with many twelfth- and thirteenth-century updates to this ancient genre adding more recently acquired information.

Bestiaries, today among the most well-known books from the Middle Ages, provided another source of information. The tradition of bestiaries can be traced back to a popular Greek treatise called the *Physiologus,* which contained descriptions of about forty animals. The bestiaries expanded this total to over 100 animals, accruing more information from the encyclopedic tradition, and sometimes adding extensive illustrations. The description of each animal usually consisted of a derivation of the animal's name and distinctive features and behavior distilled for the purpose of biblical exegesis and moralization. Like much of the information in the encyclopedias, this mixture of etymology, fact, myth, and moralization would not have withstood philosophical standards of truth, nor were they intended to.

The disparate facts about animals contained in these popular works were occasionally put to more philosophical use in the work of Neoplatonic naturalists. Their primary goal was not necessarily to understand nature for its own sake; rather they were characterized by their conviction that knowledge of the natural world was a path to speculative or divine truths. For these Chartrians, Plato's *Timaeus,* available in the partial translation and commentary by Calcidius, provided a conceptual framework for humans and the universe as microcosm and macrocosm. Unfortunately for the study of animals, Calcidius's partial text (containing only 17a–53b) lacked the part in which Plato discussed medicine, physiology, and the animal soul.[12] In the excluded sections (77a–c), Plato grants animals the capacity for belief, denied to them by Aristotle and others. Nevertheless, the polymath Adelard of Bath (d. ca. 1142) offered a highly sympathetic interpretation of animals in his *Questiones naturales.*[13] In question 13 about the souls of animals, Adelard considers the kind of decisions they make based on sense perception, such as the ability to immediately recognize their own master. He concludes that they have the power of discernment and even says that animal souls are immortal! Adelard would be echoed in this unusual conclusion about the potential for animal salvation by William of Auvergne in the thirteenth century. Another scholar closely associated with Chartres, William of Conches (d. after 1154), appears to have thought that Adelard gave the animals a little too much credit.

The ability to discern was, after all, one of the powers named as unique to humans by Bede in the passage above. Correcting Adelard, William argues that imagination is perfectly able to account for the recognition of a master.[14]

Much of the physiological information used by Adelard and other Chartrians came from the medical school at Salerno. Beginning in the late eleventh century, a wave of translations of Greek and Arabic medical texts considerably enriched Latin medical learning. Physicians at Salerno had direct access to the translations from the Greek from the nearby monastery of Monte Cassino. These new texts transmitted the scope of medical expertise proposed by ancient physicians and further developed by Arabic commentators over the following millennium. Where previous medicine in the Latin West had been predominately practical, the new translations communicated the full framework of Galenic medicine as both theoretical (i.e., philosophical) and practical.

For the future use of animals in philosophy, these theoretical texts were important in two regards. First, they provided a physiological basis for understanding all living creatures. Before the Aristotelian conception of the soul became widely known, a Platonic or, more properly, Augustinian notion of the soul was predominant. This conception entailed a threefold distinction in the parts of the soul, dividing the soul into memory, intellect, and will (or irascible, desiring, and rational parts for Plato). Ambitious scholars in Chartres and Salerno used the newly translated medical information to explain psychological processes.[15] With the powers of the soul conceived materially, animals slowly became more relevant for study of the human soul.

Secondly, medical theory stimulated interest in Aristotle's natural philosophy. Although Paris is more commonly associated with the reception of the Aristotelian corpus in its Latin form, the desire to understand the philosophy imbedded in the medical texts contributed perhaps the first impulse in the West to locate and translate Aristotle's physical works. Because of direct references to Aristotle in the new medical works, readers recognized that Aristotle's natural philosophy, including the works on animals, would be essential for understanding ancient medical theory.[16] The reception of this natural philosophy is the subject of the next section.

THE APPROPRIATION OF ARISTOTLE'S NATURAL PHILOSOPHY

The Rediscovery of Aristotle's Natural Philosophy

The most important event for the study of animals in the medieval period was the translation and appropriation of Aristotle's natural philosophy. Until the twelfth century only his logical works were available in the Latin translation by Boethius. Yet, in this and the next centuries, almost the whole *Corpus*

Aristotelicum as well as several commentaries on it were translated into Latin, from the Greek or from the Arabic.[17] The philosophical beliefs in these texts enriched the existing hierarchical classification of the soul, offering a richer account of the psychological capacities of humans and animals than that of the twelfth century.

With respect to animals, the most important collection was known in the Middle Ages as the *De animalibus*, which contained Aristotle's three major zoological works, the *History of Animals, On the Parts of Animals*, and *On Generation of Animals*. They were first translated from an Arabic translation into Latin by Michael Scot around 1220, who also translated Avicenna's *Book of the Natures of Animals*.[18] A second translation of these texts was made some forty years later, this time from the Greek, by the Flemish Dominican William of Moerbeke (d. 1286). William also completed the zoological corpus by translating two other texts on animals, *On the Movement of Animals* and *On the Progression of Animals*, which until then had scarcely received any attention. These were the texts entirely devoted to animals that would play a role in the reception of Aristotle's thought. Two other, anonymous translations were never spread widely; a translation of *De partibus animalium*, preserved in one manuscript (Padova, Bibl. Antoniana, MS 370), and another of *De motu animalium*, which is only known through Albert the Great's paraphrase of it, On the principles of progressive movement (*De principiis motus processivi*).[19] (See Figure 6.3.)

Other texts that provided zoological information were those of the *Parva naturalia* (Short treatises on natural science). This generic title stands for a collection of texts that describe the characteristics common to the soul and the body and highly relevant to the study of the sensitive powers. These treatises fall into two categories: on the one hand, the psychological *Parva naturalia* deals with sensation and sensible things, memory and recollection, sleep and waking, dreams, and prophecy in sleep; on the other hand, the more physiological texts concern the length and shortness of life, youth and old age, life and

FIGURE 6.3: Aristotle studying the movements of animals, Aristotle, *On the movement of animals*, trans. William of Moerbeke, Eisenbibliothek, Schlatt, Stiftung der Georg Fischer AG, MS 20, fol. 22r.

death, and respiration and inspiration. All these texts were translated twice from Greek into Latin in the twelfth and thirteenth centuries. On the contrary, no Arabic–Latin translation of the Aristotelian text has come to us. Yet, Averroes's paraphrase of some of the *Parva naturalia* (the psychological ones and the *De longitudine et brevitate vitae*) was translated twice into Latin and is known to have deeply influenced the reception of these texts in the Medieval West.[20] As a rule, these texts were read as amplifications of particular parts of the framework provided by Aristotle's *De anima* and the Arabic commentaries by Avicenna and Averroes.[21]

Aristotle's Animals in Medieval Taxonomies of Knowledge

The rediscovery of Aristotle's philosophical corpus provided medieval philosophers with the conceptual instruments for a systematic understanding of the physical world. By reflecting on how the Aristotelian corpus was structured they reflected simultaneously on the structure of the world itself. The study of animals and, more generally, of animated bodies was situated within the study of natural science in general.[22] It implied above all the study of the soul and of the animated bodies in so far as they are animated (*De anima*). This was followed by the study of the *Parva naturalia*, inclusive of *De motu animalium* and *De progressu animalium*, which discussed the different faculties of the soul. Generally speaking, the physiological *Parva naturalia* were said to deal with the vegetative, the psychological ones with the sensitive soul, and the two texts on locomotion with the faculty that enables local movement. After the *De anima* and the *Parva naturalia* came the *De animalibus* as well as the *De plantis*. They discussed the actual animated beings, the ones endowed with a sensitive (animals) and those with a vegetative soul (plants) in a more descriptive way and with attention to the different species. By their attention to particular plants and animals, they were considered as the final part of Aristotle's natural science in general.

It was a topic of discussion among medieval authors as to whether the *De animalibus* should also be considered a place for anthropological discourse.[23] Some authors, such as Peter of Spain and Gérard de Breuil, did believe Aristotle also wanted to discuss humans in this text (see following section). Yet, others thought of the work as dealing exclusively with animals in the strict sense, suggesting that discourse about humans should be sought in medicine or in the treatise on the soul.

Related to this, the question was raised about the *Parva naturalia*; did they also discuss the intellective soul—which is typical for humans? Some authors held that Aristotle dealt with it in his *De memoria et reminiscentia*,[24] whereas Albert the Great completed his *Parva naturalia* with a self-written treatise *De intellectu et intelligibili*. Thomas Aquinas just remarked that Aristotle wrote no book on this topic and that, if he had written it, it would not be a part of natural science but rather of metaphysics.

Aristotle's Commentators

The order of the books of natural science reveals an emphasis on theoretical considerations rather than on specific data, and with respect to animated beings, on the soul rather than on the body. It is thus not surprising that the *De animalibus,* due to its emphasis on the particular animals, was considered as the last book—or at least one of the very last—in a hierarchy of knowledge that privileged abstract theory. For this reason it is not surprising that there is no extensive commentary tradition on Aristotle's *De animalibus.* There are, however, notable exceptions. Those who did decide to comment on the *De animalibus* were probably influenced by their conviction that these texts were not only about animals but also about humans.

The oldest extant Latin commentary is probably that of Peter of Spain, written from 1246–1249 in Sienna.[25] His commentary is a collection of 822 questions based on material from seventeen of the nineteen books. It clearly belongs to a medical context: Peter is most concerned with physiological material, using Galen extensively and pointing out disagreements between Galenic and Aristotelian physiology.

The most famous—and also the most popular—commentary is a monumental work in twenty-six books written by Albert the Great in the middle of the thirteenth century, which is called *De animalibus.*[26] The first nineteen books of this work, of which more than forty manuscripts including the autograph are extant, are basically a paraphrase of Michael Scot's translation from the Arabic. Books 20–21 are a general consideration of levels of animal perfection from the lowest animal up to man. The remaining five books each treat a different category of animal: walking animals (bk. 22), flying animals (bk. 23), swimming animals (bk. 24), crawling animals (bk. 25), and worms and insects (bk. 26). Albert arranged the animals alphabetically within each category and systematically listed each animal's characteristics. His concern for the similarities and differences between animals and humans is apparent in these descriptions. He consistently points out quasi-human abilities such as the ability to learn or make use of art and speech. Some animals possess a single almost human characteristic, such as the prudence of bees or ants. Apart from the *De animalibus,* we also have a smaller set of questions on animals that result from Albert's teaching at Cologne in 1258.[27] Albert exhibits in his work also the great philosophical and scientific interest in his subject that has made him the patron saint for the study of the natural world.

Moerbeke's translation (from the Greek) was commented by Gérard de Breuil in the late thirteenth century. This commentary must have had some success, as it is preserved in about ten manuscripts, yet it still does not witness a profound interest in zoology. It is also probable that Roger Bacon (d. ca. 1294), another prominent figure in philosophy, worked on these texts, but if so his writing is not extant.

In turn, the glosses in the manuscripts of Scot's translation reveal that the readers' approach to the text was often allegorical and moralizing in character and related to biblical exegesis rather than philosophy.[28] From a codicological point of view, it is interesting to note that Moerbeke's translation of *De historia animalium* (almost always together with the other zoological works) occurs isolated in the majority of the manuscripts or in combination with texts that have nothing to do with Aristotle's natural philosophy.[29] Still, there appears to be a somewhat privileged relation with the pseudo-Aristotelian *Problemata physica*—which in itself was difficult to classify.[30] Like *De animalibus*, the *Problemata* had a high level of particularity and a close association with medical learning.

The preference of medieval philosophers toward more elevated subjects than animals is, however, most strikingly illustrated by the difference in the reception of Aristotle's *De motu animalium* and *De progressu animalium*. From the moment it was translated, the *De motu animalium* was read, excerpted, and commented upon. Both literal and *Questiones* commentaries were written, some of them by leading figures of medieval scholasticism (Albert the Great, Peter of Auvergne, John of Jandun, John Buridan) and often in combination with commentaries on other texts of the *Parva naturalia*.[31] The *De progressu animalium* was only commented once, by an anonymous author whose work is preserved in only one manuscript. Although the content of the manuscript reveals some interest of the copyist in zoology in general and in the problem of movement more concretely, this commentary is for the most part nothing more than a superficial paraphrase of Moerbeke's translation, embellished with some scarce references to other texts, mainly to the *History of Animals* and Isidore's *Etymologiae*.[32]

Undoubtedly the explanation for this phenomenon must be sought in the profound difference between the two texts on locomotion. *De motu animalium* is a more general treatise that seeks to explain how local movement is made possible. It discusses topics of major philosophical relevance, such as the appropriate roles of intellect and desire in action or in the construction of practical syllogisms. It also situates animal movement in a larger framework, drawing an analogy between the movement of the universe and that of animals. In contrast, the *De progressu animalium* describes how the different sorts of animals move. The general outlines of Aristotelian philosophy—such as teleology—are just the background for a very technical treatment of this subject. It is this difference that inspired Peter of Auvergne (d. 1304) to write in his *Sententia super de motibus animalium* that the former deals with the form and the latter with the matter of local movement.[33]

If most medieval authors were not interested in specific zoological data, we should ask in which philosophical contexts animals played a role. The major observation is that many of the questions raised about living beings witness an interest in definition and classification. Commentators were not much interested in the characteristics of individual animals, but rather in the distinctive characteristics of plants, animals, or men in general. They thus ask if characteristics that we spontaneously consider as typical for one category can also be applied to another category—for example, do plants sleep? Do animals other than men perceive smells as being pleasant *in se*? Or, can certain features be said of all creatures that belong to a given category—for example, do all animals move? Do all living beings have memory? Do all animals have a voice?[34] If specific zoological data are mentioned it is mainly as an illustration of the subject that is under discussion; logically, these illustrations are not far-fetched, quoting very exotic species, but standard examples—quadrupeds are horses, animals that hardly move (see subsequent section) are shellfish, etcetera.

In view of the fact that the focus was on classification, it comes not as a surprise that commentators paid special attention to those animals situated on the transition from plants to animals or from animals to human beings. By addressing these twilight zones, medieval commentators tried to get a better insight into the ontological status of animals and in their distinctive characteristics. We will, therefore, ask what the minimal distinction between plants and animals was, and whether or not animals were endowed with an intellect.

Local Movement and Imperfect Animals

As we have seen, according to Aristotle the distinction between plants and animals is the presence or absence of the sensitive soul. A living being can be said to be animal if, and only if, it has sensation. Like the animals, the senses themselves are hierarchically ordered. The most basic sense is touch. As a consequence, a living being can be said to be an animal when it has at least the sense of touch. The other senses belong to the higher animals and are related to the faculty of local movement. Aristotle explains that these animals seek their food from distant places, and that, for their safety, they must possess senses other than touch. Only by these senses they are able to make the distinction between what is convenient and inconvenient and thus between what is potentially harmful and useful.[35]

In the Middle Ages, some authors subtly redefine this distinction between plants and animals. They still consider sensation as the principal way to separate plants from animals. Yet, in agreement with what Avicenna wrote in his *De anima*, they elaborate the notion of local movement in such a way that it could be applied to all animals. Latin authors who explicitly dwell on this subject are, among others, Albert the Great—who draws attention to the difference between Avicenna and Aristotle—Peter of Auvergne, and other commentators concerned with the classification of the faculties of the soul.[36]

They make a distinction between motion on place (*motus in loco*) and motion from one place to another (*motus ad locum, motus processivus*). Of these, the latter is what is commonly understood under local movement. The former is a more basic sort of local motion that can be applied to all animals. The animal that moves in this way perceives something harmful or something convenient by the sense of touch and then moves by, respectively, constriction or by dilatation. An analogous movement is found in the heart, which also moves by constriction and dilatation. The standard examples are shellfish (*conchylia*), oysters, and sponges. By this redefinition, locomotion itself joins sensation as a distinctive characteristic for animals in general, contrary to plants.

Nevertheless, these authors acknowledge that motion *in loco* is not the standard type of locomotion. Rather is it typical for zoophytes, which are labeled as imperfect animals (*animalia imperfecta*). Imperfect here is not the Aristotelian notion of the absence of something that normally should be present. Thomas Aquinas, in his commentary on Aristotle's *De anima,* explicitly denies that these (relatively) immobile animals resemble monsters that are against nature and asserts that they are perfect in their species,[37] whereas Albert the Great's anatomical description shows that they are perfectly designed according to their place between plants and animals. Whereas in their capacity for (limited) locomotion and sensation they resemble animals, their body is so designed that it serves the specific needs that result from the limitations of these capacities. Apart from their apparent immobility, it is in the design of their body that the resemblance to plants is manifest.

This is illustrated by the anatomical structure of their mouth. Every animal necessarily must be fed. Since an imperfect animal cannot move to another place, it finds its food at the place where it is located; as a consequence its mouth is turned toward and attached to the place where the food is found. Moreover, since the food that it extracts from this place is impure and mixed with earth—which would rather harm than feed its substance—it does not have an open mouth; it rather sucks its food through small pores. Both in the position and functioning, its mouth thus resembles the roots of a plant.[38]

If not with respect to its own constitution, the shellfish and other similar animals are called imperfect in comparison to animals that are higher on the scale of nature, and ultimately, to humans. With respect to Albert the Great, the term *zoological anthropocentrism* has been used to describe the way in which all living creatures are compared to and measured with humans.[39] Book 21 of his *De animalibus,* which is "on perfect and imperfect animals and the reason for their perfection and imperfection," is entirely based on the idea that "the human is the most perfect animal not only by virtue of the addition of reason but also in terms of all the powers and the manner of the carrying out of the powers, both sensible and rational."[40] This anthropocentrism—which is to a certain extent already present in Aristotle—enabled the redefinition of all living beings on the scale of nature in terms of being more or less imperfect than another animal and than man. The most imperfect animal is then the animal that lacks—or better, seems to lack—locomotion: "it seems that it is a certain plant participating in something of animality."[41] It is labeled as imperfect since it participates imperfectly in the powers of the soul.

It is unsurprising that Thomas Aquinas's treatment of the connection between locomotion and imperfect animals is less developed than Albert's. Whereas Albert shows a genuine interest in biology, Aquinas is scarcely interested in it, and even depreciated it.[42] He distinguishes four grades of living, and thus of living beings: plants, imperfect animals, perfect animals, and humans:

> He here intends to distinguish ways of being alive in accord with the grades of living things, which these four ways distinguish. For in some living things (in plants, that is) we find only nourishment, growth, and deterioration, whereas in others we find, along with these, sense without local motion. (This is the case in incomplete animals, like oysters.) In certain others we also find local motion, as is the case in complete animals, which are moved progressively (like an ox or horse). In still others (in human beings) we find, along with all these, intellect.[43]

Thomas is, here as elsewhere, less explicit in distinguishing two types of locomotion than Albert and Peter of Auvergne. In the present passage, the only indication that he knows—and to a certain extent agrees with—the Avicennian theory is the redefinition of local movement as "progressive movement" when he talks about perfect animals. In other passages he does recognize that imperfect animals move, but adds that this is only in an inordinate way. More striking is the fact that Thomas considers the imperfect animals as representing a separate level of living beings. One of the advantages of considering contraction and dilatation as local movement was exactly that locomotion could become a distinctive characteristic of all animals. Thomas appears to refuse this option; when it comes to local motion, rather than underlining all animals' common feature he opts for stressing the difference.

Intellect and Animals

As we have seen before, medieval authors considered the intellect as the fundamental distinction between animals and humans. Basically, this is also the situation with Aristotle. When the Stagirite credits animals with technical knowledge and thought in the *History of Animals*, this must be seen—Richard Sorabji argues—as a casual everyday description that we all find hard to avoid applying to animals. In his more authoritative theoretical statements, Aristotle limits intellect to humans, whereas in animals only a "sort of thinking" is said to occur.[44]

Important for our present purpose is the distinction Aristotle makes between theoretical and practical intellect; the former is concerned with knowing and understanding, the latter with planning action. Whether animals had anything to do with the former was not topic of discussion. Yet, because animals seem to move purposefully, for example, in order to get food or to fly away from the danger, it became a topic of some discussion how animal action should be explained and to what extent animals might have a practical intellect.

In purposive actions, both of animals and men, Aristotle states, at least two faculties are implicated. The first of these is desire: both humans and animals act because they have a desire to achieve something. Yet, desire always functions—or should function—in combination with a second faculty, which in humans is the practical intellect. The practical intellect causes us to act by forming a practical syllogism, which takes the form of a major premise, for example, "sweet things are good" and a minor premise, provided by the presence of a particular sweet thing: "here is a sweet thing." If desire is also present, a person will eat the sweet thing. In animals, the faculty that comes closest to the practical intellect is the *phantasia,* the highest of the sensitive powers. Presumably, *phantasia* and desire might function in a similar manner in animals, as practical intellect and desire do in humans.[45]

The two main texts that bring this topic up for discussion are *De anima* and *De motu animalium.* The latter is especially interesting, as here Aristotle comes closest to granting reason to animals.[46] This ambivalence might be due to the fact that, whereas the title suggests that the text is about animal movement in general, Aristotle appears to have written some sections with solely human movement in mind. Moreover, "animals" and "intellect" are mentioned a few times in the same phrase. For medieval commentators on *De motu animalium,* for whom the authority of Aristotle was not something that was easily neglected, such phrases provoked the question whether "animals are moved by the intellect."

Generally speaking, this question was answered in two ways. Some commentators chose the easiest solution; they skipped the animals and focused entirely on the relation between movement and intellect in the strict sense. "Skipped" should be taken literally: the word *animal* does not occur in their answer to this question. The authors limit themselves to making the undisputed distinction between theoretical and practical intellect and saying that only the latter is involved in actions. Other commentators accepted the challenge to try to reconcile the pairing of animals and intellect, referring to Aristotle himself and to the Arabic interpretative tradition. The Aristotelian part of their answer consists in the specification that intellect should be understood in a wider sense, namely, as *phantasia*. *Phantasia*, aided by the other sensitive powers, is said to "comprehend the unperceived perceptions": when an animal perceives something, *phantasia* is the faculty that allows it to discern whether something is friendly or hostile, helpful or harmful.[47]

To understand this definition of *phantasia* it is important to know that Aristotle's description of the sensitive soul—especially its internal faculties—was immediately amplified by Avicenna's outline in his own *De anima,* along with other works in circulation before Aristotle's account. Where Aristotle was ambiguous, Avicenna identified precise physical and psychological loci for sensitive capacities. Through these capacities, Avicenna gave animals the ability to perform such advanced functions as distinguishing universal categories, learning, and making judgments based on limited data, while nevertheless maintaining a sharp distinction between humans and animals.

Using the faculty psychology of Avicenna and Aristotle, philosophers generally categorized the operations of the sensitive soul into the powers of apprehension and movement. (See Figure 6.2.) The latter produced motion through an appetitive faculty and an executive faculty. The appetitive faculty desires to either attain something (in which case it is called concupiscible) or to repel something (irascible). These desires are physically manifest in emotions shared by the body and soul and spread through the organism by the heart and blood. The executive faculty, infused throughout the nerves and muscles, reacts to these desires and commands the appropriate movement. In animals it is often the case that the executive power simply follows an instinct that bypasses the appetitive process altogether.

The power of apprehension is again twofold, divided into the external and internal senses. The five external senses are familiar to us as the five senses of sight, hearing, smell, taste, and touch. These senses collect sense perceptions from external objects—hence their name—in the form of primary qualities, that is, hot, cold, wet, and dry, along with the secondary qualities derived from them, for example, hard, soft, bitter, and sweet.

The internal senses attend to the sense perceptions from the external senses to accomplish progressively more refined and abstract operations, storing perceptions for future use, recalling them on request, and gleaning new information. The exact number and the division of labor for the internal senses varied from author to author, but most scholars proposed five senses. It is most likely that philosophers did not intend to make the divisions between these capacities as rigid as they appear at first sight. This fact helps account for the confusion in naming the different senses and also explains why authors could posit, for example, four, six, or seven internal senses with little hint of controversy. After all, Aristotle himself seems to name only two, the common sense and the *phantasia*. It is probably more useful to understand the internal senses holistically as a series of passive and active states: they alternate between receiving impressions and acting on those impressions to create new information, which can once again be stored and treated. The apparent rigidity is a by-product of the act of exposition. The following description is intended more to show the options available for differentiating the internal senses than to present any single author's position.

Most scholars were in agreement about the existence of first and last internal senses in the hierarchy: the common sense and the memory. The common sense sorts and compares the initial sense perceptions. In doing this it perceives common sensibles like motion, shape, and extension that are not exclusive to any single sense; it also makes us aware of our own act of sensation, for which it is sometimes associated with the modern notion of consciousness. Memory stores information and offers one distinction between animals and humans. Inspired by Aristotle's *De memoria et reminiscentia*, some scholars divided memory into three types. The highest type of memory stored universal knowledge to be used by the reason and was only attributed to humans.[48] There was less agreement about the senses between common sense and memory, which correspond with Aristotle's *phantasia*. Imagination usually came first. The *imaginatio* is a retentive power that stores these particular sense perceptions, so that a dog can imagine the exact bone that was just removed from her presence. Sometimes scholars also posited an additional, and higher, power of the *phantasia* with a more active role than the imagination; others considered this to be identical with the imagination. In the next group of virtues are the powers that act on the images in the imagination. One of these powers is what is usually called the *cogitatio* in humans. It combines and separates the images into infinite configurations and thus prepares for the judging activity of practical reasoning. Some interpreters, following the interpretation of Averroes, even endowed the cogitation itself with something resembling practical reasoning about particular cases.[49] An example used by Jean de Jandun is as follows: when a doctor recognizes a particular symptom in a patient, compares this to other times he has seen the same symptom, remembers what happened to these earlier patients, and then guesses that the same thing will happen again, this process is attributed to the cogitation.[50] In conjunction with the imagination or *phantasia*, the cogitation also creates more abstract intentions to be stored in the *memoria*. The power equivalent to the cogitation in animals was usually called the imaginative virtue (Avicenna), in order to exclude some of the higher functions of the cogitation and fantasy. Another internal sense is the estimative power. Avicenna gave the estimation the responsibility for apprehending intentions provided by the imagination. Intentions were quasi-material entities that contain information imperceptible to the external senses, such as hostility and friendship. For Avicenna, the estimation was also the power used by a sheep to recognize danger in a wolf.

Discussion of animal intellect focused on these internal senses.[51] When the above commentators on *De motu animalium* granted animals an intellect, they provided this intellect with the functions of cogitation, estimation, and *phantasia*—without sharply distinguishing among them. Since it was not a matter of debate that most, if not all animals, have *phantasia*, the question of whether animals are moved by intellect could be answered positively. Yet, interpreters did not give all animals an equally robust fantasy, as is exemplified in Jean de Jandun's (d. 1328) question: "utrum fantasia sit idem cum sensu" (if *phantasia* is identical with sensation).[52] Jean here discusses, among other things, the passage of *De anima* in which Aristotle appears to say that ants and bees do not possess fantasy (*De anima*, 428a9sqq), and proposes two interpretations.

The first interpretation Jean explicitly borrows from Albert the Great. According to Albert, the behavior of ants and bees clearly illustrates that they possess fantasy or imaginative power; he thus believes that the translation of *De anima* must be wrong at this point. Clearly the translator did not understand which animals Aristotle was talking about and therefore replaced them with bees and ants—this solution still implies that there are two animals that do not have fantasy. Jean's second solution—and the solution he appears to prefer—is that ants and bees do not possess fantasy in the same way other animals do. Only the latter possess a determinate fantasy, that is, a fantasy that can be in act in absence of the sensible object. From what follows, it becomes clear that it is opposed to indeterminate fantasy, which is only activated in the presence of a sensible object and thus can be qualified as an imperfect or diminished fantasy. Even this indeterminate fantasy can be divided into several levels. The lowest level is that of the animals discussed in the previous section, the (most) imperfect animals that only move on place by dilatation and constriction. By adopting this interpretation, Jean thus attributes some level of *phantasia* to every animal; no matter how imperfect the *phantasia* is, it still allows the animal to determine what is convenient or inconvenient, friendly or hostile, and thus serves the purpose of self-preservation.

Discussions of this kind helped to clarify the functions of sensitive powers and the practical intellect and thus the connection between animals and humans. At the same time, these discussions about the formal characteristics of the soul—namely, what each part does—were often united to physiological characteristics to form a multifaceted explanatory system. Cogitation was best served by a hot middle ventricle of the brain to carry out its subtle processes. Emotions can be defined by their physiology to explain their power to produce desire. Because memories were quite literally impressed in the brain—a damp brain (specifically the rear ventricle) would be good for short-term memory because impressions can be made easily on a wet surface; a dry brain would yield longer-lasting impressions. Presumably, this is what allowed bees and ants, both extremely dry, to retain a fixed idea of their future plans, while we can imagine that fish have terrible long-term memories. Some aspects of this physiology are addressed in the final section.

Whatever sensitive or physiological components of psychology we share with animals, it should be emphasized that moral behavior remained the exclusive domain of humans. It was in the area of morality that philosophers insisted the greatest distinction can be made between humans and animals. Indeed, the necessity of this distinction reveals one of the motivations for the study of animals. Animals helped to isolate the immaterial human soul and therefore the source of truly free thought and free will. If humans and animals share behavior and the web of physiological forces that produce it, humans can be held morally accountable for their actions where animals are not.

ANIMALS AND LATER MEDIEVAL NATURALISM

In the generation after the assimilation of Aristotelian natural philosophy the role of animals in different styles of philosophy became more distinct, reflecting growing divisions between the scholastic disciplines. As always, the study of animals was deemed most useful by naturalists, who increasingly regarded the sensitive (animal) part of the soul as the key to human nature.[53] We suggested earlier that the theoretical medical traditions revived at Salerno helped stimulate physiological interests for which animals would be very important. Indeed Aristotle's works on animals were not only studied at the Arts faculty but also considered as a medical authority from the thirteenth century onward.[54] Among scholastic physicians, we should distinguish between their use of the animal texts for strictly medical purposes and for more philosophical purposes aimed at explaining anthropology through physical and natural modes, which are of more interest here.

The situation was very different in other areas of speculation. Animals are largely absent from the problems that most preoccupied theologians around the turn of the fourteenth century.[55] When animals do appear in theological work, it is as a tactic to define human nature before being discarded for more pressing issues. For some of the greatest Franciscan scholars of the thirteenth and fourteenth centuries, the contrast with their patron saint is especially stark: in place of the naturalism of Francis, who is often depicted preaching to the birds, we find disinterest and even contempt toward animals in his later followers in the schools.[56] Animals did not seem relevant for philosophical preoccupations with the highest reaches of human rational capabilities or in supernatural interests.[57]

Before we lament the neglect of animals by theologians compared to naturalists, it is worth considering the textual basis for this disparity. As we have already mentioned, different texts in the Aristotelian corpus portrayed different levels of similarity between humans and animals. The texts that were central to the education of theologians and metaphysicians argue a more well defined break between humans and animals. Meanwhile, in the works studied in the medical curriculum, and presumably by other natural philosophers, gradual-ism is more apparent. It would not be too much of an exaggeration to say that two (or more) versions of Aristotelianism emerged at this time: one that was more metaphysical—and more familiar to modern students of philosophy—and another with a more materialistic and naturalistic bent. For this second style of Aristotelianism, the works on animals, the *Meteorologica,* and to a lesser extent, Pseudo-Aristotelian works such as the *Problemata physica* and the *Physiognomia* became central texts.

One prominent example of this latter naturalism is the thought of Peter of Abano (d. 1316). Peter is remembered today as a physician as much as a philosopher, and his anthropological doctrines certainly reflect his medical emphases.[58] Compared to other philosophers, his anthropology pays unusual attention to particular and physiological aspects of human nature. Because the anthropological problems that interested him most were situated in the animal part of the soul, works on animals play a large role in his work, even if he did not comment on them directly.

In the course of his work Peter also made many observations about animals that go beyond the mere repetition of examples from his sources and show in-terest in animals for their own sake. Sometimes these observations even modify authoritative statements about the nature of animals. One example of this is found in his commentary to problem 28, 7 of the *Problemata physica.* Here Peter takes issue with Aristotle's opinion that "though there are five senses, the other animals only derive pleasure from the two we have mentioned," namely taste and touch.[59] (The senses are hierarchically arranged from highest to low-est: sight, hearing, smell, taste, and touch). Animals only use the higher senses expecting to taste or touch something. Thus a lion enjoys neither the sight nor the sound of his victim, but only the taste. This opinion transmitted an ancient trope that the enjoyment of the higher senses of smell, hearing, and sight is ex-clusively human because only humans are able to recognize beauty. Neverthe-less, Peter takes issue with Aristotle's judgment, offering examples of animals enjoying smell, hearing, and sight for their own sake. Every divergence from Aristotle of this kind is notable because of the great weight of his authority. In such comments, Peter takes a decidedly more animal friendly approach than many of his contemporaries.

Beyond these particular observations, Peter's work also exemplifies a man-ner of thought that employed more systematic and synthetic use of doctrines about animals. Of particular importance here, his materialistic approach to anthropology shows the influence of two traditions that were largely neglected by most philosophers and theologians: complexion theory and physiognomy. These are notable for the history of philosophical thought about animals because information derived from animals is fully imbedded within both traditions.

Complexion is the sum of the mixture of hot, cold, wet, and dry qualities in a body. Because every natural body has a complexion, it had universal explanatory power in the natural world and could be applied equally to animals and humans. For example, bees are cold and dry, horses are hot and dry, fish are cold and wet, and humans have both the hottest and most balanced complexion of the animals. Every variation in physiological, emotional, or psychological state was accompanied by an equivalent variation in complexion. As a whole, animals are cooler, denser, and less likely to act against the impulse of the gross matter of which they are composed.[60] The fact that humans are hotter than animals is most clearly manifest in the fact that humans stand erect because our heat holds us up. For animals, a notable property of this theory is that it places humans and animals together on the same natural scale; differences in complexion are qualitative differences of more or less, not differences in category. In the Galenic text translated by Burgundio of Pisa as *De complexionibus* (otherwise known as *De temperamentis*), Galen frequently draws examples from the animal world to explain complexion. Galen's comparative approach is illustrated in the scale of complexions from Peter of Abano's *Conciliator*. The center contains a perfect complexion *ad pondus,* which is unattainable for any living creature. Beyond this, the rings indicate various states of health and illness in humans and the qualitative disproportions that mark different animals (fish, ants, horses). Even the complexion of figs is included. (See Figure 6.4.)

If complexion theory implied similarity with animals, it was also a vehicle for the competing impulse to attribute a fundamental distinction between humans and beasts. Avicenna's influential version of complexion theory transmits the idea that although humans and animals can be described in the same fundamental qualitative terms, nevertheless, the human complexion is incommensurable with animal complexion in an important way: the exceptional balance of human complexion would not ordinarily be possible in nature without divine—and celestial—intervention.[61] To this extent the human complexion is almost supernatural. Galen, who was not constrained by religious doctrines about man's essential difference, had not put the difference between humans and animals in such stark terms.

Complexion theory was complemented by the physiognomic tradition, transmitted most prominently in the Pseudo-Aristotelian *Physiognomy,* as well as other ancient and Arabic physiognomic texts.[62] The aim of physiognomy was to identify innate characteristics of the soul through the appearance of the body. Typically, a physiognomic text listed the parts of the body from head to foot, along with other natural operations, such as the way someone breathes or laughs. For example, ears that are narrow and oblong reveal an envious character; a hairy back indicates bravery. Animals are liberally dispersed throughout physiognomic texts because their features were linked to their character and then used to understand human behavior. Deer and rabbits

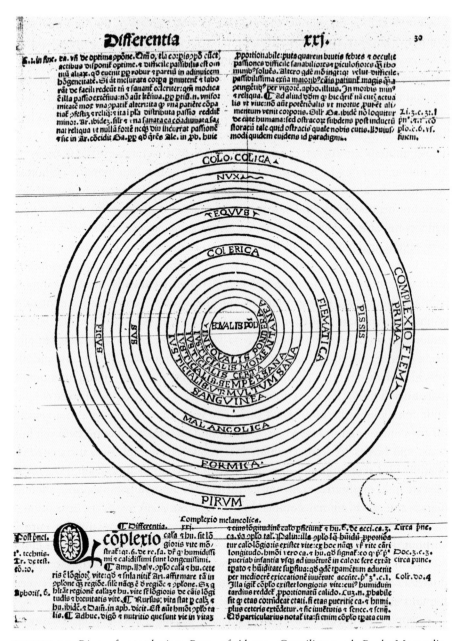

FIGURE 6.4: *Ring of complexion*, Peter of Abano, *Conciliator*, ed. B. de Morandis, 1523, p. 30.

were recognized to be timid creatures; therefore deerlike or rabbitlike features in a person were trusted to be sign of innate timidity. On the other hand, lion-like features signify bravery. Males are like lions, females are like horses. This use of animals is pervasive.[63] The appearance of animals made a particularly fruitful area for the study of innate character because the traits of animals were taken to be constant; unlike humans, who could overcome innate tendencies, animals were bound to their character.

Physiognomy and complexion are just two aspects of an eclectic genre of medieval naturalism that merged with the study of Aristotle's books on animals and the other *libri naturales* to take a serious interest in the nature of animals. It is important to distinguish this naturalism from the moral and analogical uses of animals mentioned at the beginning of this chapter. Although physiognomy, for example, certainly had moral purposes, the characteristics of animals are not moralized. Instead, physiognomy strove to derive factual information about the appearance and character of animals to inform thinking about human nature. All of these texts contributed to the naturalist project—with both theoretical and practical dimensions—to articulate a physiological and psychological framework for all living creatures.

In this chapter we have mainly focused on how an inclusive understanding of psychology enabled medieval natural philosophers to envision living creatures within the sublunary world and to define a place for animals within a hierarchy headed by humans. Even when philosophers were very serious about learning the nature of animals, they were most often studied for the sake of man. In other areas of speculation, the focus on humans was even more apparent. In bestiaries animals were discussed as moral exempla, from whose behavior humans could learn. Theologians used animals mainly to define human nature as signifiers of divine purpose but discarded the animals themselves as intrinsically uninteresting. This philosophical anthropocentrism explains why there was hardly any discussion about the treatment of animals, or animal rights. It is only in later time periods that the case for the proper treatment of animals, which had already been defended by some Greek thinkers, reemerged.

This chapter also necessarily reflects our current understanding of animals in philosophical discourse. We have a good sense of the process of translation and commentary of ancient texts explicitly about animals, recounted previously. However, we know that these commentaries do not tell the whole story about the use of the animal texts. Because the direct commentary tradition is somewhat lacking, we must look elsewhere to understand the depth of the influence of philosophical work on animals. As we suggest in the final section, it is possible that a closer study of the way naturalists actually incorporated animals into their doctrines may give us a richer understanding of medieval thought about animals.

CHAPTER SEVEN

Beyond the Ark

Animals in Medieval Art

BRIGITTE RESL

"Animals are good to think [with]."[1] This is one of the reasons why animals provide many of the most popular motifs in medieval art, especially in the religious sphere from which the majority of the surviving artwork from the period derives. The Bible is, of course, replete with animal metaphors, while texts such as the *Physiologus*, the bestiary genre, and encyclopedias contain moral allegories specifically shaped around animals. Preachers routinely used these analogies in sermons in order to instruct their audiences and to provide them with recognizable mnemonic tools. The visualization of meaningful animals also helped to fix these messages in Christian minds. In consequence, manuscripts produced by and for the clergy are full of depictions of animals, while churches and liturgical objects are decorated with animals in a wide variety of media. Animals were deployed in such contexts as signs loaded with spiritual and moral meanings; it is often this rather than the appreciation of the animals themselves that determines the species selected and the form in which they are presented by learned elites, who were drawing on long-established artistic traditions. To understand the role of animals in medieval religious art it is therefore essential to relate them to earlier defining moments in the Christian use of artistic imagery. For the principles developed in late antiquity were adhered to throughout the early medieval period, and it was these that were reconsidered during the controversy over art of the early twelfth century.[2]

However, the enthusiasm for the use of animal imagery in medieval art did not derive exclusively from the symbolic significance of its subjects. It is abundantly clear that medieval Europeans simply enjoyed looking at animals and that their artistic representation had no other purpose than to delight, even in artworks produced in explicitly religious contexts, such as the illustrations in Bibles or the decorations on liturgical vessels or vestments. Furthermore, the style of animal portrayals in art between 1000 and 1400 varies according to context or purpose. The reduction of the animal image to an icon enhances its symbolic power, which helps to explain why some forms of depiction are rigidly standardized and do not appear to change much over centuries. From the thirteenth century, however, individual depictions of animals based on study and observation begin to increase in number, expressing the growth of interest in their subjects for their own sake, and not just as vehicles for allegorical messages. Both forms of representation—allegorical and naturalistic—then coexist for some considerable time, and artists can often combine both styles within the same piece of work. In general, even so, the context of the work in question normally carries significant implications for its form and style. In manuscript illuminations, for example, bestiaries and encyclopedias that depend on instant recognition of their animal subjects as mnemonic and didactic tools prefer the easy familiarity of standardized, iconic depictions long into the thirteenth and fourteenth centuries. At the same time, hunting manuals and medical texts that are more concerned with the description of such matters as the behavior and welfare of animals, or their pharmaceutical uses, prefer to adopt a more naturalistic style of representation.

The topic of animals in medieval art is an enormous one, and a long-established field of scholarly enquiry and publication.[3] This chapter can only concern itself with a few key aspects selected to give a flavor of the breadth and variety of the subject. Most research has concentrated on the analysis of the symbolic meanings of animals, especially in the religious sphere; we need to begin, therefore, by outlining why animals were considered particularly attractive vehicles for the communication of religious and moral messages. Artistic representations of animals in medieval religious works served primarily as didactic and mnemonic tools, much as art in general was intended to serve within Christian contexts. The foundations of this tradition had been established in late antiquity by church fathers such as Augustine (354–430), who emphasized the didactic function of animals in his *De doctrina Christiana* (On Christian teaching). Here he stressed the importance of knowing the figurative as well as literal meanings of biblical animals in order to achieve a fuller understanding of Holy Scripture and to employ animal metaphors as meaningful signs. Authoritative statements such as these only encouraged the depiction of animals within the fast-emerging context of Christian iconography. One of the defining moments in the ongoing evolution of this tradition then occurred under

Pope Gregory I, the Great (590–604). Among his numerous contributions to the shaping of medieval Christianity, Pope Gregory upheld the legitimacy of using art in the ecclesiastical sphere in precise terms. In July 599 he wrote a letter to Bishop Serenus of Marseille admonishing him for the destruction of images in his church in response to their adoration by some members of his congregation. Gregory reminded the zealous bishop that "a picture is provided in churches for the reason that those who are illiterate may at least read by looking at the walls what they cannot read in books."[4] When Serenus dared to insist on the validity of his actions by reference to the divine commandment against image worship—in a letter that sadly does not survive—Gregory was provoked into explaining in more detail the distinction between worshipping an image and reading it: "For the worship of a picture is one thing but learning what should be worshipped through the story of a picture is something else."[5] His opinion about the didactic value of art would regularly be cited throughout the medieval period to justify the value of artistic representations in ecclesiastical contexts, and sometimes with specific reference to animal imagery, for example in Hugh of Fouilloy's *Aviarium* and in bestiaries.

Gregory the Great also provided a rationale for the practice of endowing animals with meaning in his *Moralia,* a commentary on the Book of Job that would become one of the most copied texts of the Middle Ages. In the Bible story, Job was striving to come to terms with the sudden string of catastrophes ruining his life when he received the advice to "ask the beasts, and they will teach you; the birds of the air, and they will tell you; or the plants of the earth, and they will teach you; and the fish of the sea will declare to you."[6] For Pope Gregory this biblical passage showed how the natural world was full of meaningful signs, so its careful observation could be a source of valuable moral lessons. This viewpoint came to be appreciated not only by church authorities but also by lay instructors, especially within the context of education in elite households. It is exemplified in the ninth-century manual written by the Carolingian noblewoman Dhuoda for the edification of William, her absent son, in which, like Saint Augustine and Pope Gregory before her, she stressed the importance of recognizing the exemplary value of animals. Encouraging William to "[l]ove, venerate, welcome, and honor everyone, so that you may deserve the enjoyment of a reciprocal benefit ...," she holds up the stag, as discussed by Augustine in his commentary on Psalm 41, as an exemplar. Dhuoda further illustrates this by reference to an account derived from Pliny's *Natural History* of the "fraternal creaturely kindness" seen in herds of stags in swimming across water, when they take it in turns to swim at the front, in a manner akin to that of modern cycle racers. She concludes this powerful admonition by quoting the advice given to Job to ask the beasts of burden and the birds of the sky for advice.[7]

Some animals derived their religious symbolic meanings directly from their appearances in biblical contexts. Those species that feature most frequently or prominently in the Bible, such as sheep, lions, and serpents, are those that are emphasized in exegetical interpretation, and, by extension, this ensured that they recur particularly often as conveyers of meaning in medieval religious art. The lamb, as a symbol of Christ in particular or of salvation more generally is, for example, a standard motif in Romanesque church decoration, where it is often found in central positions, whether depicted on a tympanum above the entrance or as the keystone of the chancel vault.[8] (See Figure 7.1.)

Sheep, lambs, and rams were relatively easy to interpret, since they carried only positive meanings, whether as symbols of Christ, the faithful crowd, or sacrifice. Other animals, such as lions, could be read antithetically as representations of evil, as in scriptural narratives such as Daniel's adventure in the lions' den or Samson's fight with the lion. In both cases the heroes' ability to escape unscathed from their confrontations with these fierce beasts allowed these episodes to function as reminders to the faithful that the eternal struggle between good and evil would ultimately be resolved in salvation. This potent message guaranteed that the Daniel motif in particular would often feature in religious ornament, as for example in the sculpted decoration of the column capitals of Romanesque churches. In such contexts the identical motif is sometimes repeated more than once within a single building, or within just one area of a church, even in small structures that offered limited scope for artistic decoration, or in those with very few specimens of such artwork. In some cases

FIGURE 7.1: *Agnus Dei*. Besse. © Brigitte Resl.

this might reflect the limitations of the sculptor's repertoire, but it also suggests that the motif was especially valued for its figurative meaning, rather than as a literal reminder of the individual Bible episode.

Lions are nevertheless more complicated in their meanings than sheep. Although they can stand for evil or the devil, they can equally serve as symbols of Christ, as in the highly influential *Physiologus,* where the significance of the creature is enhanced by its placing at the head of all the more common versions of the text.[9] Lions can therefore serve as a salutary reminder of the inconvenient fact that animals' symbolic meanings were frequently ambiguous, and necessarily subject to context. Augustine had already taken pains to point this out when he warned that things could have various meanings, "either contrary or just different. By contrary I mean cases in which a particular thing is used sometimes in a good sense and sometimes in a bad one, ... [an] example is 'lion,' which signifies Christ in the passage 'The lion from the tribe of Judah has conquered' [Rev. 5:5], but 'devil' in the passage 'Your enemy walks like a roaring lion, seeking someone to devour' [1 Pet. 5:8]."[10] The dominant reading of any particular creature was also susceptible to change over time. In the earlier Middle Ages good and bad lions occurred side by side, but from the eleventh century onward lions are increasingly found in positive contexts, while leopards supersede them as felines with negative connotations.[11]

The latter development is also bound up with the eventual expansion in the range of animals employed in Christian art. Before the twelfth century the repertoire of symbolic animals was largely confined to sheep, lions, serpents, and dragons, and to the other animals that appear in the *Physiologus,* such as the stag, pelican, unicorn, phoenix, and elephant. With the exception of the sheep that feature in so many biblical episodes, all of these are wild animals—in the sense that they had not been domesticated; indeed, most of them are exotic, and sometimes wholly imaginary. Anthropologists have argued that the particular power of mythical beasts as symbols can be explained by the fact that the boundaries between them and humans are more readily accepted. The selection of animals in the *Physiologus* and portrayed most frequently in religious art, especially before the twelfth century, appears to confirm this viewpoint.[12] The omnipresence of dragons and unicorns, for example, ensures that they remain the animals instinctively associated with medieval culture in the popular imagination today. These creatures appear in the *Physiologus* and in bestiaries as symbols respectively of evil and of Christ, both derived from their appearances in Scripture. Unicorns found their way into the Bible through a misunderstanding. In the Latin Vulgate, the Hebrew word for a type of cattle, *re'em,* was translated by a word derived from natural histories that described a particularly ferocious horned creature, the unicorn. The *Physiologus* then explained this by linking its horn with Christ through the gospel passage " ... he has visited and redeemed his people, and has raised up a horn of salvation for

us in the house of his servant David" (Luke 1:68–69). The medieval concept of
the dragon also has its roots in biblical terminology. The Latin word *draco*—a
huge serpent—was used in the Vulgate to describe the beast, and by extension
Satan, in the book of Revelation, but came also to be applied to the humble
serpens who tempted Eve in paradise. Initially the devil had been represented
in the latter form, as a snake; the *Physiologus* accordingly features snakes in
various forms, but no dragons. By the time of the emergence of the expanded
bestiaries in the twelfth century, however, dragons have frequently replaced
snakes, and they gradually assume the image of an elaborate hybrid beast that
increasingly exhibits the features of dragons with which we are still familiar:
a prominent jaw with sharp teeth, pointy ears, birds' or bats' wings attached
to a reptile's body and tail, and birds' or lions' feet. These standard traits can
vary significantly in detail, as in an ink-drawn dragon that forms the initial
S in a thirteenth-century breviary from Seckau (Austria), which has a rather
unusual fish tail, but otherwise features all the key characteristics of the species
that would have made it recognizable to contemporaries and moderns alike.
(See Figure 7.2.)

   The more general proliferation in the range of animals that could be deployed with symbolic purposes from the twelfth century onward can best
be observed through the development of the bestiary genre. Although this
evolved directly out of the *Physiologus*, it rapidly expanded upon it both
quantitatively—by steadily increasing the number of animal examples—and
qualitatively—whether by offering more accurate descriptions of animals or
deriving from them not only spiritual interpretations but explicit moral guidelines.[13] The bestiaries also emphasize the importance of visualization as a means
of reinforcing the didactic function of the moralizations and of expanding the
audience of such messages to include the illiterate. Illustrations had already
begun to be incorporated alongside the Latin text of the *Physiologus* by the
ninth century at the latest, when they are present in manuscript 318 of the
Bürgerbibliothek in Berne, one of its earliest surviving versions. (See Figure 6.1
in chapter 6.) By the twelfth century, representations of most of the *Physiologus* and bestiary animals had turned into standardized icons designed to convey moral messages and spiritual truths, along the lines that had been justified
by Gregory the Great many centuries earlier. Hugh of Fouilloy (d. ca. 1172)
duly repeated the pope's instructions about the didactic value of images in the
prologue to his *Aviarium*:

   I decided to paint the dove whose wings are *silvered and the hinderparts
   of the back in pale gold* (Ps. 67:14), and by a picture to instruct the minds
   of simple folk, so that what the intellect of the simple folk could scarcely
   comprehend with the mind's eye, it might at least discern with the physical eye: and what their hearing could scarcely perceive, their sight might

FIGURE 7.2: *Dragon*. Initial, Breviary (thirteenth century), Chorherrenstift Seckau, Universitätsbibliothek Graz, MS 789, fol. 305r. © Institut für Realienkunden—ÖAW.

do so. I wished not only to paint the dove physically, but also to outline it verbally, so that by the text I may represent a picture; for instance, whom the simplicity of the picture would not please, at least the moral teaching of the text might do so.[14]

He explains his intention in greater detail further on in the passage:

Because I must write for the unlettered, the diligent reader should not wonder that, for the instruction of the unlettered, I say simple things about subtle matters. Nor should he attribute it to levity that I paint a hawk or a dove, because the blessed Job and the prophet David bequeathed to us birds of this sort for our edification. For what Scripture means to the teachers, the picture means to simple folk. For just as the learned man delights in the subtlety of the written word, so the intellect of simple folk is engaged by the simplicity of a picture.[15]

The author of the Aberdeen Bestiary, a good example of the development of the genre in its second generation, had much the same in mind and copied the passage around 1200 in his work. By this stage, the range of animal examples that could be included had expanded not only in number, but in meaning and significance. The newly introduced animals are mostly familiar and included wild animals of an everyday nature such as beavers and badgers alongside domesticated ones such as horses, sheep, cats, and dogs, as well as numerous birds, derived in this case from Hugh of Fouilloy's *Aviarium*. The aforementioned examples of the dove and the hawk can serve to show how such creatures could now be used for other purposes than merely to suggest spiritual meanings, since they are employed allegorically to instruct different members of a monastic community about correct behavior. The dove stands for a converted clergyman and the hawk for a converted knight both sharing "the monastic life together."[16] Both birds are selected for this exemplary purpose because of their natural attributes. Even so, the fundamental function of the visual representation of these creatures remains the same as ever; they are intended as texts to be read by the illiterate in the sense explained by Gregory the Great.

The proliferation of species included in bestiaries is also found in other media, such as the sculptural decoration of churches. In the Poitou, for example, the arch over the northern entrance to the church of Saint-Junien in Lusignan, dating from the twelfth century, is divided into twenty-three segments that feature an intriguing assortment of animals. Here the wild beasts familiar from the *Physiologus* tradition, such as the elephant, or a beaver castrating itself, alternate with domestic animals such as cats, bovines, and a pig; the latter now outnumber their wild counterparts. Perhaps surprisingly, the camel that

FIGURE 7.3: *Saint-Junien, Lusignan.* © Brigitte Resl.

is depicted here can also be legitimately regarded as falling into the domestic category. Its inclusion in bestiaries coincided with the expanding horizons of the period of the Crusades, when the animal became increasingly familiar as a beast of burden. Given that the lords of Lusignan had strong links with the Near East and were firmly committed to the crusading movement, the inclusion of a camel among the beasts of the Saint-Junien portal may well be specifically linked with their patronage of the church. Naturally, camels had acquired a generic spiritual significance too; they were supposed to remind the onlooker of "the humility of Christ, who bears all our sins, or of the Gentiles converted to the Christian faith."[17] (See Figure 7.3.)

In stylistic terms, the decorative composition of the arch over the north door of Saint-Junien is not altogether different from that of other contemporary churches in the region in its blend of the familiar and the exotic, juxtaposing domestic and wild animals with more fabulous beasts. It is distinguished, however, by the unusually wide variety of animals on display, and because the mythical or fabricated hybrid creatures among them are in the minority. Wild and mythical animals more frequently predominate, and it is quite common for the latter to be composites, constructed out of the body parts of various different creatures, as in the equally fascinating assortment of beasts that can be seen sculpted in relief in the outer register of the celebrated southern portal of the church of Saint-Pierre in Aulnay, in the Saintonge, dating from the first half of the twelfth century. (See Figure 7.4.)

This parade of animals, unlike that at Saint-Junien, is dominated by hybrid and imaginary creatures. But the choice of several of them can similarly be explained by reference to the significance that is ascribed to them in the *Phys-*

FIGURE 7.4: *Saint-Pierre, Aulnay*. © Brigitte Resl.

iologus or in bestiaries, as for example in the case of centaurs and sirens. In the *Physiologus* the moralizing interpretation of both creatures builds on the fact that they are hybrids: "There are some in the church who have the form of piety but deny its force, and though they are in the church as men, when they depart from the church they become beasts."[18] In bestiaries the hybrid nature of centaurs is usually commented upon in accounts of horses, while sirens convey a warning message about the lures of sensual pleasures: some people "expend their intellectual energy entirely on comedies, tragedies, and various musical compositions, and all at once they become eagerly sought-after prey of their enemies."[19] It should be noted, even so, that the form in which these creatures are depicted at Aulnay bears no resemblance whatsoever to the conventional iconography of the bestiaries, and that many of the other monstrous beings that feature on the arch are complex hybrids without any obvious correspondents in established visual or textual traditions. The most striking of these, perhaps, are a series of native quadrupeds that are familiar in nature, but extraordinary in the manner in which they are portrayed: walking on their hind legs, like humans. Their apparent transgression of the conventional boundaries between man and beast—intensified by the portrayal of some of these creatures in clerical guise—arguably renders them more monstrous in their deviation from the norm than the stereotypical monsters themselves. Francis Klingender referred to this beastly assembly as a carnival procession, and the musical ass

FIGURE 7.5: *Ram bishop*. Saint-Pierre, Aulnay. © Brigitte Resl.

and the dancing deer are certainly reminiscent of figures that are known to have paraded in festival pageants of the period.[20] As in the cases of humans dressing as animals, the intention may have been to convey a similar notion of the world turned upside-down. Indeed, the ram bishop and his sheep minister call to mind another favorite carnival costume of contemporary layfolk, namely clerical dress; here, however, in some kind of double inversion, it would seem that the animals are mimicking lay humans who dress up as men of the church.[21] (See Figure 7.5.)

Motifs such as those found at Saint-Pierre in Aulnay were common elements of decoration in Romanesque ecclesiastical architecture throughout western Europe at the time, whether in monastic contexts or not. However, it could be said that the suitability and meaning of such motifs when depicted within spaces that were exclusively reserved for the monastic life presents a particular problem for the modern scholar. It certainly generated considerable controversy among contemporaries in the twelfth century. Bernard of Clairvaux vehemently rejected the appearance of such monstrosities in the cloister:

in the cloisters, before the eyes of the brothers while they read—what is that ridiculous monstrosity doing ...? What are the filthy apes doing there? The fierce lions? The monstrous centaurs? The creatures, part man and part beast? The striped tigers? The fighting soldiers? The hunters blowing horns? You may see many bodies under one head, and conversely many heads on one body. On one side the tail of a serpent is seen on a quadruped, on the other side, the head of a quadruped is on the body of a fish. Over there an animal has a horse for the front half and a goat for the back; here a creature which is horned in front is equine behind.[22]

At first sight this reads as a condemnation of the artistic representation of wild animals in general, and hybrid creatures in particular. However, this statement needs to be understood in the context of the twelfth-century monastic reform movement and the Cistercian repudiation of the accumulation of wealth and indulgence in luxury that the reformers alleged were characteristic of Benedictine communities. Bernard was not criticizing the monstrosities on display per se, but questioning their appropriateness for a space that was reserved for contemplation by the monks. While he found the use of such decoration in the architecture of the cloister disturbing, he did not question its didactic function in those areas of religious buildings that were accessible to the laity.[23] If, however, one chooses to interpret these wild and hybrid creatures as symbols of sin and evil it could, of course, be argued that the presentation of such inner demons in material form could prove equally constructive for the meditating monks.[24] It must be emphasized, moreover, that Bernard's doubts on this subject are only a minor element in his wider critique of excessive expenditure on religious art. In the preceding chapter of his *Apologia*, Bernard had just condemned such spending in those areas of churches that were accessible to the laity; here, however, he objects specifically to such things as ornate liturgical vessels, and does not criticize paintings or sculptural decoration.[25] His strident opposition to the depiction of animals was thus context specific, and limited in its significance. In overseeing the rebuilding of his monastic church at much the same time, Abbot Suger was meanwhile reiterating the common justification for additional expenditure on works of art in the context of religious architecture by adapting Pope Gregory the Great's famous words: "The dull mind rises to the truth through material things ... "[26] Even Bernard of Clairvaux did not really disagree that decorative art could fulfill an important function in religious architecture. Despite opposition to the intrusion of the lurid and fantastic into what some regarded as particularly inappropriate settings, the fundamental notion that animals and even monsters conveyed meaning was never disputed, and nor was the didactic value of these representations.

It is impossible to argue that any linear or particular development in the perception of animals had taken place by the thirteenth and fourteenth centuries; instead, the later medieval period is characterized by the proliferation of a much greater variety of attitudes.[27] In general, differences in both perception and representation depend principally on the context. The depiction of

animals in religious art remained subject to convention when intended to provide moral and spiritual allegories, although less so when used for more straight-
forwardly illustrative purposes, as we shall see. In other contexts, however, the
understanding and interpretation of animals was undergoing more substantial
changes. By the thirteenth century, the study of animals was becoming not just
a means to a higher spiritual end, but a worthy topic of intellectual inquiry in
its own right. No example better serves to illustrate this than Matthew Paris's
famous drawings of Henry III's elephant.[28] In 1255 Louis IX of France had
presented the beast to his brother-in-law as a gift that, as so often in such cases,
was intended primarily to display his own status. The monk and chronicler
Matthew Paris recounts how he found the arrival of the poor elephant in the
Tower menagerie sufficiently fascinating for him to make the journey from
Saint-Albans to the capital in order to draw the creature from life. He was
by no means alone in his desire to see the exotic arrival at firsthand, since, as
he notes in his chronicle, "people flocked together to see the novel sight."[29]
While it is debatable whether Matthew Paris did in fact enjoy the opportunity
to sketch the elephant from life or whether he only claimed to have done so in
order to enhance the value of a copy he had made from someone else's drawing,
it is indisputable that he made considerable effort in the depiction that he included in his chronicle to achieve a naturalistic effect, to the extent of including
"Henry the beast-keeper" within it in order to give his audience some idea of
the creature's enormous size. After all, while people might have known what
an elephant looked like from the familiar representations of such creatures in
bestiaries and church decorations, these would not necessarily have given them
any sense of its remarkable scale.[30]

   The depiction of the elephant by Matthew Paris is frequently compared
by scholars with the equally celebrated drawings of animals by the northern
French artist Villard de Honnecourt, in the first quarter of the thirteenth century, and in particular with that of the lion, about which the artist comments:
"here is a lion as one sees it from the front, please bear in mind that he was
drawn from life."[31] (See Figure 7.6.) In each of these cases, exotic beasts that
were conceptually recognizable but had never been seen in the flesh by the vast
majority of the artists' audiences inspired representations that were explicitly
based on examples from life rather than the conventional stereotypes. Matthew Paris and Villard de Honnecourt may well have been driven by a desire
to observe and accurately to characterize species that for all practical purposes
were hitherto unfamiliar. If so, however, the impact of firsthand knowledge of
this type remained particular and limited; it did not change the ways in which
these creatures were typically represented. Elephants in bestiaries, for example,
continued to be drawn in the conventional, iconic manner.[32] After all, their
primary function in such works was to remind the viewer of the moral allegory
associated with the creature; what mattered first and foremost, therefore, was

FIGURE 7.6: *Lion.* Nicholas de Honnecourt, Sketchbook (ca. 1230), BnF, Paris, MS Français 19093, fol. 24v.

ease of recognition. In such a context it was more important for the subject to look typical than realistic.

The thirteenth-century traveler Marco Polo displayed a similar but far more sustained interest in the observation of exotic fauna during his travels through

FIGURE 7.7: *Fauna of Eli*. Marco Polo, *Devisament du Monde*, BnF, Paris, MS Français 2810, fol. 85r.

Asia. His audience wanted to be entertained as much as informed, however, and their enjoyment was dependent upon a certain level of familiarity if they were to be able to appreciate his account. In a fourteenth-century manuscript of Polo's report from Paris, the illustrations allow a glimpse of the problems imposed upon artists by the audience's expectations and the limits of its imagination.[33] While Polo frequently dismisses common stereotypes about the marvelous animals of the East in his account, the accompanying illuminations make no attempt to portray what the text explains but to simply reproduce the familiar stereotypes instead. While Marco Polo's description of his encounter with a rhinoceros on Java sadly failed to inspire an illumination in this work, his account of the fauna of the kingdom of Eli on the coast of Malabar did.[34] Polo had been thoroughly astonished by the remarkable differences between the animals he saw there and those he knew from Europe.[35] However, he failed dismally to report any sighting of the mythical creatures that readers of courtly literature such as the Alexander romances would have instinctively associated with the East. The illustrator rectified this obvious flaw in his account by supplying what was missing from the text. At the center of the illustration of the fauna of Eli, he depicted the most popular of these imaginary beasts, the unicorn, in full and glorious stride. (See Figure 7.7.)

In so doing, even so, the illustrator need not, as one might imagine, have been simply indifferent to or ignorant of the content of the adjacent text. In his account Marco Polo mentioned only that there are "lions and other wild beasts" in Eli and that "[t]here is abundance of game, both beasts and birds."[36] According to contemporary bestiaries and encyclopedias alike, the wildest of all the beasts was the unicorn, so the artist and his audience might immediately have called that creature to mind when reading or hearing Marco Polo's story, despite the disappointing absence of any specific reference to it in the text.[37] In support of this interpretation it is worth noting that the illustrator does interpret Polo's allusion to "game, both beasts and birds" more or less literally. The swans, boar, bear, and fox that feature in the illustration were not only common game at the time, but the inspiration for the way in which they are depicted here is likely to have been derived from an illustrated hunting manual, a genre in which animals were often depicted in their natural habitat in realistic poses. Polo's assertion in his introduction to the Malabar Coast that the animals found there were wholly different from European species was a concept altogether too complicated and elusive to be readily transferable into pictorial form. Instead a lion and a unicorn were pasted into an otherwise familiar scene in order to signify the more exotic elements in his account.

The aforementioned hunting manuals are an emerging manuscript genre of the thirteenth and fourteenth centuries that is often richly illustrated. The text of such works typically elaborates on the animals' habits, their outer appearance, how they breed, and what food they prefer, bringing together a substantial amount of knowledge drawn directly from observation of the behavioral characteristics of the various species concerned. The accompanying illustrations show a similar tendency toward realism, and it is in this context that animals are routinely portrayed for the first time in a style that suggests the images are informed by firsthand knowledge of the animals and their habitats. Not all of these depictions are naturalistic or taken from life, of course; as so often, some of them are merely copied from existing examples. At some stage, even so, those models were developed on the basis of observation, and, just as significantly, the artists who copied them became increasingly able to discriminate between the animals they found in different manuscript contexts in order to match them with the style of representation most appropriate to the genre in which they were working. (See Figure 1.1 in chapter 1.) The animals depicted in a thirteenth-century series of illuminated manuscripts of the dietetic manual *Tacuinum sanitatis* are similarly shown in everyday situations.[38] Although in such texts they are considered in the context of their value as foodstuffs and medicines, the essential emphasis is still on the animals themselves, if only as a commodity, and not on their underlying significances. As in the case of the hunting manuals, this functional approach encouraged a new style of representation.

Meanwhile, the texts emerging as a result of advances in zoological knowledge, such as the translations of Aristotle's *Historia animalium,* often remain disappointingly devoid of illustrations, or are accompanied only by conventional depictions of animals based on the exemplars found in bestiaries and model books. One example of this can be found in an illuminated initial in an early copy of William of Moerbeke's translation of Aristotle's *De motu animalium* (On the movement of animals) in a manuscript from the late thirteenth century. (See Figure 6.3 in chapter 6.). It shows the natural philosopher at work by depicting Aristotle studying the movements of animals. The three chosen exemplars—dog, bird, and snake—stand for the various categories of species. They are clearly shown as if in motion, not in any attempt at naturalistic representation, but rather by the way in which they are arranged within the letter *d*, and in other respects they conform to the formulaic conventions of their depictions in bestiaries.[39] This conservatism of image, if not text, has led to speculation that the addition of traditional Christian iconography to what could be regarded as revolutionary knowledge might have been deliberately designed to make its reception less unpalatable.[40] In the light of the frequent dislocations between image and text that have already been discussed, a simpler explanation might be that in the context of natural science and philosophy the conventional stereotypical representations of animals remained the preferred mode of visualization in this period principally because they were the most easily recognizable. This facilitated the efficient attribution of the new knowledge to the appropriate categories without risk of error. After all, in such contexts the animals were being studied not out of interest in the creatures as such, but as a means to better understand humans.[41] In this regard, at least, the aim was not so very different from the motives of traditional Christian iconography.

It is not the case, in any event, that all the animals portrayed in religious art have to be interpreted symbolically. Often, they are simply participants in defining moments of the biblical narrative in both the Old and New Testaments. From the story of the creation and Noah's ark, via Christ's entry to Jerusalem on the back of a donkey, to the terrible beast of the apocalypse, animals and monsters are frequently mentioned in scripture and, as a result, are familiar presences in the illustration of such stories in painting, sculpture, and manuscript illumination. (See Figure 7.8.) For much of the medieval period, the visual representations of religious narratives were constrained by convention in various ways. By the later Middle Ages, however, the nature and portrayal of the animals populating these scenes increasingly reveals the influence of the prevailing cultural trends described previously.

The book of Genesis was particularly central to the understanding of medieval church doctrine concerning the relationship between humans and animals, as established during the creation of all living beings. On the fifth day of creation, God filled the waters with "swarms of living beings" and the sky with birds (Gen. 1:20–23). On the following day, God created "living creatures of every kind": wild animals, cattle, and creeping things (Gen. 1:24–25). This distinction introduces the basic taxonomic system that distinguished animals into those living in the air or in the water from those dwelling upon the earth. The establishment of human dominion over the whole of creation is next expressed through reference to the same basic categories: "Then God said, 'Let us make man in our image, after our likeness; and let them have dominion over the fish of the sea, and over the birds of the air, and over the cattle, and over all the earth, and over every creeping thing that creeps upon the earth'" (Gen. 1:26). Human superiority over the rest of creation is subsequently reiterated by Adam's assigning of names to all creatures. (Gen. 2:19–20).

FIGURE 7.8: *Entry to Jerusalem.* Bible (fifteenth century), Zisterzienserkloster Neuberg, Universitätsbibliothek Graz. © Institut für Realienkunden—ÖAW.

The particular significance of this narrative for medieval audiences can be measured by the frequency with which it was visualized. A genre in which the events of the creation story were routinely depicted in the later Middle Ages was that of the illustrated Bible. Sometimes the whole sequence of the creation of living beings is condensed into a single image, as for example in one version

FIGURE 7.9: *Creation of birds and fish.* Guiard des Moulins, *Bible historiale* (first half of fourteenth century), BnF, Paris, MS Français 156, fol. 5v.

of Guiard des Moulins's *Bible historiale* from the first half of the fourteenth century. (See Figure 7.9.) This depiction accompanies the biblical account of the creation of birds and fish, but the quadrupeds are included in the picture as well, as if to make up for the fact that their own entrance into the world will not otherwise be independently portrayed. In other contemporary instances, the various stages of the process are illustrated in sequence in multiple frames, as in another manuscript of the same text from the early fourteenth century.[42] This contains illuminations that in turn depict the creation of birds and fish, of quadrupeds, and of the other terrestrial animals. The first of these snapshots of the birth of life depicts God releasing a big fish into the sea under the watchful observation of birds sitting in the trees above. (See cover illustration.) The next image illustrates the creation of terrestrial animals by showing God standing in the middle of a flock of sheep and goats.[43] But despite the fact that these ruminants were only introduced to the world in this second stage of the process, their appearance had been anticipated in the previous image, where the sheep have already served as casual bystanders to God's creation of the birds of the sky and the fish of the sea. In representing these momentous events, the illuminator of the manuscript was not strictly bound by the sequence of the text, but felt able to allow himself a measure of artistic license.

The gaps in the creation story left more obvious scope for interpretation. Nowhere in the account of the creation of living beings does Scripture specifically mention any particular species except humankind. As a result, the animals that were selected to illustrate this episode vary widely across the medieval period in accordance with particular artistic contexts.[44] Representations of creation scenes are influenced in particular by the medium in which they are depicted and differ accordingly between manuscript illustrations, mosaics, and stone carvings. These variations tend to confirm that the appearance of animals in these scenes was generically intended to support the ready identification of the biblical story being presented, not to convey the symbolic meanings that might be associated with individual animal participants.

The same tendency can be seen in the portrayal of another frequently depicted episode in Genesis in which animals play a leading role, the story of Noah's Ark. The boarding and the leaving of the ark are favored as suitable moments to serve as reminders of the whole narrative of the Flood but, as in the case of creation, the specific selection of animals and the style in which they are depicted depends primarily on the artistic context. By the thirteenth and fourteenth centuries, as one might expect, such illustrations tend to incorporate a wider range of species, and they begin to present them in ways that are indicative of the growing interest in the naturalistic observation of animals. Another version of Guiard des Moulins's *Bible historiale* from the early fifteenth century can serve to illustrate the more advanced levels of observation that have by this stage come to inform the depiction of the different species on display.[45] (See Figure 7.10.) The boars in the foreground, for example, share all the characteristics of their equivalents in bestiaries. Their bodies appear static, such that only the hint of movement in their legs gives any suggestion that they are approaching the ark. The horses, on the other hand, are depicted with far more attention to the finer points of their physiognomy, so that they appear far more mobile; their legs and thighs seem caught in motion, and one of them turns its head slightly on entry to the ark. As for the dogs at the right-hand margin of the illustration, their depiction lies somewhere in between; although less expressive than that of the horses, it is not simply generic either. Indeed, the animals shown are not strictly a pair at all, as one might expect, but two different breeds of hunting dogs that were popular at the time. Meanwhile, there is but a solitary fox, but one depicted in vivid manner and naturalistic pose; perhaps his missing companion should be assumed to have sneaked into the ark already, which may help to explain his furtive air. This is not necessarily to suggest that the artist studied horses, dogs, or foxes directly before portraying them, although this could easily have been the case. It is perhaps more likely that the various animals were copied from different models, as was frequently the case in the later Middle Ages, so that the artist combined more naturalistic and formulaic representations within the same work, under the inspiration of the diverse styles available to him in such sources as hunting manuals and bestiaries.[46] In any event, religious art was often conventional,

FIGURE 7.10: *Animals entering the ark*. Guiard des Moulins, *Bible historiale* (early fifteenth century), BnF, Paris, MS Français 9, fol. 15r.

but never static, and thus it could offer a forum for the display of evolving attitudes to animals.

One further possibility is that the artist simply took greater pleasure in portraying certain species. The spiritual or moral messages carried by animals certainly account for much of their prominence in medieval religious art, and this was matched, in the secular sphere, by their uses in heraldry.[47] In the images that accompany hunting and medical manuals, meanwhile, one can see the practical value of the careful depiction of animals as objects of inquiry in their own right. But in numerous instances, finally, it seems likely that animals were portrayed in medieval art for no other reason than the fulfillment of aesthetic desire. Examples of this enthusiasm for animal motifs can be found in all areas of medieval culture, including the ecclesiastical sphere. Religious vestments, for example, could be embroidered with animal motifs that did not carry any obvious symbolic meaning, unless perhaps a heraldic one. (See Figure 7.11.). A

FIGURE 7.11: *Parrot, cock, rabbit, and bird.* Fragment of liturgical vestment (mid-thirteenth century), Klosterneuburg, Stiftsgalerie. © Institut für Realienkunden—ÖAW.

cloth fragment of a liturgical vestment of Italian origin kept in Klosterneuburg from the middle of the thirteenth century, for example, shows parrots, cockerels, rabbits, birds, plants and lilies arranged decoratively to form a pattern that is repeated across the whole piece. The lily is shown in its heraldic version, but none of the other elements are, and even if the selected animals may have some personal meaning for the patron who commissioned the piece, this would presumably have been lost on his successors.

It is equally doubtful whether every one of the thousands of animals carved in stone as part of the sculptural decoration of churches was intended to bear the heavy symbolic weight of an allegorical message. But the most obvious illustrations of animals with no apparent meaning whatsoever are those that litter the margins of medieval manuscripts. All genres of writing, from holy texts and prayer books to legal texts and cartularies, can include more or less elaborate marginal drawings. In some cases the animals that so frequently appear in these illustrations do bear a specific relationship to the adjacent text, for example by playing punningly upon its content, as Michael Camille has abundantly demonstrated.[48] More often, however, there is no evident link between the text and the marginal images, and the latter seem to be there for nothing other than the entertainment of the artist or the reader. In luxury psalter manuscripts from the fourteenth century long narratives can be played out along the borders by animal actors, or the routine practices of animal husbandry are portrayed in

FIGURE 7.12: *Bears*. Ulrich von Albeck, *Promptuarium iuris*, 1429, Chorherrenstift Seckau, Universitätsbibliothek Graz, MS 23, II, fol. 27v. © Institut für Realienkunden— ÖAW.

ways that would otherwise remain unknown.[49] Even the margins of dry legal texts could be decorated with beasts, as for example atop an initial in an early fifteenth-century copy of Ulrich von Albeck's *Promptuarium iuris*—a juristic encyclopedia—where a bear happily cavorts before his seated friend. (See Figure 7.12.) Although examples of this type survive from throughout the medieval period, they increase considerably in number in the later thirteenth and fourteenth centuries. More than anything else, they illustrate the extent to which, by the later Middle Ages, animals had become not only good to think with, but also a pleasure and a joy to look at.

NOTES

Introduction

1. R. Delort, *Les animaux ont une histoire* (Paris: Éditions du Seuil, 1984), pp. 101–184.
2. Cf. P. De Leemans and M. Klemm, chapter 6, this volume.
3. C. Dyer, for example, used such records to reconstruct the numbers of animals held by late medieval peasants: C. Dyer, *Standards of Living in the Later Middle Ages* (Cambridge: Cambridge University Press, 1989).
4. Cf. L. J. Kiser, chapter 4, this volume.
5. Cf. E. Pascua, chapter 3, this volume.
6. W. Wattenbach, ed., "Continuatio Claustroneoburgensis III," in *Monumenta Germaniae Historica, Scriptores 9* (Hanover: MGH, 1851), pp. 613–624, at p. 619.
7. W. Wattenbach, ed., "Historia Annorum 1264–1279," in *Monumenta Germaniae Historica, Scriptores 9* (Hanover: MGH, 1851), pp. 649–654, at p. 652.
8. W. Wattenbach, ed., "Continuatio Novimontensis," *Monumenta Germaniae Historica, Scriptores 9* (Hanover: MGH, 1851), pp. 669–677, at pp. 671–672.
9. W. Wattenbach, ed., "Continuatio Sancrucensis II," in *Monumenta Germaniae Historica, Scriptores 9* (Hanover: MGH, 1851), pp. 637–646, at p. 641.
10. B. A. Henisch, *Fast and Feast: Food in Medieval Society* (University Park: Pennsylvania State University Press, 1976), pp. 28–50, at p. 47.
11. B. Pohl-Resl, *Rechnen mit der Ewigkeit. Das Wiener Bürgerspital im späten Mittelalter* (Vienna: Oldenbourg, 1996), pp. 97–110.
12. Gottfried von Strassburg, *Tristan*, trans. A. T. Hatto (1960: repr., London: Penguin, 1967).
13. J. Cummins, *The Hound and the Hawk: The Art of Medieval Hunting* (London: Phoenix Press, 2001), p. 121.
14. A. Pluskowski, *Wolves and the Wilderness in the Middle Ages* (Woodbridge, UK: Boydell, 2006), pp. 73–109.
15. Cf. the detailed overview by A. Smets and B. van den Abeele, chapter 2, this volume.
16. Cummins, *The Hound and the Hawk*, p. 207, with quotation from the *Boke of St. Albans* regarding weasels and polecats.

17. H. J. Schroeder, *Disciplinary Decrees of the General Councils: Text, Translation and Commentary* (St. Louis, MO: B. Herder, 1937), pp. 236–296.

18. Cf. E. Pascua, chapter 3, this volume.

19. Cf. E. M. Veale, *The English Fur Trade in the Later Middle Ages* (1966; repr., Oxford: Oxford University Press, 2003).

20. A. Luders and others, eds., *Statutes of the Realm*, 9 vols. (1810–1822; repr., London: Dawson, 1963), vol. 1, p. 381 (1363). Cf. D. Serjeantson, "Animal Remains and the Tanning Trade," in *Diet and Crafts in Towns: The Evidence of Animal Remains from the Roman to the Post-Medieval periods*, BAR British Series 199, ed. D. Serjeantson and T. Waldron (Oxford, BAR, 1989), pp. 129–146, esp. 130–133.

21. T. Dean, trans. and ed., *The Towns of Italy in the Later Middle Ages* (Manchester: Manchester University Press, 2000), no. 89, pp. 202–205, at p. 204.

22. William of Malmesbury, *De gestis pontificum Anglorum*, in *Wholly Animals: A Book of Beastly Tales*, D. N. Bell, trans. (Kalamazoo, MI: Cistercian Publications, 1992), pp. 122–123, at p. 123.

23. R. Reed, *The Nature and Making of Parchment* (Leeds: Elmete Press, 1975).

24. I. Ventura, "The *Curae ex animalibus* in the Medical Literature of the Middle Ages: the Example of the Illustrated Herbals," in *Bestiaires médiévaux. Nouvelles perspectives et les traditions textuelles*, ed. B. Van den Abeele (Louvain-la-Neuve: Université Catholique de Louvain, 2005), pp. 213–248, at p. 221. For animals in medieval magic cf. S. Page, chapter 1, this volume.

25. J. Gray, *Straw Dogs: Thoughts on Humans and Other Animals* (London: Granta Books, 2002), pp. 3–4. Addresses the different views on this subject found in Christianity and other world religions.

26. Pliny, *Natural History*, trans. and ed. H. Rackham (Cambridge, MA: Harvard University Press, 1983), vol. 3, bk. VIII, 1, pp. 2–3.

27. Isidore, *Etymologiae XII, 1, 1*, in *The Etymologies of Isidore of Seville*, trans. S. A. Barney and others (Cambridge: Cambridge University Press, 2006), p. 247.

28. Ibid.

29. Isidore, *Etymologiae I, 7, 5*, in *The Etymologies of Isidore of Seville*, trans. S. A. Barney and others (Cambridge: Cambridge University Press, 2006), p. 42.

30. C. T. Onions, *Oxford Dictionary of English Etymology* (Oxford: Clarendon Press, 1966), pp. 38, 83; F. Kluge, *Etymologisches Wörterbuch der deutschen Sprache*, 7th ed. (Strassburg: Trubner, 1910), p. 729. Cf. also B. Resl, *Understanding Animals, 1150–1350* (Basingstoke: Palgrave Macmillan, forthcoming).

31. Augustine, *On Christian Teaching*, trans. R. P. H. Green (Oxford: Oxford University Press, 1997), p. 44.

32. N. Henkel, *Studien zum Physiologus im Mittelalter* (Tübingen, Germany: Niemeyer, 1976).

33. D. Sperber, "Why are Perfect Animals, Hybrids and Monsters Food for Symbolic Thought?" *Method and Theory in the Study of Religion* 8, no. 2 (1996): 143–169.

34. M. R. James, *The Bestiary* (Oxford: Roxburghe Club, 1928); F. McCulloch, *Medieval Latin and French Bestiaries*, rev. ed. (Chapel Hill: University of North Carolina Press, 1962); cf. R. Baxter, *Bestiaries and Their Users in the Middle Ages* (Stroud: Sutton Publishing, 1998), pp. 83–143; and W. B. Clark, *A Medieval Book of Beasts. The Second-Family Bestiary: Commentary, Art, Text and Translation* (Woodbridge, UK: Boydell Press, 2006), pp. 7–20.

35. R. Barber, *Bestiary* (Woodbridge, UK: Boydell Press, 1999), pp. 80–81 (translation of Oxford, MS Bodley 764, mid-thirteenth century).

36. Ibid., p. 81.
37. Aberdeen University Library MS 24, fols. 20v–21r. http://www.abdn.ac.uk/bestiary/ (accessed May 22, 2007).
38. Clark, *A Medieval Book of Beasts*, pp. 15–20.
39. J. E. Salisbury, *The Beast Within: Animals in the Middle Ages* (New York: Routledge, 1994), pp. 1–11, 103–136.
40. Ibid., p. 103.
41. The poem is translated by J. Ziolkowsky, *Talking Animals: Medieval Latin Beast Poetry, 750–1150* (Philadelphia: University of Philadelphia Press, 1993), p. 241. Cf. ibid., pp. 48–49.
42. Ibid., p. 50.
43. Ibid., pp. 69–79, and translation of the poem, pp. 262–265.
44. Salisbury, *The Beast Within*, p. 122.
45. Ibid., p. 125.
46. Venantius Fortunatus, "Vita s. Hilarii," in *Monumenta Germaniae Historica, Scriptores rerum Merovingicarum*, 4, 2, ed. B. Krusch (Hanover: MGH, 1902), p. 55.
47. J. Voisenet, *Bêtes et hommes dans le monde médiévale. Le bestiaire des clercs du Ve au XIIe siècle* (Turnhout, Belgium: Brepols, 2000), p. 173.
48. J. Le Goff, "Ecclesiastical Culture and Folklore in the Middle Ages: Saint Marcellus of Paris and the Dragon," in idem, *Time, Work and Culture in the Middle Ages* (Chicago: University of Chicago Press, 1980), pp. 159–188, at p. 172.
49. R. Grant, *Early Christians and Animals* (New York: Routledge, 1999), pp. 37–38.
50. See L. J. Kiser, chapter 4, this volume.
51. See B. Resl, chapter 7, this volume.
52. R. Wittkower, "Marvels of the East: a Study in the History of Monsters," *Journal of the Warburg and Courtauld Institutes* 5 (1942): 159–197.
53. Marco Polo, *The Travels*, trans. A. Ricci (London: Routledge, 1931), p. 283.
54. U. Eco, *Kant and the Platypus. Essays on Language and Cognition* (London: Secker and Warburg, 1999), pp. 57–59.
55. Cf. Resl, *Understanding Animals* (forthcoming).
56. Marco Polo, *Travels,* p. 304.
57. Ibid.
58. E. P. Evans, *The Criminal Prosecution and Capital Punishment of Animals* (1906; repr., Boston: Faber and Faber, 1987), esp. pp. 140–145, and appendix I, pp. 290–291.
59. J. P. J. Goldberg, "Pigs and Prostitutes: Streetwalking in Comparative Perspective," in *Young Medieval Women*, ed. K. Lewis, N. J. Menuge, and K. M. Phillips (Stroud, UK: Sutton Publishing, 1999), pp. 172–193, at p. 172.
60. Evans, *Criminal Prosecution*, p. 142.
61. Alexander Neckam, *De naturis rerum et De laudibus divinae sapientiae*, ed. T. Wright (London: Longman, Green, 1863), pp. 232–252.
62. See P. Beullens, chapter 5, and P. De Leemans and M. Klemm, chapter 6, this volume.
63. Albertus Magnus, *On Animals*, 2 vols., trans. K. F. Kitchell Jr. and I. M. Resnick (Baltimore: John Hopkins University Press), bk. 22, tract 1, chap. 1, p. 1440. Cf. C. Hünemörder, "Die Zoologie des Albertus Magnus," in *Albertus Magnus. Doctor Universalis, 2180/1980*, ed. G. Meyer and A. Zimmermann (Mainz, Germany: Matthias-Grünewald-Verlag, 1980), pp. 235–248, at p. 242.

64. Albertus Magnus, *On Animals*, bk. 24, chap. 1, p. 1668.
65. Ibid., bk. 8, tract 2, chap. 6, p. 716; P. Hoßfeld, *Albertus Magnus als Naturphilosoph und Naturwissenschaftler* (Bonn: Albertus-Magnus-Institut, 1983), p. 87.
66. Albertus Magnus, *On Animals*, bk. 7, tract 1, chap. 6, p. 614 (fish in Danube).
67. Ibid., bk. 1, tract 2, chap. 3, p. 98. Cf. K. F. Kitchell Jr. and I. M. Resnick, "Introduction," in Albertus Magnus, *On Animals*, p. 30.
68. Ibid., p. 31; L. Thorndike, *The History of Magic and Experimental Science*, vol. 4 (New York: Columbia University Press, 1933), pp. 540–541.
69. Albertus Magnus, *On Animals*, bk. 23, p. 1554.
70. Ibid., p. 1603.
71. Ibid., p. 1607.
72. Kathleen Walker-Meikle provides ample proof of this in her doctoral thesis: "Late Medieval Pet-Keeping: Gender, Status and Emotions" (PhD diss., University College London, forthcoming).
73. Clark, *Book of Beasts*, p. 54 (camels), p. 120 (lions), p. 122 (tigress).
74. Ibid., p. 132 (apes) and p. 145 (dogs).
75. Alexander Neckam, *De naturis rerum*, pp. 253–255.
76. Salisbury, *The Beast Within*, pp. 32–36.
77. J.-C. Schmitt, *The Holy Greyhound: Guinefort, Healer of Children since the Thirteenth Century* (Cambridge: Cambridge University Press, 1983).

Chapter 1

1. J. H. Pitman, trans., *The Anglo-Saxon Physiologus* (New Haven: Yale University Press, 1921), p. 3.
2. T. Ingold, *What Is an Animal?* (New York: Routledge, 1994), p. xxiii.
3. Gerald of Wales, *Topographica hibernica*, pt. II, chap. 54, trans. J. O'Meara (London: Penguin, 1982), pp. 73–74.
4. Adelard of Bath, *Questiones naturales*, quest. 46, trans. and ed. C. Burnett (Cambridge: Cambridge University Press, 1998), p. 177.
5. Gervase of Tilbury, *Otia imperialia*, bk. II, chap. 12, trans. and ed. S. E. Banks and J. W. Binns (Oxford: Oxford University Press, 2002), pp. 332–335.
6. Marco Polo, *The Travels*, trans. R. Latham (London: Penguin, 1958), chap. 6, pp. 230–231.
7. There are a few exceptions to this position, for example, Adelard of Bath argued that animals had immortal souls in his *Questiones naturales*, quest. 14, p. 119.
8. See, for example, J. T. McNeill and H. M. Gamer, *The Medieval Handbooks of Penance* (New York: Columbia University Press, 1990), pp. 276–277, 293, 305, 318, 334–335.
9. Aquinas, *Summa theologica*, pt. 1, quest. 96, art. 1.
10. Genesis 1:26–30; Aquinas, *Summa theologica*, 2.1, quest. 102, art. 6.
11. Augustine, *Enarratio in psalmos*, 145.13–14, 34.1.6, qtd. in R. Sorabji, *Animal Minds and Human Morals* (Ithaca, NY: Cornell University Press, 1993), pp.168, 195.
12. Bonaventure, *Major Life of St Francis*, chap. 12, in *St Francis of Assisi: Writings and Early Biographies*, ed. M. A. Habig (Chicago: Franciscan Herald Press, 1983), p. 723.
13. Gerald of Wales, *Topographica hibernica*, pt. II, chap. 52, pp. 69–72.

14. The story first appears in Jerome's *Life of St. Paulus* (written in 374 or 375).

15. C.W.R.D. Moseley, trans., *The Travels of Sir John Mandeville* (London: Penguin, 1983), chap. 7, p. 64.

16. Ibid.

17. The earliest mention of the legend of the dog-headed saint is in the Gnostic *Acts of St. Bartholomew*, originating in fourth-century Egypt. His cult was most popular in the Eastern Church but also occasionally spread into the West.

18. Romans 1:20.

19. P. Dronke, trans., *De Coelesti Hierarchia*, chap. 2, in *Fabula: Explorations into the Uses of Myth in Medieval Platonism*, (Leiden, the Netherlands: Brill, 1974), p. 44.

20. *De Coelesti Hierarchia*, chap. 2, 144B, and chap. 15, 337B, trans. C. Luibheid and P. Rorem, in *Pseudo-Dionysius, The Complete Works* (New York: Paulist Press, 1987), pp. 152, 189.

21. Commentary on Macrobius's *Commentarii in somnium Scipionis*, trans. Dronke, *Fabula*, p. 43.

22. A. Davril and T. M. Thibodeau, eds., *Rationale divinorum officiorum* (Turnhout, Belgium: Brepols, 1995), bk. 1, chap. 3, sec. 6, p. 37.

23. Matthew 10:16.

24. Augustine, *De doctrina christiana*, bk. 2, sec. 61, trans. and ed. R.P.H. Green (Oxford: Clarendon Press, 1995), pp. 84–85.

25. Cambridge, Trinity College MS R.17.1, fol. 109v.

26. Quotations from the Bible cite the King James version.

27. Chrétien de Troyes, *Le Chevalier au Lion*. In the *Queste del Saint Graal* Perceval also saves a lion from a serpent.

28. William Durandus, *Rationale divinorum officiorum*, ed. A. Davril and T. M. Thibodeau (Turnhout, Belgium: Brepols, 1995) bk. 1, chap. 3, sec. 9, p. 38.

29. The story is told in Guibert de Nogent's *De vita sua sive monodiarum*, bk. III, chap. 13.

30. Marco Polo, *Travels*, chap. 2, pp. 54–55.

31. Marco Polo, *Travels*, chap. 4, pp. 153–155.

32. C. Rudolph, trans. and ed., *Apologia ad Guillelmum Abbatem*, XII, 29, in *The "Things of Greater Importance"* (Philadelphia: University of Pennsylvania Press, 1990), pp. 282–283.

33. R. Mellinkoff, *Averting Demons: The Protective Power of Medieval Visual Motifs and Themes* (Los Angeles: Ruth Mellinkoff Publications, 2004).

34. J. F. Hamburger, *The Rothschild Canticles: Art and Mysticism in Flanders and the Rhineland circa 1300* (New Haven: Yale University Press, 1990), pp. 35–42.

35. R. Willis, ed., *Signifying Animals* (London: Routledge, 1994), p. 18.

36. E.O.G. Turville-Petre, *Myth and Religion of the North: The Religion of Ancient Scandinavia* (London: Weidenfeld and Nicolson, 1964), pp. 227–230; H. R. Ellis Davidson, "Shape-changing in the Old Norse Sagas," in *Animals in Folklore*, ed. J. R. Porter and W.M.S. Russell (Cambridge: D.S. Brewer, 1978), pp. 126–142.

37. R. O'Connor, trans., *Icelandic Histories and Romances* (Stroud, UK: Tempus, 2002), pp. 96–97.

38. Merlin disguises himself as a stag in the *Estoire de Merlin*; Nectanebus transforms himself into a dragon–ram hybrid to seduce Queen Olympias in the Alexander Romance.

39. O. Cavallar, S. Degenring, and J. Kirshner, eds., *A Grammar of Signs: Bartolo da Sassoferrato's Tract on Insignia and the Coat of Arms* (University of California Press: Berkeley, 1994), p.115.

40. See, for example, Pseudo-Albertus Magnus, *Liber aggregationis* and *De mirabilibus mundi;* Albertus Magnus, *De animalibus*, bks. 22–26; and Bartholomaeus Anglicus, *De proprietatibus rerum*, bk. 18.

41. For heraldic beast identification in Chrétien de Troyes, see M. Neumeyer, "Le bestiaire héraldique. Un miroir de la chevalerie," in *Il mondo animale* (Florence: Sismel, 2000), vol. 1, pp. 145–164, at pp. 151–154. On the use of animal heraldic devices to signify the bestial qualities of non-Christian enemies, see D. H. Strickland, *Saracens, Demons, and Jews* (Princeton: Princeton University Press, 2003), pp. 180–182.

42. Saints associated with particular animals include Saint Anthony and a pig, Saint Hubert and a stag, Saint Roch with his dog, Saint Francis and birds, and Saint Jerome and a lion.

43. In the *Mabinogion*, Arawn, king of Annwfn (the Celtic afterlife) has white hunting dogs that lure Pwyll, lord of Dyfed into his sphere, and the partly supernatural Rhiannon rides a snow white horse. Supernatural white animals are also found in *Erec et Enide, Floriant et Florete,* and *Sir Orfeo.*

44. On the recto side of the Wilton Diptych the mediating quality of white hart is signaled by its presence on the dresses of the eleven angels surrounding the Virgin Mary, to whom the king is being presented.

45. R. Dennys, *The Heraldic Imagination* (London: Barrie and Jenkins, 1975), p. 69.

46. C. G. Walker, "An Edition with Introduction and Commentary of John Blount's English Translation of Nicholas Upton's *De Studio Militari*" (PhD diss., University of Oxford, 1998).

47. C. M. Edsman, "The Story of the Bear Wife," *Ethnos* 1–2 (1956): 36–56; Davidson, "Shape-changing in the Old Norse Sagas."

48. J. Le Goff and E. Le Roy Ladurie, "Mélusine maternelle et défricheuse," *Annales. Economies, Sociétés, Civilisations* 26 (1971): 587–622, at 601, where reference is made to the legend of Mélusine bringing lands, castles, towns, and lineage to the family patrimony of her knightly descendents.

49. The Duc de Berry's bears are often depicted in the marginal illuminations of his celebrated manuscripts such as *Les Très Riches Heures.*

50. See T. Dean, trans. and ed., *The Towns of Italy in the Later Middle Ages*, Manchester: Manchester University Press, 2000, pp. 47–48.

51. Marco Polo, *The Travels*, chap. 7, pp. 261–262.

52. Free Library of Philadelphia, Lewis MS E201.

53. E. Cohen, "Animals in Mediaeval Perceptions: The Image of the Ubiquitous Other," in *Animals and Human Society. Changing Perspectives*, ed. A. Manning and J. Serpell (London: Routledge, 1994), pp. 59–80, at pp. 65–68.

54. R. Mellinkoff, "Riding Backwards: Theme of Humiliation and Symbol of Evil," *Viator* 4 (1973): 154–66.

55. S. Y. Edgerton, *Pictures and Punishment: Art and Criminal Prosecution during the Florentine Renaissance* (New York: Cornell University Press, 1985), chap. 2.

56. Ælfric, *Lives of Three English Saints,* ed. G. I. Needham (London: Methuen and Co., 1966), pp. 43–59, p. 52.

57. *La Passiun de Seint Edmund,* l. 266, ed. J. Grant (London: Anglo-Norman Text Society, 1978), p. 101.

58. Aquinas, *Summa Theologica*, pt. 1, quest. 96, art.1.
59. A. Lecoy de la Marche, ed., *Tractatus de diversis materiis praedicabilibus*, in *Anecdotes historiques, légendes et apologues* (Paris: Librairie Renouard, 1877), pp. 325–328. Cf. J.-C. Schmitt, *The Holy Greyhound* (Cambridge: University of Cambridge Press, 1983).
60. S. Lipton, "Jews, Heretics, and the Sign of the Cat in the *Bible moralisée*," *Word and Image* 8 (1992): 362–377.
61. Marco Polo, *The Travels*, chap. 7, p. 253.
62. *The Travels of John of Mandeville*, chap. 18, p. 121, and chap. 21, p. 134; London, British Library, Harley MS 3954, fol. 40v.
63. J. Duvernoy, ed., *Le Registre d'inquisition de Jacques Fournier (1318–1325)*, 3 vols. (Toulouse: Édouard Privat, 1965), 39d. See also 98b.
64. Ibid., 123b, 202c, 253a, 269a.
65. Ibid., 76 a, b.
66. J. Hansen, *Quellen und Untersuchungen zur Geschichte des Hexenwahns und der Hexenverfolgung im Mittelalter* (Bonn: Georgi, 1901), pp. 39, 40–41.
67. See, for example, Aquinas, *Summa theologica*, pt. 1, quest. 114, art. 4.
68. M. Summers, trans., *Malleus maleficarum* (1928; repr. New York: Dover Publications, 1971), pt. 1, quest. 10 and pt. II, quest. 1, chap. 8, pp. 61–65 and 122–124.
69. S. Clark, "Glamours: Demons and Virtual Worlds," in *Vanities of the Eye: Vision in Early Modern European Culture* (Oxford: Oxford University Press, 2007), chap. 4, pp. 123–160.
70. Caesarius of Heisterbach, *The Dialogue on Miracles*, trans. H. von E. Scott and C. C. Swinton Bland, 2 vols. (London: Routledge, 1929), vol. 1, bk. 5, chaps. 6, 44, 47, 50, and 56.
71. M. R. James, ed., "Twelve Medieval Ghost Stories," *English Historical Review* 37 (1922): 413–422, at 415–418.
72. Ibid., p. 421.
73. Jacobus de Clusa, *De animabus exutis in corporibus* (cologne, 1496).
74. D. McKitterick, ed., *The Trinity Apocalypse* (London: The British Library, 2005), fig. 84.
75. John of Salisbury, *Policraticus*, bk. 1, chap. 13; Tobias 11:9.
76. Gerald of Wales, *Topographia hibernica*, pt. II, chap. 43, p. 65.
77. J. Shinners, trans., *Medieval Popular Religion, 1000–1500* (Peterborough, Ontario: Broadview, 1997), p. 449.
78. Lecoy de la Marche, *Tractatus de diversis materiis praedicabilibus*, 356, p. 315.
79. Ibid., 353, p. 314.
80. C. Burnett, "Arabic Divinatory Texts and Celtic Folklore: A Comment on the Theory and Practice of Scapulimancy in Western Europe," *Cambridge Medieval Celtic Studies* 6 (1983): 31–42, at 35.
81. M. C. Seymour and others, ed., *John Trevisa's Translation of Bartholomaus Anglicus "De proprietatibus rerum"* (New York: Clarendon Press, 1988), vol. 2, pp. 1149–1150.
82. D. Wilkins, *Concilia Maguae Britanniae et Hiberniae, 446–1717* (Brussels, 1964), vol. 1, p. 363.
83. Summers, *Malleus maleficarum*, pt. II, quest. 1, chap. 14, p. 146.
84. A. Sannino, "Ermete mago e alchimista nelle biblioteche di Guglielmo d'Alvernia e Ruggero Bacone," *Studi Medievali* 41 (2000): 151–209, at 185.
85. William of Auvergne, *De universo*, pt. II, chap. 76 in *Opera omnia* (Paris, 1674), vol. 2.

86. T. O. Cockayne, *Leechdoms, Wortcunning and Starcraft of Early England* (London: Longman, 1864), vol. 1, pp. 386–389. The remedy for sick sheep in this manuscript is simpler: just give them a bit of ale!

87. Ibid., p. 384. Translation by Lea Olsan.

88. London, British Library, Add. MS 35,179, fol. 87v.

89. W. L. Braekman, ed., *Studies on Alchemy, Diet, Medecine [sic] and Prognostication in Middle English* (Brussels: Omirel, 1986), p. 130.

90. *De legibus*, chap. 27, in *Opera*, vol. I, (Paris, 1674).

91. N. Weill-Parot, *Les "images astrologiques" au Moyen Âge et à la Renaissance*, (Paris: Honoré Champion, 2002), chap. 9.

92. *Liber lune*, Oxford Corpus Christi 125, 61–67, at fol. 66v.

93. *Liber lune*, Oxford Corpus Christi 125, 66–67.

94. Cohen, "Animals in Mediaeval Perceptions," pp. 65–71.

95. *Picatrix Latinus*, bk. III, chap. vii, 31, 33, 38, ed. D. Pingree (London: The Warburg Institute, 1986), pp. 132, 135, 136.

96. Al-kindi, *De radiis*, ch. 9, ed. M.-T. d'Alverny and F. Hudry, *Archives d'histoire doctrinale et litteraire du moyen age*, 41 (1974): 139–260, at pp. 254–257.

97. See, for example, R. Kieckhefer, *Forbidden Rites: A Necromancer's Manual of the Fifteenth Century* (Pennsylvania: Penn State University Press, 1997).

98. *Les Grandes Chroniques de France* (Paris: Librairie ancienne Honoré Champion 1937), vol. 5, p. 269.

99. Gervase of Tilbury, *Otia Imperialia*, pt. III, chap. 92, pp. 738–743.

100. M.-D. Chenu, *Nature, Man and Society in the Twelfth Century* (Chicago: University of Chicago Press, 1968), pp. 1–48.

Chapter 2

1. See H. J. Epstein, "The Origin and the Earliest History of Falconry," *Isis* 34 (1942–1943): 497–509, and C. Dobiat, "Zur Herkunft der Falknerei aus archäologisch-historischer Sicht," *Alma Mater Philippina* (WS1995–1996): 10–14.

2. For details on birds and techniques, cf. B. Van den Abeele, *La fauconnerie au Moyen Âge. Connaissance, affaitage et médecine des oiseaux de chasse d'après les traités latins* (Paris: Klincksieck, 1994).

3. On the different kinds of dogs, see J. Bugnion, *Les chasses médiévales. Le brachet, le lévrier, l'épagneul, leur nomenclature, leur métier, leur typologie* (Paris: Edition Folio, 2005).

4. J. Cummins, *The Hound and the Hawk. The Art of Medieval Hunting* (London: Phoenix Press, 2001), pp. 32–46.

5. For the cultural image of boar hunting, see M. Pastoureau, "La chasse au sanglier: histoire d'une dévalorisation (IVe–XIVe siècle)," in *La chasse au Moyen Age. Société, traités, symboles*, ed. A. Paràvicini Bagliani and B. Van den Abeele (Firenze: Sismel, 2000), pp. 7–24.

6. Cummins, *The Hound*, p. 58. For French examples, see F. Duceppe-Lamarre, "Les réserves cynégétiques en France septentrionale, seconde moitié du XIIe siècle-fin XVe siècle," in *Forêt et chasse, Xe–XXe siècle*, ed. A. Orvol (Paris: L'Harmattan, 2006), pp. 29–42.

7. Bugnion, *Les chasses*, pp. 27–49, 51.

8. See C. Gaier, "Quand l'arbalète était une nouveauté. Réflexions sur son rôle militaire du Xᵉ au XIIIᵉ siècle," *Le Moyen Age* 101 (1995): 137–144.

9. Cummins, *The Hound*, p. 49.

10. C. Gasser, "Attività venatoria e documentazione scritta nel Medioevo. L'esempio dell'uccellagione," in *Los libros de caza*, ed. J. M. Fradejas Rueda (Tordesillas, Spain: Seminario de Filología Medieval, 2005), pp. 69–82.

11. For more information on bird catching, see Gasser, "Attività venatoria"; for the catching and exportation of falcons, see A.E.H. Swaen, *De valkerij in de Nederlanden* (Zutphen: W. J. Thieme & Cie, 1936); and F. Morenzoni, "La capture et le commerce des faucons dans les Alpes occidentales au XIVe siècle," in *Milieux naturels, espaces sociaux. Etudes offertes à Robert Delort*, ed. E. Mornet and F. Morenzoni (Paris: Publications de la Sorbonne, 1997), pp. 287–298.

12. See H. H. Müller, "Falconry in Central Europe in the Middle Ages," in *Exploitation des animaux sauvages à travers le temps* (Juan-les-Pins, France: Editions APDCA, 1993), pp. 431–437.

13. Epstein, "The Origin."

14. D. Jenkins, "Hawk and Hound: Hunting in the Laws of Court," in *The Welsh King and His Court*, ed. T. C. Edwards and others (Cardiff: University of Wales Press, 2000), pp. 255–280.

15. W. Linnard, "The Nine Huntings: A Re-examination of *Y Naw Helwriaeth*," *The Bulletin of the Board of Celtic Studies* 31 (1984): 119–132.

16. Reproduction of the Brussels MS BR 9169, with transcription and commentary by L. Pérez Martínez and others, *Jaime III Rey de Mallorca. Leyes Palatinas* (Palma de Mallorca, Spain: Olañeta, 1991).

17. R. S. Oggins, *The Kings and the Hawks. Falconry in Medieval England* (New Haven: Yale University Press, 2004).

18. C. Niedermann, *Das Jagdwesen am Hofe Herzog Phillipps des Guten von Burgund* (Brussels: Archives et Bibliothèques de Belgique, 1995).

19. J. Bover, "La cetrería en las Islas Baleares: siglos XIII–XIV," in *Los libros de caza*, ed. Fradejas Rueda, pp. 9–20.

20. D. Dalby, *Lexicon of the Mediaeval German Hunt* (Berlin: de Gruyter, 1965).

21. G. Malacarne, *Le cacce del principe. L'ars venandi nella terra dei Gonzaga* (Modena: Il Bullino, 1998); G. Malacarne, *I Signori del cielo. La falconeria a Mantova al tempo dei Gonzaga*, (Mantova, Italy: Artiglio Editore, 2003).

22. G. Hoffmann, "Falkenjagd und Falkenhandel in den nordischen Ländern während des Mittelalters," *Zeitschrift für deutsches Altertum* 88 (1957): 115–149.

23. Oggins, *Kings*, pp. 82–108.

24. Cf. the biography by W. Stürner, *Friedrich II, Teil 2. Der Kaiser, 1220–1250* (Darmstadt: Wissenschaftliche Buchgesellschaft, 2000), p. 574.

25. See B. Van den Abeele, *La littérature cynégétique* (Turnhout: Brepols, 1996), and for the Latin texts see also Van den Abeele (*La fauconnerie*); for the French treatises see A. Smets and B. Van den Abeele, "Manuscrits et traités de chasse français du Moyen Âge. Recensement et perspectives de recherche," *Romania* 116 (1998): 316–367; and for the Spanish tradition, see J. M. Fradejas Rueda, *Bibliotheca cinegetica hispanica: bibliografía crítica de los libros de cetrería y montería hispano-portugueses anteriores a 1799* (London: Grant & Cutler, 1991); and J. M. Fradejas Rueda, *Suplemento 1* (London: Tamesis, 2003), as well as J. M. Fradejas Rueda, *Literatura cetrera de la Edad media y el Renacimiento español* (London: Department of Hispanic Studies, Queen Mary and Westfield College, 1998).

26. Cf. Van den Abeele, *La fauconnerie*, pp. 17–37, for a presentation of twenty-eight texts preserved in sixty-five manuscripts, with references of existing editions. Only more recent references are indicated in the present text.

27. A. Smets, ed., *Le "Liber accipitrum" de Grimaldus: un traité d'autourserie du haut Moyen Âge* (Nogent-le-Roi, France: J. Laget – LAME, 1999).

28. See C. Burnett and others, eds., *Adelard of Bath, Conversations with his Nephew: On the Same and the Different, Questions on Natural Science, and on Birds* (Cambridge: Cambridge University Press, 1998).

29. A. L. Trombetti Budriesi, Federico II di Svevia, *De arte venandi cum avibus* (Rome: Editori Laterza, 2000); C. A. Wood and F. M. Fyfe, trans., *The Art of Falconry, Being the "De arte venandi cum avibus" of Frederick II of Hohenstaufen* (Stanford, CA: University Press, 1943).

30. See B. Van den Abeele and J. Loncke, "Les traités médiévaux sur le soin des chiens: une littérature technique méconnue," in *Inquirens subtilia diversa. Dietrich Lohrmann zum 65. Geburtstag*, ed. H. Kranz and L. Falkenstein (Aachen, Germany: Shaker, 2002), pp. 281–296, at pp. 286–293.

31. An edition of these two texts by J. Loncke will appear shortly in the series *Bibliotheca cynegetica* (Editions J. Laget).

32. W. Richter and R. Richter-Bergmeier, eds., *Petrus de Crescentiis, Ruralia commoda. Das Wissen des vollkommenen Landwirts um 1300* (Heidelberg: C. Winter, 1995–1998), vol. III, pp. 169–210.

33. Van den Abeele, *La littérature cynégétique*, pp. 40–41.

34. Smets and Van den Abeele, "Manuscrits et traités." A complement to this article will appear in the near future. Unless otherwise indicated, we refer to this article for the edition(s) of the texts mentioned in the present contribution.

35. For a presentation of these translations, see A. Smets, "Les traductions françaises médiévales des traités de fauconnerie latins: vue d'ensemble," in *Le bestiaire, le lapidaire, la flore*, ed. G. Di Stefano and R. M. Bidler (Montréal: CERES, 2004–2005), pp. 299–318.

36. Four different Middle French translations of the *De falconibus* are known (cf. A. Smets, "Des faucons: les quatre traductions en moyen français du De falconibus d'Albert le Grand. Analyse lexicale d'un dossier inédit," (PhD diss., Leuven, Belgium, K.U. Leuven, 2003); the editions will be published in the series Bibliotheca cynegetica.

37. Partial printed version: *L'art d'archerie. Sur les traces du premier livre d'archerie*, 2nd ed. (St-Egrève, France: Emotion Primitive, 2002).

38. On this topic, see A. Strubel, "Le débat entre fauconniers et veneurs: un témoignage sur l'imaginaire de la chasse à la fin du moyen âge," *Travaux de littérature* 10 (1997): 49–64.

39. See Fradejas Rueda, *Literatura cetrera* and *Bibliotheca cinegetica hispanica*; J. M. Abalo Buceta, "Literatura cinegética peninsular. La montería: contrastes y peculiaridades frente a otras tradiciones literarias europeas," in *Los libros de caza*, ed. Fradejas Rueda, pp. 9–28, and other articles in this volume.

40. Van den Abeele, *La littérature cynégétique*, p. 50. Ibid., pp. 51–52, contains references to the editions of the Italian texts mentioned here.

41. D. Scott-MacNab, *A Sporting Lexicon of the Fifteenth Century* (The J. B. Treatise, Oxford: The Society for the Study of Medieval Languages and Literature, 2003). See also Van den Abeele, *La littérature cynégétique*, pp. 54–56, for the editions of the English texts.

42. K. Lindner, "Die Anfänge der deutschen Jagdliteratur. Ihre Entwicklung vom 14. Jahrhundert bis zur Zeit der Reformation," *Zeitschrift für Jagdwissenschaft* X (1964): 41–51. See Van den Abeele, *La littérature cynégétique*, pp. 52–53, for references of the texts cited here.

43. For references of the Dutch texts, see Van den Abeele, *La littérature cynégétique*, p. 54.

44. For the courtly aspects of hunting, see W. Rösener, ed., *Jagd und höfische Kultur im Mittelalter* (Göttingen, Germany: Vandenhoeck & Ruprecht, 1997).

45. For the Old French examples quoted below, see B. Van den Abeele, *La fauconnerie dans les lettres françaises du XIIe au XIVe siècle* (Leuven, Belgium: Leuven University Press, 1990).

46. A. Rooney, *Hunting in Middle English Literature* (Rochester: Boydell Press, 1993), and R. Weick, *Der Habicht in der deutschen Dichtung des 12. bis 16. Jahrhunderts* (Göppingen: Kümmerle Verlag, 1993). For Spanish literature, cf. the bibliography of Fradejas Rueda, *Bibliotheca cinegetica hispanica*.

47. See Fradejas Rueda, *Bibliotheca cinegetica hispanica*, for references.

48. T. Saly, "Tristan chasseur," in *La Chasse au Moyen Age*, pp. 436–441.

49. E. Williams, "Hunting the Deer: Some Uses of a Motif-Complex in Middle English Romance and Saint's Life," in *Romance in Medieval England*, ed. M. Mills and others (Cambridge: D.S. Brewer, 1991), pp. 187–206.

50. R. Harris, "The White Stag in Chrétien's *Erec et Enide*," *French Studies* 10 (1956): 55–61.

51. Rooney, *Hunting*, pp. 159–193.

52. Bugnion, *Les chasses médiévales*, pp. 29–30, 44–45, 82–83, and 110. For other examples, see Bugnion, pp. 30, 32, 45–48, 54, 127–129.

53. Saly, "Tristan chasseur."

54. Oggins, *Kings*, p. 109.

55. M. Thiebaux, *The Stag of Love: The Chase in Medieval Literature* (Ithaca, NY: Cornell University Press, 1974).

56. See U. Steckelberg, *Hadamar von Laber 'Jagd'. Überlieferung, Textstrukturen und allegorische Sinnbindungsverfahren* (Tübingen, Germany: Niemeyer, 1998).

57. See A. Smets, "L'image ambiguë du chien à travers la littérature didactique latine et française (XIIe–XIVe siècles)," *Reinardus* 14 (2001): 243–253.

58. Oggins, *The Kings*, pp. 120–126; T. Szabo, "Die Kritik der Jagd. Von der Antike zum Mittelalter," in *Jagd*, ed. W. Rösener, pp. 167–230.

59. D. Boccassini, *Il volo della menta. Falconeria e Sofia nel mondo mediterraneo. Islam, Federico II, Dante* (Ravenna, Italy: Longo Editore, 2003).

60. See J. Cummins, "*Aqueste lance divino*: San Juan's Falconry Images," in *What's Past Is Prologue: A Collection of Essays in Honour of L.J. Woodward*, ed. S. Bacarisse and others (Edinburgh: Scottish Academy Press, 1984), pp. 28–32 and 155–156.

61. Oggins, *Kings*, p. 134.

62. See M. Bath, *The Image of the Stag. Iconographic Themes in Western Art* (Baden-Baden: V. Koerner, 1992); Cummins, *Hound*, pp. 68–83, chap. "The Symbolism of the Deer."

63. See L. Thorpe, "Tristewell et les autres chiens de l'enfer," in *J. Misrahi Memorial Volume: Studies in Medieval Literature*, ed. H. R. Hunte, H. Niedzielski, and W. L. Hendrickson (New York: Columbia University Press, 1977), pp. 115–135.

64. G. Tilander, *Les Livres du Roy Modus et de la Royne Ratio* (Paris: SATF, 1932), vol. I, pp. 307–309.

65. Cf. Rooney, *Hunting*, pp. 24–34.

66. There is no general study of the iconography of hunting in the Middle Ages, but several inquiries limited to themes or regions have been published, see, for example, H. Peters, "Falke, Falkenjagd, Falkner und Falkenbuch," in *Reallexikon zur Deutschen Kunstgeschichte*, VI (Munich: A. Druckenmüller, 1971), col. 1261–1366.

67. Several reproductions of this manuscript exist, by ADEVA (Graz, 1969 and 2000) and in pocket by Harenberg (Dortmund, Germany, 1980). Ultimately, with Spanish translation and commentary by J. M. Fradejas Rueda, *El arte de Cetrería de Federico II* (Vaticano-Madrid: Testimonio, 2004).

68. Cf. B. Yapp, "The Illustrations of Birds in the Vatican Manuscript of 'De arte venandi cum avibus' of Frederick II," *Annals of Science* 40 (1983): 597–534.

69. See B. Van den Abeele, "Falken auf Goldgrund. Illuminierte Handschriften lateinischer Jagdtraktate des Mittelalters," *Librarium* 47 (2004): 2–19.

70. Some codices of these texts exist in facsimilé: the Gaston Phebus of Paris, BnF, MS fr. 616, and of New York, PML, M 1044; the *Livres du Roy Modus* of Brussels, BR, 10218–19.

71. Figures prepared by B. Van den Abeele for the Léopold Delisle conferences at the Paris BNF in December 2005 (publication foreseen).

72. Many examples in Burgundian manuscripts.

73. See G. Siebert, "Falkner und Beizjagd in den Miniaturen der Grossen Heidelberger Liederhandschrift," *Deutscher Falkenorden Jahrbuch* (1968): 89–95, and D. Walz, "Falkenjagd – Falkensymbolik," in *Codex Manesse, Katalog zur Ausstellung*, ed. E. Mittler and W. Werner (Heidelberg: Braus, 1988), pp. 350–371.

74. See the corpus reproduced by L. Randall, *Images in the Margins of Gothic Manuscripts* (Berkeley: University of California Press, 1966).

75. This hunting cycle is reproduced and commented on by K. Lindner, *Queen Mary's Psalter* (Berlin: Paul Parey, 1966).

76. One very interesting case is the late fifteenth-century Bavarian book of hours preserved in London, BL, Egerton 1146; most of the calendar pages are reproduced in R. Almond, *Medieval Hunting* (Stroud, UK: Sutton Publishing, 2003).

77. See M. Friedman, "The Falcon and the Hunt: Symbolic Love Imagery in Medieval and Renaissance Art," in *Poetics of Love in the Middle Ages. Texts and Context*, ed. M. Lazar and N. Lacy (Fairfax, VA: George Mason University Press, 1989), pp. 157–175.

78. For the various meanings of this motif, see B. Van den Abeele, "Le faucon sur la main. Un parcours iconographique médiéval," in *La chasse au Moyen Age*, pp. 87–109 and pls. 1–12.

79. See F. Garnier, "Les significations symboliques du faucon dans l'illustration des Bibles moralisées de la première moitié du 13e siècle," in *La chasse au vol au fil des temps* (Gien, France: Editions du Musée International de la Chasse, 1994), pp. 135–142; H. Wolter-von dem Knesebeck, "Aspekte der höfischen Jagd und ihrer Kritik in Bildzeugnissen des Hochmittelalters," in *Jagd und höfische Kultur*, ed. W. Rösener, pp. 493–572.

80. See G. W. Digby, *The Devonshire Hunting Tapestries* (London: Victoria and Albert Museum, 1971); A. Claxton, "The Sign of the Dog: An Examination of the Devonshire Hunting Tapestries," *Journal of Medieval History* 14 (1988): 127–179.

81. Complete reproduction and study in A. Balis, K. De Jonge, G. Delmarcel, and A. Lefébure, *Les chasses de Maximilien* (Paris: Musée du Louvre, 1993).

82. A beautifully illustrated book has been published on this corpus by C. Gasser and H. Stampfer, *La caccia nell'arte del Tirolo* (Bolzano, Italy: Athesia, 1995).

83. For Roncolo, see C. Gasser, "Imago venationis. Jagd und Fischerei im Spätmittelalter zwischen Anspruch und Wirklichkeit," in *Schloss Runkelstein. Die Bilderburg*, Bozen/Bolzano: Athesia, 2000, pp. 411–430. For Schifanoia, complete reproductions *Atlante di Schifanoia*, ed. R. Varese (Modena, Italy: Francesco Cosimo Panini, 1989).

Chapter 3

1. J. Voisenet, "L'espace domestique chez les auteurs du Moyen Ages, d'Isidore de Séville a Brunetto Latini," in *L'homme, l'animal domestique et l'environnement du Moyen Age au XVIIIe siècle*, ed. R. Durand (Nantes, France: Ouest Éditions, 1993), p. 42.

2. R. Bartlett, *England under the Norman and Angevin Kings 1075–1225* (Oxford: Clarendon Press, 2000), p. 667; J.-P. Digard, "Perspectives anthropologiques sur la relation homme-animal domestique et sur son évolution," in *L'homme, l'animal domestique et l'environnement du Moyen Age au XVIIIe siècle*, ed. R. Durand (Nantes, France: Ouest Éditions, 1993), pp. 22–23.

3. B. Jennings, *Yorkshire Monasteries: Cloister, Land and People* (Otley, UK: Smith Settle, 1999), p. 158.

4. J. Thrupp, "On the Domestication of Certain Animals in England between 7th and the 11th Centuries," *Transactions of the Ethnological Society of London* 4 (1866): 164–172; V. Fumagalli, "Gli Animali e L'Agricoltura," in *L'uomo di fronte al mondo animale nell'Alto Medioevo*, Settimane di Studio del Centro Italiano di studi sull'Alto Medioevo XXXI (1985), vol. I, pp. 579–609, at p. 584.

5. M. L. Ryder, "The History of Sheep Breeds in Britain," *Agricultural History Review* XII (1964): 1–12, 65–82, at 6; T. H. Lloyd, "Husbandry Practices and Disease in Medieval Sheep Flocks," *Veterinary History* 10 (1977–1978): 3–14, at 3.

6. S.J.M. Davis, *The Archaeology of Animals* (New Haven: Batsford, 1987), p. 19.

7. F. E. Zeuner, *A History of Domesticated Animals* (London: Hutchinson, 1963), p. 214; S. Bokonyi, "The Development and History of Domestic Animals in Hungary: The Neolithic through the Middle Ages," *American Anthropologist* 73 (1971): 640–674, at 652–660, 669; F. Audoin-Rouzeau, "Les modifications du bétail et de sa consommation en Europe médiévale et moderne: le témoignage des ossements animaux archéologiques," in *L'homme, l'animal domestique et l'environnement du Moyen Age au XVIIIe siècle*, ed. R. Durand (Nantes, France: Ouest Éditions, 1993), pp. 109–126, at pp. 111–113.

8. M. Montanari, "Gli animali e l'Alimentazione umana," in *L'uomo di fronte al mondo animale nell'Alto Medioevo*, Settimane di Studio del Centro Italiano di studi sull'Alto Medioevo XXXI (Spoleto, Italy: La Sede del Centro, 1985), vol. I, pp. 619–663, at pp. 635–636.

9. Davis, *Archaeology*, p. 189.

10. Zeuner, *History*, p. 267.

11. Montanari, "Gli animali," p. 623.

12. J. Wiseman, *The Pig. A British History* (London: Duckworth, 2000), p. 3.

13. J. Clutton-Brock, *Domesticated Animals from Early Times* (London: Heinemann, 1981); Davis, *The Archaeology*, p. 187.

14. Wiseman, *The Pig*, p. 8.

15. Fumagalli, "Gli animali," p. 589.
16. Bokonyi, "The Development," p. 664.
17. Bartlett, *England*, pp. 306–307.
18. A. Grant, "Animal Resources," in *The Countryside of Medieval England*, ed. G. Astill and A. Grant (Oxford: Basil Blackwell, 1988), pp. 149–187, at p. 152.
19. B. Levitan, "Medieval Animal Husbandry in South West England," in *Studies in the Palaeoeconomy and Environment of South West England*, BAR British Series, 181, ed. N. D. Balaam and others (Oxford: B.A.R., 1987), pp. 51–80.
20. C. Wickham, "Pastoralism and Underdevelopment in the Early Middle Ages," in *L'Uomo di fronte al mondo animale nell'Alto Medioevo*, Settimane di Studio del Centro Italiano di Studi sull'Alto Medioevo XXXI (Spoleto, Italy: La Sede del Centro, 1985), pp. 401–451, at pp. 437–439.
21. H. E. Hallam, *Rural England, 1066–1348* (Glasgow, UK: Fontana, 1981), p. 26.
22. Zeuner, *History*, p. 385.
23. P. L. Armitage, "A Preliminary Description of British Cattle from the Late 12th to the Early 16th Century," *The Ark* 7 (1980): 405–412; P. L. Armitage, "Developments in British Cattle Husbandry from the Romano-British Period to Early Modern Times," *The Ark* 9 (1982): 50–54.
24. T. P. O'Connor, "The Archaeozoological Interpretation of Morphometric Variability in British Sheep Limb Bones" (PhD diss., University of London, 1982).
25. J. Rackham, "Physical Remains of Medieval Horses," in J. Clark (ed.), *The Medieval Horse and Its Equipment, c. 1150–c. 1450* (London: HMSQ, 1995), pp. 19–32, at p. 22; Ibid., "Appendix: Skeletal Evidence of Medieval Horses from London Sites," pp. 169–174, at p. 170.
26. H. S. Bennet, *Life on the English Manor. A Study on Peasant Conditions, 1150–1400* (Cambridge: Cambridge University Press, 1937), pp. 78, 94.
27. E. Sabine, "City Cleaning in Medieval London," *Speculum* XII (1937): 24–25.
28. Bennet, *Life*, p. 92.
29. Zeuner, *History*, p. 244; Bennet, *Life*, p. 91.
30. D. Oschinsky, *"Walter of Henley" and Other Treatises on Estate Management* (London: Clarendon Press, 1971), p. 319.
31. A. Hyland, *The Horse in the Middle Ages* (Stroud, UK: Sutton Publishing, 1999), pp. 1, 43.
32. Hyland, *Horse*, p. 1.
33. Rackham, "Physical Remains," p. 20; F. Audoin-Rouzeau, "Les ossements du cheptel medieval," *Ethnozootechnie* 59 (1997): 69–67.
34. J. H. Moore, "The Ox in the Middle Ages," *Agricultural History* 35, 2 (1961): 90–93, at 93.
35. Hyland, *Horse*, p. 56.
36. W. C. Jordan, *The Great Famine: Northern Europe in the Early Fourteenth Century* (Princeton: Princeton University Press, 1996), p. 35.
37. R. M. Stecher and L. Gross, "Ankylosing Lesions of the Spine," *Journal of Veterinary Medical Association* 138 (1961): 248–265; Hyland, *Horse*, p. 53.
38. Rackham, "Appendix," p. 173.
39. J. Langdon, *Horses, Oxen and Technological Innovation: The Use of Draught Animals in English Farming from 1066–1500* (Cambridge: Cambridge University Press, 1986), p. 17.
40. Langdon, *Horses*, pp. 34–35; P. Contamine, "Jalons pour une histoire du cheval dans l'économie rurale lorraine à la fin du Moyen Age," *Ethnozootechnie* 59 (1997): 51–59; Moore, "The Ox," p. 91.

41. R. Fossier, "L'élevage médiéval. Bilan d'un problème," *Ethnozootechnie* 59 (1997): 9–20.

42. Oschinsky, *Walter of Henley,* pp. 289, 325, 427, 429; Lloyd, "Husbandry Practices," pp. 4–5.

43. Lloyd, "Husbandry Practices," p. 10.

44. Davis, *Archaeology,* pp. 186–187.

45. Lloyd, "Husbandry Practices," p. 7.

46. Ibid., p. 8.

47. M. Riu y Riu, "Agricultura y ganadería en el Fuero de Cuenca," *Estudios en memoria del Professor D. Salvador de Moxó,* vol. II (1982): 369–386, at 380.

48. C. J. Biskho, "El Castellano hombre de llanura. La explotación ganadera en el área fronteriza de La Mancha y Extremadura en la Edad Media," *Homenaje a Jaime Vicens Vives* (Barcelona: Universidad de Barcelona, 1967), vol. I, pp. 201–218.

49. J. Klein, *The Mesta: A Study in Spanish Economic History, 1273–1836* (Cambridge, MA: Harvard University Press, 1920), pp. 31–46.

50. P. García Martín, coord., *Cañadas, cordeles y veredas* (Valladolid, Spain: Junta de Castilla y Leon, 2000).

51. M. Cordero del Campillo, "Veterinary Medicine in the Medieval Period: The Christian Kingdoms in Spain," *Historia Medicinae Veterinariae* 22 (1997): 73–104, at 86.

52. Zeuner, *History,* pp. 194–195.

53. A. Sánchez-Belda and M. C. Sánchez Trujillano, *Razas ovinas españolas* (Madrid: Ministerio de Agricultura, 1989); and E. Laguna Sanz, *Historia del Merino* (Madrid: Ministerio de Agricultura, 1986); Cordero del Campillo, "Veterinary Medicine," p. 86.

54. K. Biddick, "Pig Husbandry on the Peterborough Abbey Estate from the Twelfth to the Fourteenth century A.D.," in *Animals and Archaeology: Husbandry in Europe,* B.A.R. International Series 227, ed. C. Grigson and J. Clutton-Brock (Oxford: B.A.R., 1984), pp. 161–178, at p. 176; Bennet, *Life,* p. 92.

55. Wiseman, *The Pig,* pp. XVII, 1; Bokonyi, "The Development," p. 671.

56. Zeuner, *History,* pp. 194–195, 410.

57. J. Arnold, "L'élevage du lapin au Moyen Age," *Ethnozootechnie* 59 (1997): 61–68.

58. J. Bond, "Rabbits: The Case for Their Medieval Introduction to Britain," *Local History* 18 (1988): 53–57; Bartlett, *England,* p. 672.

59. Zeuner, *History,* pp. 194–195, 414.

60. Davis, *Archaeology,* p. 190.

61. E. Jamroziak, "Rievaulx Abbey as a Wool Producer in the Late Thirteenth Century: Cistercians, Sheep and Debts," *Northern History* XL, 2 (2003): 197–218; Lloyd, "Husbandry Practices," p. 11.

62. Lloyd, "Husbandry Practices," pp. 12–13.

63. Oschinsky, *Walter of Henley,* pp. 275, 381.

64. Lloyd, "Husbandry Practices," p. 12.

65. Jordan, *The Great Famine,* p. 37.

66. Ibid.

67. Lloyd, "Husbandry Practices," p.11.

68. Zeuner, *History,* pp. 270–271.

69. Armitage, "Preliminary," pp. 405–413; M. L. Ryder, "Livestock Remains from Four Medieval Sites in Yorkshire," *Agricultural History Review* IX (1961): 105–110.

70. Armitage, "Preliminary," pp. 409–411.

71. Langdon, *Horses*, p. 18.
72. Audoin-Rouzeau, "Les modifications," pp. 120–121; C. Dyer, *Everyday Life in Medieval England* (London: Hambledon, 2000), p. 85.
73. Dyer, *Everyday Life*, p. 89; Audoin-Rouzeau, "Les modifications," p. 114; Bokonyi, "The Development," p. 651.
74. Dyer, *Everyday Life*, p. 4.
75. Bokonyi, "The Development," p. 651.
76. Hyland, *Horse*, p. 44.
77. Davis, *Archaeology*, p. 186.
78. Wiseman, *The Pig*, pp. 8–9.
79. Biddick, "Pig Husbandry," p. 176.
80. Clark, *The Medieval Horse*, pp. 10–11.
81. Rackham, "Physical Remains," pp. 27–28.
82. Clark, *The Medieval Horse*, p. 90.
83. Hyland, *Horse*, pp. 19–23.
84. Cordero del Campillo, "Veterinary Medicine," p. 91; L. Bartosiewicz, ed., *Animals in the Urban Landscape in the Wake of the Middle Ages: A Case Study from Vác, Hungary* B.A.R. 609 (Oxford: B.A.R., 1995), pp. 71–87.
85. R. Muchembled, *Popular Culture and Elite Culture in France, 1400–1750* (1985; repr., Baton Rouge: Louisiana State University Press, 2004), p. 23.
86. Clark, *The Medieval Horse*, pp. 16, 18.
87. Bartlett, *England*, pp. 584–588.
88. Bokonyi, "The Development," p. 673.
89. T. U. Holmes, *Daily Living in the Twelfth Century: Based on the Observations of Alexander Neckam in London and Paris* (Madison: University of Wisconsin Press, 1952), pp. 231–232.
90. E. Powers, *Medieval English Nunneries c. 1275–1535* (Cambridge: Cambridge University Press, 1922), pp. 305–309, 412–413.
91. Ibid., p. 306, n. 3.
92. Ibid., p. 662.
93. F. Santi, "Cani e gatti, grandi battaglie. Origini storiche di un conflitto ancora aperto," *Micrologus* 8 (2000): pp. 31–40.
94. L. Bobis, "L'évolution de la place du chat dans l'espace social et l'imaginaire occidental, du Moyen Age au XVIIIe siecle," in *L'homme, l'animal domestique et l'environnement du Moyen Age au XVIIIe siècle*, ed. R. Durand (Nantes, France: Ouest Editions, 1993), pp. 73–84, at p. 73.
95. Ibid., p. 74.
96. Bokonyi, "The Development," p. 673.
97. Bobis, "L'évolution," pp. 73–75.

Chapter 4

1. John Trevisa, *On the Properties of Things: John Trevisa's Translation of Bartholomaeus Anglicus. De Proprietatibus Rerum*, ed. M. C. Seymour, 3 vols. (Oxford: Oxford University Press, 1975), vol. 2, p. 1110. St. John Damascene (d. 749), in *De fide orthodoxa* 24.24–8, uses three of these categories, and Robert Grosseteste (ca. 1225) uses all four in *Hexaemeron* (7.14.8).

2. G. Loisel, *Histoire des menageries de l'antiquité a nos jours*, 3 vols. (Paris: Octave Doin et Fils, 1912), vol. I, p. 142.

3. Ibid., pp. 162–163.

4. See R. Bartlett, *England under the Norman and Angevin Kings, 1075–1225* (Oxford: Clarendon Press, 2000), p. 670.

5. Scandinavian rulers had polar bears in the eleventh century; see H. Pálsson, trans., *Hrafnkel's Saga and Other Icelandic Stories* (Harmondsworth, UK: Penguin, 1971), p. 28.

6. Loisel, *Histoire des menageries*, vol. I, p. 154–155. For Edward II's lion and Edward III's menagerie, see C. Shenton, "Edward III and the Symbol of the Leopard," in *Heraldry, Pageantry and Social Display in Medieval England*, ed. P. Coss and M. Keen (Woodbridge, UK: Boydell, 2002), pp. 76–77, and Loisel, *Histoire des menageries*, vol. I, p. 155. Edward I's animal acquisitions and Richard II's camel: D. Hahn, *The Tower Menagerie: The Amazing 600-Year History of the Royal Collection of Wild and Ferocious Beasts Kept at the Tower of London* (New York: Penguin Group, 2004), p. 48. The Tower Menagerie remained continuously operative until 1828.

7. Loisel, *Histoire des menageries*, vol. I, p. 146.

8. Ibid., pp. 149–153.

9. Ibid., pp. 148–149.

10. Ibid., pp. 168–173.

11. Ibid., pp. 170–175.

12. L. Solski, "Zoological Gardens of Central-Eastern Europe and Russia," in *Zoo and Aquarium History: Ancient Animal Collections to Zoological Gardens*, ed. V. N. Kisling (Boca Raton, FL: CRC, 2001), p. 140.

13. V. N. Kisling, ed., *Zoo and Aquarium History: Ancient Animal Collections to Zoological Gardens* (Boca Raton, FL: CRC, 2001), p. 23; H. Strehlow, "Zoological Gardens of Western Europe," in *Zoo and Aquarium History*, ed. V. N. Kisling, p. 81; Loisel, *Histoire des menageries*, vol. I, pp. 156–159.

14. Loisel, *Histoire des menageries*, vol. I, p. 157.

15. Strehlow, "Zoological Gardens," p. 79.

16. R. Delort, "Le Prince et la bête," in *Guerre, pouvoir et noblesse au Moyen Âge: Mélanges en l'honneur de Philippe Contamine*, ed. J. Paviot and J. Verger (Paris: Presses de l'Université de Paris-Sorbonne, 2000), p. 186.

17. Delort, "Le Prince et la bête," pp. 186, 194.

18. Ibid., pp. 194–195.

19. Loisel, *Histoire des menageries*, vol. I, pp. 163–164.

20. A. Wilmart, "La légende de Ste. Édith en prose et vers par le moine Goscelin," *Analecta Bollandiana* 56 (1938): 68. My thanks to Christopher A. Jones for this reference and for help in translating Goscelin's difficult Latin.

21. J. Bumke, *Courtly Culture: Literature and Society in the High Middle Ages*, trans. T. Dunlap (Berkeley: University of California Press, 1991), p. 221.

22. Ibid., p. 213.

23. Loisel, *Histoire des menageries*, vol. I, p. 46.

24. Ibid., pp. 166–168.

25. It might be profitable to see the display of Asian, Middle Eastern, and African beasts as part of the Wonders of the East tradition; see L. Daston and K. Park, eds., *Wonders and the Order of Nature, 1150–1750* (New York: Zone Books,

1998), for collections of rare natural objects, such as ostrich eggs, gemstones, magnets, whales' ribs, and unicorns' horns' in twelfth- and thirteenth-century Europe. Charlemagne received bears, lions, camels, and hawks from his Moorish counterparts according to the late eleventh-century *Chanson de Roland* (lines 30, 128, 183, 645, 847).

26. R. Barber and J. Barker, *Tournaments: Jousts, Chivalry and Pageants in the Middle Ages* (New York: Weidenfeld and Nicolson, 1989), p. 77.

27. Bumke, *Courtly Culture*, p. 214.

28. A. R. Myers, *London in the Age of Chaucer* (Norman: University of Oklahoma Press, 1972), p. 169.

29. Barber and Barker, *Tournaments*, p. 46.

30. Loisel, *Histoire des menageries*, vol. I, pp. 147–148.

31. Jean Froissart, *Chronicles*, trans. G. Brereton (Harmondsworth, UK: Penguin, 1978), p. 354.

32. J. J. Jusserand, *Les sports et jeux d'exercice dans l'ancienne France* (Paris: Plon-Nourrit, 1901), p. 12.

33. Barber and Baker, *Tournaments*, p. 14.

34. Ibid., pp. 78, 91, 103.

35. T. McLean, *The English at Play in the Middle Ages* (Windsor Forest, UK: Kensal, 1983), pp. 63–64; Jusserand, *Les sports*, pp. 78–79.

36. Bumke, *Courtly Culture*, pp. 251–257.

37. Barber and Baker, *Tournaments*, p. 191.

38. Horses had to be trained to change leads quickly on command; see C. Gillmor, "Practical Chivalry: The Training of Horses for Tournaments and Warfare," *Studies in Medieval and Renaissance History* 13, o.s. 23, 1992, pp. 8–13. Horses were trained to tolerate the noise and crowded conditions of combat and to rush headlong into the path of another oncoming horse, an action violating the animal's natural inclinations; Ibid., p. 8. For medieval descriptions of a good tournament horse, see Hartmann von Aue's *Gregorius* p. 187, Wolfram von Eschenbach's *Parzifal* pp. 93, 95, and Gottfried von Strassbourg's *Tristan*, pp. 69, 130. For scenes involving tournament horsemanship, see also the medieval biography of William Marshal: *L'Histoire de Guillaume le Maréchal, comte de Striguil et de Pembroke* [1891–1901], 3 vols., ed. P. Meyer (Paris: Société de l'histoire de France, 1891–1901), and S. Painter, *William Marshal* (Baltimore: Johns Hopkins University Press, 1933).

39. For jousting rules, see Jusserand, *Les sports*, pp. 102–107. There are no treatises on the approved styles of managing a horse and lance until the fifteenth century *Art of Good Horsemanship* (Barber and Baker, *Tournaments*, pp. 198–201). On game structure and common techniques in tournaments, see R. Barber, *The Knight and Chivalry* (London: Longmans, 1970), pp. 166–169. Techniques became increasingly stylized; see Ibid., pp. 171–178; T. S. Henricks, "Sport and Social Hierarchy in Medieval England," *Journal of Sport History* 9 (1982): 24. For variations on jousting (*pas d'armes*), see Barber, *The Knight and Chivalry*, pp. 173–174; H. Gillmeister, "Medieval Sport: Modern Methods of Research – Recent Results and Perspectives," *The International Journal of the History of Sport* 5 (1988): 53–58.

40. Barber and Barker, *Tournaments*, p. 196.

41. Jousting often took place before, during, and after tournaments. For jousting on the night before a tournament (vesper games or litigant jousts) see, for example, Wolfram von Eschenbach's *Parzifal* p. 39, and Marie de France's *Chaitivel* p. 106.

Individual jousts at the tournament of Saint-Inglevert, 1390, often included the collision of horses; see Froissart, *Chronicles*, pp. 375–376.

42. J. Clark, ed., *The Medieval Horse and its Equipment, c. 1150–c. 1450*, 2nd ed. (Woodbridge, UK: Boydell, 2004), pp. 23–29; M. Bennett, "The Medieval Warhorse Reconsidered," in *Medieval Knighthood*, ed. S. Church and R. Harvey (Woodbridge, UK: Boydell, 1995), vol. 5, p. 22.

43. Bennett, "Medieval Warhorse," p. 26; A. Hyland, *The Medieval Warhorse from Byzantium to the Crusades* (Phoenix Mill, UK: Alan Sutton, 1994), p. 57; R. H. Bautier and A.-M. Bautier, "Contribution a l'histoire de cheval au Moyen Âge: L'élevage du cheval," in *Bulletin philologique et historique du comité des travaux historiques et scientifiques, 1978* (Paris: Bibliothèque Nationale, 1980), pp. 17–24.

44. R.H.C. Davis, *The Medieval Warhorse: Origin, Development and Redevelopment* (London: Thames and Hudson, 1989), pp. 60–61.

45. Bautier and Bautier, "Contribution," p. 15.

46. Barber and Barker, *Tournaments*, p. 191.

47. Davis, *Medieval Warhorse*, pp. 101–102.

48. Ibid., p. 103.

49. For some examples of ladies as spectators, see Chretien de Troyes' *Erec and Enide*, pp. 63–64, Hartmann von Aue's *Gregorius*, p. 193, Wolfram von Eschenbach's *Parzifal*, pp. 39, 42, 192, 288, Boccaccio's *Decameron* (10:7), and *Sir Percyvell of Gales*, lines 59–60. A particularly vivid example of the erotic effect that the image of a knight on his horse could evoke is seen in Chaucer's *Troilus and Criseyde* 2:624–652 and 1261.

50. Bumke, *Courtly Culture*, p. 224; Jusserand, *Les sports*, p. 45. Pope John XXII lifted the ban on tournaments and jousting in 1316; see Barber and Barker, *Tournaments*, pp. 40, 141. For Jacques de Vitry's screed against war games, see M. Keen, *Chivalry* (New Haven: Yale University Press, 1984), p. 95. On secular rulers prohibiting tournaments and jousting, see Barber and Barker, *Tournaments*, p. 19, 40; Jusserand, *Les sports*, p. 46.

51. L. Clare, *La quintaine, la course de bague et le jeu des têtes: Étude historique et ethno-linguistique d'une famille de jeux équestres* (Paris: Centre National de la Recherche Scientifique, 1983), pp. 16, 26, 29–30.

52. J. Strutt, *The Sports and Pastimes of the People of England* (1801; repr., Bath: Firecrest, 1969), p. 109; Jusserand, *Les sports*, pp. 162–163, 167; Barber and Barker, *Tournaments*, pp. 45, 46, 60; Clare, *La quintaine*, pp. 47–48.

53. Clare, *La quintaine*, p. 77.

54. For taurine rituals in Mediterranean prehistory, see J. M. Gómez-Tabanera, "Origenes y determinantes de las fiestas taurinas in España," in *El Folklore Español*, ed. J. M. Gómez-Tabanera (Madrid: Instituto Español de Anthropologia Aplicada, 1968), pp. 269–295, and T. Mitchell, *Blood Sport: A Social History of Spanish Bullfighting* (Philadelphia: University of Pennsylvania Press, 1991), pp. 38–40.

55. A.-M. S. A. Rodrigues, "Le taureau dans les fêtes aristocratiques et populaires du Moyen Âge," in *Jeux, sports et divertissements au Moyen Âge et à l'Âge classique*, ed. J.-M. Mehl (Paris: Éditions du CTHS, 1993), p. 184.

56. A. Alvarez de Miranda, *Ritos y juegos del toro* (Madrid: Taurus, 1962), p. 49.

57. Rodrigues, "Le taureau," p. 84; M. Delgado Ruiz, *De la muerte de un dios: La fiesta de los toros en el universo simbólico de la cultura popular* (Barcelona: Nexos, 1986).

58. Rodrigues, "Le taureau," p. 185.

59. Ibid., p. 186.
60. Alvarez de Miranda, *Ritos y juegos*, pp. 108, 111.
61. Ibid., p. 49.
62. Rodrigues, "Le taureau," p. 188.
63. J. R. Conrad, *The Horn and the Sword: The History of the Bull as a Symbol of Power and Fertility* (New York: Dutton, 1957); Alvarez de Miranda, *Ritos y juegos*; Delgado Ruiz, *De la muerte de un dios.*
64. Alvarez de Miranda, *Ritos y juegos*, pp. 98–99.
65. Rodrigues, "Le taureau," p. 190. Bull-running was practiced in Northern Europe, for example in medieval Tutbury (Staffordshire), England: F. W. Hackwood, *Old English Sports* (London: T. Fisher Unwin, 1907), pp. 326–327; McLean, *The English at Play*, p. 26. On bull-running in medieval Stamford, see McLean, *The English at Play*, pp. 26, 204. On bullfighting outside of the Iberian Peninsula, especially in Italy, see Loisel, *Histoire des menageries*, vol. I, p. 148; W. Endrei and L. Zolnay, *Fun and Games in Old Europe* (Budapest: Corvina, 1986), p. 153.
66. T. Mitchell, *Violence and Piety in Spanish Folklore* (Philadelphia: University of Pennsylvania Press, 1988), pp. 151–152.
67. Rodrigues, "Le taureau," pp. 191–192.
68. A. Nicoll, *Masks, Mimes and Miracles: Studies in the Popular Theatre* (New York: Cooper Square, 1931), p. 146.
69. C. Reeves, *Pleasures and Pastimes in Medieval England* (Phoenix Mill, UK: Sutton, 1997), p. 100.
70. McLean, *The English at Play*, pp. 20–21.
71. W. Fitzstephen, *Descriptio nobilissimae civitatis Londoniae*, trans. H. E. Butler, in *Norman London,* with an essay by Sir F. Stenton (New York: Italica, 1990), pp. 53–54; B. Hanawalt, *Growing Up in Medieval London: The Experience of Childhood in History* (Oxford: Oxford University Press, 1993), p. 33.
72. Strutt, *Sports and Pastimes*, p. 33.
73. McLean, *The English at Play*, p. 209.
74. Bautier and Bautier, "Contribution," p. 43.
75. W. Heywood, *Palio and Ponte: An Account of the Sports of Central Italy from the Age of Dante to the XXth Century* (1904; rept., New York: Hacker Art Books, 1904), pp. 6–10.
76. Ibid., p. 16.
77. Ibid., pp. 62, 83.
78. Ibid., p. 12.
79. Ibid., pp. 6–10, 89.
80. Ibid., pp. 15–16.
81. Ibid., pp. 10, 19.
82. Strutt, *Sports and Pastimes*, p. 33.
83. R. Germain, "Jeux et divertissements dans le centre de la France à la fin du Moyen Âge," in *Jeux, sports et divertissements au Moyen Âge et à l'Âge classique*, ed. J.-M. Mehl (Paris: Éditions du CTHS, 1993), p. 52.
84. Delort, "Le Prince et la bête," p. 189.
85. Fitzstephen, *Descriptio*, p. 56; A. F. Leach, *The Schools of Medieval England* (London: Methuen, 1915), p. 256.
86. R. Favreau, "Fêtes et jeux en Poitou à la fin du Moyen Âge," in *Jeux, sports et divertissements au Moyen Âge et à l'Âge classique*, ed. J.-M. Mehl (Paris: Éditions du CTHS, 1993), p. 37.

87. I. Forsyth, "The Theme of Cockfighting in Burgundian Romanesque Sculpture," *Speculum* 53 (1978): 270–271.

88. Strutt, *Sports and Pastimes*, p. 244; B. Hanawalt, *The Ties That Bound: Peasant Families in Medieval England* (Oxford: Oxford University Press, 1986), p. 217.

89. On modern cockfighting in a status-based sociocultural context, see C. Geertz, "Deep Play: Notes on a Balinese Cockfight," *Daedalus* 101 (1972): 1–37.

90. Alexander Neckam, *De laudibus sapientiae divinae*, ed. T. Wright (London: Longman Green, 1863), pp. 391–392.

91. N. Orme, *Medieval Children* (New Haven: Yale University Press, 2001), p. 186, 355n.

92. R. F. Green, *Poets and Princepleasers: Literature and the English Court in the Late Middle Ages* (Toronto: University of Toronto Press, 1980), p. 55. Cf. Pliny, *Natural History*, trans. H. Rackham (Cambridge, MA: Harvard University Press, 1983), bk. 10, p. 323.

93. Bartlett, *England under the Norman and Angevin Kings*, p. 669.

94. Arnoul II of Normandy baited a bear with dogs out in public; see Loisel, *Histoire des menageries*, vol. I, p. 165.

95. Hackwood, *Old English Sports*, p. 348.

96. E. K. Chambers, *The Mediaeval Stage*, 2 vols. (Oxford: Oxford University Press, 1903), vol. I, p. 53n.

97. Fitzstephen, *Descriptio*, p. 58.

98. Strutt, *Sports and Pastimes*, pp. 205–206.

99. On bearbaiting as a popular spectacle for which bear wards would charge admission, see J. J. Jusserand, *English Wayfaring Life in the Middle Ages*, trans. L. Toulmin Smith (1889; repr., London: Methuen, 1950), p. 110. On commoners "bere baiting" and "bole-slatyng" (baiting) at large urban festivals sponsored by the royal court, see *Kyng Alisaunder*, lines 195–200.

100. K. Thomas, *Man and the Natural World: Changing Attitudes in England, 1500–1800* (Oxford: Oxford University Press, 1983), p. 144; Strutt, *Sports and Pastimes*, p. 204.

101. Thomas, *Man and the Natural World*, p. 93; Strutt, *Sports and Pastimes*, p. 207.

102. Hackwood, *Old English Sports*, pp. 297–302.

103. S. Wenzel, ed., *Fasciculus Morum: A Fourteenth-Century Preacher's Handbook* (University Park: Pennsylvania State University Press, 1989), p. 159.

104. John Trevisa, *On the Properties of Things*, vol. II, p. 1262.

105. J. D. Martin, "Sva lykr her hverju hestaðingi: Sports and Games in Icelandic Saga Literature," *Scandinavian Studies* 75 (2003): 25–44.

106. Orme, *Medieval Children*, p. 179.

107. Hackwood, *Old English Sports*, pp. 289–290.

108. Germain, "Jeux et divertissements," pp. 49–50; J. Deleito y Piñuela, *También se divierte el pueblo* (Madrid: Espasa-Calpe, 1944), p. 24.

109. Mehl, J.-M., *Les jeux au royaume de France du XIIIe au début du XVIe siècle* (Paris: Fayard, 1990), p. 479; Endrei and Zolnay, *Fun and Games*, p. 153.

110. R. Vaultier, *Le Folklore pendant la guerre de Cent Ans d'après Les Lettres de Rémission du Trésor des Chartres* (Paris: Librairie Guénégaud, 1965), pp. 189–191.

111. Thomas, *Man and the Natural World*, p. 147.

112. Mehl, *Les jeux*, p. 62; Germain, "Jeux et divertissements," p. 47; Chambers, *The Mediaeval Stage*, vol. I, p. 148.

113. Jusserand, *Les sports*, p. 28.

114. Endrei and Zolnay, *Fun and Games*, p. 128.

115. Mehl, *Les jeux*, p. 487.

116. On medieval children's hobbyhorses before the fifteenth century, see Endrei and Zolnay, *Fun and Games*, p. 20. On hobbyhorses in late medieval English rituals, see E. C. Cawte, *Ritual Animal Disguise: A Historical and Geographical Study of Animal Disguise in the British Isles* (Cambridge: D.S. Brewer, 1978), pp. 3–47.

117. Chambers, *The Mediaeval Stage*, vol. I, pp. 71–72.

118. Strutt, *Sports and Pastimes*, plates 26–28; J. Southworth, *The English Medieval Minstrel* (Woodbridge, UK: Boydell, 1989), p. 14.

119. Strutt, *Sports and Pastimes*, p. 151 and plate 25.

120. Bumke, *Courtly Culture*, p. 223.

121. B. Einarsson, ed., *Haraldskvaeði*, in *Agrip af Nóregskonunga Sogum, Fagrskinna-Noregs Konunga Tal* (Reykjavik: Islenzka Fornrit, 1985), vol. 29, p. 64.

122. Alexander Neckam, *De naturis rerum*, Rolls Series 34, ed. T. Wright, (London: Longman Green, 1863), pp. 208–211.

123. Strutt, *Sports and Pastimes*, plate 26.

124. H. W. Janson, *Apes and Ape Lore in the Middle Ages and the Renaissance* (London: Warburg Institute, 1952), p. 171.

125. T.S.R. Boase, *English Art, 1100–1216* (Oxford: Oxford University Press, 1953), plate 7c.

126. For *Ruodlieb*, cf. R. Axton, *European Drama of the Early Middle Ages* (Pittsburgh: University of Pittsburgh Press, 1974), p. 22.

127. Strutt, *Sports and Pastimes*, plate 25.

128. J. Bolland and others, eds., *Acta Sanctorum quotquot toto orbe coluntur* (1643; repr., Turnhout, Belgium: Brepols, 1966–1971), Jan II, 25.

129. Southworth, *The English Medieval Minstrel*, p. 86.

130. Janson, *Apes and Ape Lore*, p. 170.

131. Bartlett, *England under the Norman and Angevin Kings*, p. 669.

132. Jusserand, *English Wayfaring Life*, p. 116.

133. Chambers, *The Mediaeval Stage*, vol. I, p. 67.

134. Nicoll, *Masks, Mimes and Miracles*, p. 166; Chambers, *The Mediaeval Stage*, vol. I, pp. 71–72n.

135. Southworth, *The English Medieval Minstrel*, p. 17–18.

136. This manuscript is Oxford, Bodleian Library MS 264.

137. Chambers, *The Mediaeval Stage*, vol. II, pp. 290–306; V. Alford, *The Hobby Horse and Other Animal Masks* (London: Merlin, 1978), pp. 19–23; B. Filotas, *Pagan Survivals, Superstitions and Popular Cultures in Early Medieval Pastoral Literature* (Toronto: Pontifical Institute of Mediaeval Studies, 2005), pp. 56–61.

138. On ritual slayings of rams and lambs, see Chambers, *The Mediaeval Stage*, vol. I, pp. 140–141; on the display of the heads and hides of dead horses and cattle, see p. 141.

139. Cawte, *Ritual Animal Disguise*; Chambers, *The Mediaeval Stage*, vol. I, p. 42; G. Wickham, *The Medieval Theatre*, 3rd ed. (Cambridge: Cambridge University Press, 1974), p. 131.

140. Chambers, *The Mediaeval Stage*, vol. I, p. 208.

141. Axton, *European Drama*, pp. 40–41.

142. Chambers, *The Mediaeval Stage*, vol. I, pp. 287–332.

143. Ibid., p. 287.

144. Froissart, *Chronicles*, p. 359.

145. Southworth, *The English Medieval Minstrel*, p. 108; Chambers, *The Mediaeval Stage*, vol. I, p. 302n.

146. Boccaccio, *Decameron*, 2 vols., trans. J. Payne, rev. C. S. Singleton (Berkeley: University of California Press, 1982), p. 313.

147. L. J. Kiser, "Animals in Sacred Space: St. Francis and the Crib at Greccio," in *Speaking Images: Essays in Honor of V. A. Kolve*, ed, R. F. Yeager and C. C. Morse (Asheville, NC: Pegasus, 2001), pp. 55–57.

148. McLean, *The English at Play*, p. 174.

149. See especially lines 1–2, 429, 343, and 443 of the English Towneley Buffeting of Christ; lines 162–71 and 450 of the English N-Town Cycle Trial of Jesus; and lines 184–185 and 245 of the English York Buffeting of Christ; line 6439 of the French Semur Buffeting of Christ; line 20952 ff. of the French Greban Buffeting of Christ; and lines 4315–4335 of the German Eger Buffeting of Christ.

Chapter 5

1. G. Petit and J. Théodoridès, *Histoire de la zoologie des origines à Linné* (Paris: Hermann, 1962), p. 153. The passage is reproduced from the lecture "La zoologie au moyen âge" given by Théoridès at the Palais de la Découverte in Paris on 1 February 1958 and printed afterward. The only difference is the use of the term *inepties* (nonsense) instead of *balivernes*.

2. Romans 1:20.

3. J. P. Migne, ed., *Honorii Augustodunensis opera omnia*, trans. P. Beullens, Patrologiae Latinae tomus 172 (repr., Turnhout, Belgium: Brepols, 1970), bk. I, chap. 12, col. 1117C.

4. Genesis 1:28.

5. 1 Corinthians 9:9–10.

6. 588b4–10.

7. 491a22.

8. Augustine, *De doctrina Christiana*, bk. 2, chap. 16, para. 24, trans. D. W. Robertson Jr. (Indianapolis: Bobbs-Merrill, 1958).

9. Thomas Aquinas, *Summa theologiae*, pars Ia, quaest. I, art. 10, in *St Thomas Aquinas summa theologiae*, vol. I, *Christian Theology* (Ia.1), trans. T. Gilby (McGraw Hill: New York, 1964).

10. N. Henkel, *Studien zum Physiologus im Mittelalter* (Tübingen, Germany: Niemeyer, 1976).

11. F. J. Carmody, ed., *Physiologus Latinus. Éditions préliminaires versio B* (Paris: Droz, 1939).

12. F. Sbordone, ed., *Physiologus*, Milan, Genoa, Rome, Naples, 1936. D. Offermans, *Der Physiologus nach den Handschriften G und M* (Meisenheim am Glan, Germany: Hain, 1966). D. Kaimakis, *Der Physiologus nach der ersten Redaktion* (Meisenheim am Glan, Germany: Hain, 1974).

13. M. R. James, *The Bestiary* (Oxford: Roxburghe Club, 1928).

14. F. McCulloch, *Mediaeval Latin and French Bestiaries* (Chapel Hill: University of North Carolina Press, 1960).

15. W. George and B. Yapp, *The Naming of the Beasts. Natural History in the Medieval Bestiary* (London: Duckworth, 1991); R. Baxter, *Bestiaries and Their Users in the Middle Ages* (Stroud, UK: Sutton, 1998); B. Van den Abeele, ed., *Bestiaires*

médiévaux. Nouvelles perspectives sur les manuscrits et les traditions textuelles (Louvain-la-Neuve, Belgium: Université Catholique de Louvain, 2005).

16. *Etymologiae*, bk. 12, chap. 7, para. 26; bk. 12, chap. 2, para. 13.

17. W. B. Clark, trans. and ed., *The Medieval Book of Birds. Hugh of Fouilloy's Aviarium* (Binghampton, NY: MRTS, 1992).

18. Ibid., pp. 118–119.

19. B. Van den Abeele, "Trente et un nouveaux manuscrits de l'Aviarium: regards sur la diffusion de l'oeuvre d'Hugues de Fouilloy," *Scriptorium* 57 (2003): 253–271.

20. R. French and A. Cunningham, *Before Science. The Invention of the Friars' Natural Philosophy* (Aldershot, UK: Scolar, 1996).

21. Thomas Cantimpratensis, *Liber de natura rerum,* trans. P. Beullens and ed. H. Boese (Berlin: de Gruyter, 1973), p. 3, lines 16–29.

22. A. Borst, *Das Buch der Naturgeschichte. Plinius und seine Leser im Zeitalter des Pergaments* (Heidelberg: Winter, 1994).

23. J. Brams, *La riscoperta di Aristotele in occidente* (Milan: Jaca Books, 2003).

24. Aristotle, *De animalibus. Michael Scot's Arabic–Latin Translation*. Pt. 3, bks. XV–XIX, *Generation of Animals*, ed. A. van Oppenraay (New York: Brill, 1992); pt. 2, bks. XI–XIV, *Parts of Animals* (Boston: Brill, 1998); pt. 1, bks. I–X, *History of Animals* (forthcoming).

25. H. J. Drossaart Lulofs, ed., *De generatione animalium. Translatio Guillelmi de Moerbeka*, Aristoteles Latinus XVII 2.v (Paris: Brill, 1966). P. Beullens and F. Bossier, eds., *De historia animalium. Translatio Guillelmi de Morbeka*, Prima pars: lib. I–V, Aristoteles Latinus XVII 2.i.i (Boston: Brill, 2000).

26. De Leemans, ed. (Turnhout, Belgium: Brepols, forthcoming).

27. Roger Bacon, *Opera quedam hactenus inedita*, ed. J. S. Brewer (London: Longman, 1859), vol. I, p. 473.

28. The translation of *De partibus animalium* is preserved in MS Padua, Biblioteca Antoniana, scaff. XVII 370. Pieter De Leemans is preparing an edition of the translation of *De Motu Animalium* (Turnhout, Belgium: Brepols, forthcoming); see also Pieter De Leemans, "The Discovery and Use of Aristotle's *De Motu Animalium* by Albert the Great," in *Geistesleben im 13. Jahrhundert,* Miscellanea Mediaevalia 27, ed. J. A. Aertsen and A. Speer (New York: de Gruyter, 2000), pp. 170–188.

29. S. P. Lambros, ed., *Excerptorum Constantini de natura animalium libri duo. Aristophanis historiae animalium epitome* (Berlin: Reimer, 1885).

30. A. van Oppenraay, "The Reception of Aristotle's *History of Animals* in the Marginalia of Some Manuscripts of Michael Scot's Arabic-Latin Translation," *Early Science and Medicine* 8, 4 (2003): 387–403.

31. B. Van den Abeele, "Le 'De animalibus' d'Aristote dans le monde latin: modalités de sa réception médiévale," *Frühmittelalterliche Studien* 33 (1999): 287–318.

32. J. Hamesse, *Les Auctoritates Aristotelis. Un florilège médiéval* (Paris: Béatrice-Nauwelaerts, 1974); J. Hamesse, "Johannes de Fonte, compilateur des 'Parvi flores'. Le témoignage de plusieurs manuscrits conservés à la Bibliothèque Vaticane," *Archivum Franciscanum Historicum* 88 (1995): 515–531.

33. P. Beullens, "A 13th-century Florilegium from Aristotle's Books on Animals: *Auctoritates extracte de libro Aristotilis de naturis animalium,*" in *Aristotle's Animals in the Middle Ages and Renaissance,* ed. C. Steel, G. Guldentops and P. Beullens (Leuven: University Press, 1999), pp. 69–95.

34. B. Van den Abeele, "Une version moralisée du *De animalibus* d'Aristote," in *Aristotle's Animals in the Middle Ages and Renaissance*, ed. C. Steel, G. Guldentops and P. Beullens (Leuven: University Press, 1999), pp. 338–354.

35. MS Paris, Bibliothèque Nationale, lat. 14704; see P. De Leemans, "La réception du *De progressu animalium* d'Aristote au Moyen Age," in *Textes et cultures: réception, modèles, interférences*, vol. 1, *Réception de l'Antiquité*, ed. P. Nobel (Besançon, France: Presses Universitaires due Franche-Comté, 2004), pp. 165–185.

36. J. Martinez Gazquez, "El 'Liber de animalibus' de Pedro Gallego, adaptación del "Liber animalium aristotelico," in *Roma magistra mundi*, ed. J. Hamesse (Louvain-la-Neuve: FIDEM, 1998), pp. 563–574. His edition of the text (Florence: SISMEL Edizioni, del Galluzo, 2000) contains too many errors to be used as a work of reference.

37. M. De Asua, "Medicine and Philosophy in Peter of Spain's Commentary on *De animalibus*," in *Aristotle's Animals in the Middle Ages and the Renaissance*, ed. C. Steel, G. Guldentops, and P. Beullens (Leuven: Leuven University Press, 1999), pp. 189–211.

38. T. Goldstein, "Gérard du Breuil et la zoologie aristotélicienne au XIIIe siècle," *Positions des thèses de l'École des Chartes* (1969), pp. 61–68.

39. Commentary by Gerard of Breuil *ad* 570a25–31, quoted according to MS Milan, Bibliotheca Ambrosiana, Z.252.Sup, fol. 77v.

40. Bk. I, chap. 10 (ed. Duaci, p. 26), translation in French and Cummingham, *Before Science*, p. 175.

41. French and Cunningham, *Before Science*.

42. P. Aiken, "The Animal History of Albertus Magnus and Thomas of Cantimpré," *Speculum* 22, no. 2 (1947): 205–225.

43. T.-M. Nischik, *Das volkssprachliche Naturbuch im späten Mittelalter. Sachkunde und Dinginterpretation bei Jacob van Maerlant und Konrad von Megenberg* (Tübingen, Germany: Niemeyer, 1986); A. Berteloot and D. Hellfaier, *Jacob van Maerlants "Der naturen bloeme" und das Umfeld: Vorläufer, Redaktionen, Rezeption* (Münster, Germany: Waxmann, 2001); F. van Oostrom, *Maerlants wereld* (Amsterdam: Prometheus, 1996).

44. C. M. Stutvoet-Joanknecht, *Der byen boeck. De Middelnederlandse vertalingen van Bonum universale de apibus van Thomas van Cantimpré en hun achtergrond* (Amsterdam: VU, 1990).

45. B. Smalley, "Thomas Waleys O.P.," *Archivum Fratrum Praedicatorum* 24 (1954): 50–107, in particular 81.

46. From the collection of Lawrence J. Schoenberg, MS LJS 477. A more detailed description can be found in the catalog of the Sotheby's sale in London on July 5, 2005. The author received Mr. Schoenberg's permission to see the manuscript in Paris on August 2, 2005.

47. Preserved in MS Munich, Staatsbibliothek, lat. 18141.

48. *Friderici Romanorum imperatoris secundi De arte venandi cum avibus*, ed. C. A. Willemsen, 2 vols. (Leipzig, Germany: In aedibus Insulae, 1942).

49. B. Prévot, *La Science du cheval au moyen âge. Le* Traité d'hippiatrie de Jordauus Rufus (Paris: Klincksieck, 1991).

50. K. Sudhoff, "Die erste Tieranatomie von Salerno und ein neuer salernitanischer Anatomietext," in *Archiv für Geschichte der Mathematik, der Naturwissenschaften und der Technik* 10 (1927): 136–154; Y. V. O'Neill, "Another Look at the 'Auatomia Porci'," Viator I (1970), pp. 115–124.

51. Albertus Magnus, *On Animals*, 22, 16. Thomas of Cantimpré in his *De natura rerum* writes that Frederick received the animal as a gift from the Persian sultan, but he cites the story under a variant name of the giraffe: ed. H. Boese (Berlin: de Gruyter, 1973), 4, 84, 9–11.

52. Albertus Magnus, *De vegetabilibus* bk. VI, tract 1, chap. 1, in *Opera omnia*, ed. A. Borgnet (Paris: Vives, 1890–1899), vol. X, p. 160.

53. *Alberti Magni quaestiones super De animalibus.* ed. E. Filthaut (Münster: Aschendorff, 1955).

54. Albertus Magnus, *On animals*.

55. Albertus Magnus, *Physica.* Pars I, Libri 1–4, ed. P. Hoßfeld (Münster, Germany: Monasterii Westfalorum, 1987), pp. 578, 20–27.

56. H. Balss, *Albertus Magnus als Biologe* (Stuttgart: Wissenschaftliche Verlagsgesellschaft 1947).

57. P. Hoßfeld, *Albertus Magnus als Naturphilosoph und Naturwissenschaftler* (Bonn: Albertus-Magnus-Institut, 1983).

58. Aiken, "The Animal History."

Chapter 6

1. Aristotle, *Parts of Animals* with an English translation by A. L. Peck; *Movement of Animals, Progression of Animals* with an English translation by E. S. Forster (Loeb Classical Library) (Cambridge, MA: Harvard University Press, 1945), p. 101.

2. Isidore of Seville's account of beavers (*Etymologiae* XII, 21) is moralized in bestiaries; cf. S. A. Barney, W. J. Lewis, J. A. Beach, and O. Berghof, trans., *The Etymologies of Isidore of Seville* (Cambridge: Cambridge University Press, 2006), p. 252.

3. S. Marrone, "Medieval Philosophy in Context," in *The Cambridge Companion to Medieval Philosophy*, ed. A. S. McGrade (Cambridge: Cambridge University Press, 2003), pp. 10–43.

4. M.-T. d'Alverny, "Translations and Translators," in *Renaissance and Renewal in the Twelfth Century,* ed. R. Benson and G. Constable (Cambridge, MA: Harvard University Press, 1982), pp. 421–462.

5. K. Park, "The Organic Soul," in *The Cambridge History of Renaissance Philosophy*, ed. C. B. Schmidt and Q. Skinner (Cambridge: Cambridge University Press, 1988), pp. 464–484.

6. Beda Venerabilis, *Libri Quatuor in principium Genesis usque ad nativitatem Isaac et eiectionem Ismahelis adnotationum*, cura et studio Ch. W. Jones (Turnhout, Belgium: Brepols, 1967), p. 56 (quoting Augustine's *De genesi contra Manichaeos*).

7. Aristotle, *History of Animals.* Bks. VII–X, trans. and ed. D. M. Balme, prep. publ. A. Gotthelf (Loeb Classical Library 439) (Cambridge, MA: Harvard University Press, 1991), pp. 62–63.

8. M. D. Chenu, *Nature, Man, and Society in the Twelfth Century: Essays on New Theological Perspectives in the Latin* West (Chicago: University of Chicago Press, 1968); Benson and Constable, eds., *Renaissance and Renewal.*

9. L. White Jr., *Medieval Technology and Social Change* (Oxford: Clarendon, 1962).

10. R. W. Southern, "The Schools of Paris and the School of Chartres," in *Renaissance and Renewal,* ed. R. Benson and G. Constable (Cambridge, MA: Harvard University Press), pp. 113–137.

11. P. O. Kristeller, "The School of Salerno: Its Development and Its Contribution to the History of Learning," *Bulletin of the History of Medicine* 17 (1945): 138–194; P. O. Kristeller, "Bartholomaeus, Musandinus, and Maurus of Salerno and Other Early Commentators of the *Articella* with a Tentative List of Texts and Manuscripts," *Italia medioevale et umanistica* 19 (1976): 57–87.

12. J. H. Waszink, ed., *Timaeus a Calcidio translatus commentarioque instructus*, (London: Warburg-Brill, 1962).

13. C. Burnett, trans. and ed., *Adelard of Bath, Conversations with His Nephew: On the Same and the Different, Questions on Natural Science, and On Birds* (Cambridge: Cambridge University Press, 1998).

14. William of Conches, *Dragmaticon philosophiae*, ed. I. Ronca (Turnhout, Belgium: Brepols, 1997), VI.24, p. 261.

15. M. Jordan, "The Construction of a Philosophical Medicine: Exegesis and Argument in Salernitan Teaching on the Soul," *Osiris,* second series 6 (1990): 42–61.

16. A. Birkenmajer, ed., "Le rôle joué par les médecins et les naturalistes dans la réception d'Aristote au XIIe et XIIIe siècles," in *Études d'histoire des sciences et de la philosophie du Moyen Age* (Wrocław: Zakład narodowy im. Ossolinskich, 1970), pp. 73–87; D. Jacquart, "Aristotelian Thought in Salerno," in P. Dronke (ed.), *A History of Twelfth-Century Western Philosophy* (Cambridge: Cambridge University Press, 1988), pp. 407–428.

17. J. Brams, *La riscoperta di Aristotele in occidente* (Milan: Jaca Books, 2003).

18. Edition (in progress) by Van Oppenraay.

19. A critical text of William's translation of all zoological work is available on *Aristoteles Latinus Database Release 2/2006* (Turnhout, Belgium: Brepols Publishers, 2006).

20. The *translatio vetus* of the *Parva Naturalia* is the work of James of Venice and of some anonymous authors. The *tr. nova* is the work of William of Moerbeke.

21. Aristotle's *De anima* was translated from the Greek by James of Venice and by William of Moerbeke. Averroes's long commentary on *De anima* together with the Aristotelian text itself was translated in the early thirteenth century (ed. Stuart). Avicenna's *De anima* (alias *Liber sextus de naturalibus*), was translated in the twelfth century (ed. Van Riet); see also D. N. Hasse, *Avicenna's De Anima in the Latin West. The Formation of a Peripatetic Philosophy of the Soul 1160–1300* (London: Warburg Institute, 2000).

22. Cf. Peter of Auvergne, *Questions on Aristotle's* De Caelo. *A Critical Edition with an Interpretative Essay by G. Galle* (Leuven, Belgium: Leuven University Press, 2003). T. W. Köhler, *Grundlagen des philosophisch-anthropologischen Diskurses im dreizehnten Jahrhundert. Die Erkenntais bemühung um den Menschen im zeitgenössischen Verständnis* (Boston: Brill, 2000).

23. Köhler, *Grundlagen*, esp. III.3., pp. 306–335.

24. Ibid., p. 380.

25. M. De Asua, "Medicine and Philosophy in Peter of Spain's Commentary on *De animalibus*," in *Aristotle's Animals in the Middle Ages and the Renaissance*, ed. C. Steel, G. Guldentops, and P. Beullens. (Leuven, Belgium: Leuven University Press, 1999), pp. 189–211; M. De Asua, "Peter of Spain, Albert the Great and the *Quaestiones de animalibus*," *Physis* 34 (1997): 1–30.

26. Albertus Magnus, *De Animalibus Libri XXVI*. Nach der Cölner Urschrift, ed. H. Stadler (Beiträge zur Geschichte der Philosophie des Mittelalters. Texte und Untersuchungen XV–XVI) (Münster: Aschendorff, 1916–1921).

27. Albertus Magnus, *On Animals. A Medieval Summa Zoologica,* trans. K. F. Kitchell Jr. and I. M. Resnick, 2 vols. (Baltimore: The Johns Hopkins University Press, 1999).

28. A. Van Oppenraay, "The Reception of Aristotle's History of Animals in the Marginalia of Some Latin Manuscripts of Michael Scot's Arabic–Latin Translation," *Early Science and Medicine* 8, 4 (2003): 387–403.

29. List of manuscripts in *De historia animalium. Translatio Guillelmi de Morbeka,* ed. P. Beullens and F. Bossier (Aristoteles Latinus XVII 2.I 1) (Boston: Brill, 2000).

30. J. Cadden, "Preliminary Observations on the Place of the *Problemata* in Medieval Learning," in *Aristotle's Problemata in Different Times and Tongues,* ed. P. De Leemans and M. Goyens (Leuven, Belgium: Leuven University Press, 2006), p. 6.

31. Cf. P. De Leemans, "Medieval Latin Commentaries on Aristotle's *De Motu Animalium:* A Contribution to the *Corpus commentariorum medii aevi in Aristotelem Latinorum,*" *Recherches de Théologie et Philosophie Médiévales* LXVII, 2 (2000): 272–360.

32. P. De Leemans, "Aristotle's *De progressu animalium* in the Middle Ages: Translation and Interpretation," in *Frontiers in the Middle Ages,* ed. O. Merisalo (Louvain-la-Neuve, Belgium: Fédération internationale des instituts d'études médiévales, 2006), pp. 525–541, esp. pp. 533–541.

33. P. De Leemans, "Peter of Auvergne on Aristotle's *De motu animalium* and the ms." Oxford, Merton College, 275, *Archives d'Histoire doctrinale et littéraire du moyen âge* 71 (2004); 129–202, at 188.

34. Examples taken from K. White, "Two Studies Related to St. Thomas Aquinas' Commentary on Aristotle's *De sensu et sensato,* Together with an Edition of Peter of Auvergne's *Quaestiones super Parva Naturalia*" (PhD diss., University of Ottawa, 1986).

35. Cf. Aristotle, *De anima,* e.g., bk. II, chap. 2, and bk. III, chap. 12.

36. For Albert the Great see *Liber de principiis motus processivi,* ed. B. Geyer (Alberti Magni Opera Omnia XII, 2) (Münster, Germany: Aschendorff, 1955), pp. 47–48; Peter of Auvergne (?), *Questiones in de motu animalium.* Unedited commentary, preserved in the mss. Oxford, Merton College, 275 and Roma, Bibl. Angelica, 549, quest. 3; Hasse, *Avicenna's De Anima in the Latin West.* pp. 92–98.

37. Thomas Aquinas, *Sentencia libri de sensu et sensato,* cura et studio fratrum Praedicatorum, ed. R. A. Gauthier (Sancti Thomae de Aquino Opera omnia XLV,2) (Rome and Paris: Commissio Leonina-Vrin, 1985), p. 243.

38. Cf. Albertus Magnus, *Liber de principiis motus processivi,* ed. B. Geyer, p. 47; discussed in similar terms by Peter of Auvergne (cf. n. 59).

39. G. Guldentops, "Albert the Great's Zoological Anthropocentrism," in *Micrologus* 8 (2000), pp. 217–236.

40. Albertus Magnus, *On Animals,* p. 1411.

41. Ibid., p. 1433.

42. Cf. C. Hünemörder, "Thomas von Aquin und die Tiere," in *Thomas von Aquin. Werk und Wirkung im Licht neuerer Forschungen,* ed. A. Zimmermann and C. Kopp (New York: De Gruyter, 1988), p. 210.

43. Thomas Aquinas. *A Commentary on Aristotle's De Anima,* trans. R. Pasnau (New York: Yale University Press, 1999), pp. 137–138.

44. Cf. R. Sorabji, *Animal Minds and Human Morals. The Origins of the Western Debate* (London: Duckworth, 1993).

45. *Nicomachean Ethics*, 1147a24ff. Aristotle discusses the practical syllogism also in his *De motu animalium* and *De anima*: M. C. Nussbaum, *Aristotle's De Motu Animalium*, 2nd ed. (Princeton: Princeton University Press, 1985), pp. 165–220.

46. Sorabji, *Animal Minds*, p. 16.

47. P. De Leemans, "Internal Senses, Intellect, and Movement. Peter of Auvergne (?) on Aristotle's *De motu animalium*," in *Corpo e anima, sensi interni e intelletto dai secoli XIII–XIV ai post-cartesiani e spinoziani*, ed. G. Vescovini, V. Sorge, and C. Vinti (Turnhout, Belgium: Brepols, 2006), pp. 139–160.

48. Cf. Peter of Abano, *Conciliator*, diff. 57, fol. 83v, 2F.

49. Cf. F. Stuart, ed., *Averrois Cordubensis Commentarium Magnum in Aristotelis De anima libros*, (Corpus commentariorum Averrois in Aristotelem Versionum Latinarum VI, 1, Cambridge, MA: Medieval Academy of America, 1953), pp. 415–416. Averroes names only four internal senses: the common sense, imagination, cogitation, and memory.

50. Jean de Jandun, *Questiones super libros de anima* (Venice, 1480), *Liber* II, *Quaestio* 37, fol. 79rv (consulted on http://gallica.bnf.fr).

51. E. Mahony, "Sense, Intellect, and Imagination in Albert, Thomas, and Siger," in *The Cambridge History of Later Medieval Philosophy: From the rediscovery of Aristotle to the Disintegration of Scholasticism 1100–1600*, ed. N. Kretzmann, A. Kenny, and J. Pinborg (Cambridge: Cambridge University Press, 1982), pp. 602–622.

52. Jean de Jandun, *Questiones super libros de anima* (Venice, 1480), *Liber* II, *Quaestio* 37, fol. 80rv.

53. K. Boughan, "Beyond Diet, Drugs, and Surgery: Italian Scholastic Medical Theorists on the Animal Soul, 1270–1400" (PhD diss., University of Iowa, 2006).

54. D. Jaquart's intervention in O. Boulnois, "Rapport de la table ronde sur le nouvel Aristote," in *L'enseignement des disciplines à la Faculté des arts (Paris et Oxford, XIIIe–XVe siècles)*, ed. O. Weijers and L. Holtz (Turnhout, Belgium: Brepols, 1997), pp. 330–331, and L. Cova's reaction on it (on p. 332).

55. A. Boureau, "L'animal scolastique," in *L'animal exemplaire au Moyen Âge (Ve–XVe siècle)*, ed. J. Berlioz and M. A. Polo de Beaulieu (Rennes, France: Presses Universitaires de Rennes, 1990), pp. 99–109.

56. M. E. Reina, "Un Abbozzo di polemica sulla psicologia animale: Gregorio da Rimini contro Adamo Wodeham," in *L'homme et son univers au moyen âge*, ed. C. Wenin (Louvain-la-Neuve, Belgium: Éditions de l'Institut supérieur de philosophie, 1986), pp. 598–609.

57. L. Bianchi, "La felicità intellettuale come professione nella Parigi del Duecento," *Rivista di filosofia* 78 (1987): 181–199.

58. M. Klemm, "Medicine and Moral Virtue in the *Expositio Problematum Aristotelis*," *Early Science and Medicine* 11 (2006): 302–335 (with further literature).

59. Aristotle, *Problems*, ed. W. S. Hett, 2 vols. (Loeb Classical Library) (Cambridge, MA: Harvard University Press, 1926), p. 133.

60. See Peter's *Conciliator*, diff. 3: cf. E. Riondato and L. Olivieri, eds., *Pietro d'Abano, Conciliator. Ristampa fotomeccanica dell'edizione Venetiis apud Iuntas 1565* (Padua, Italy: Editrice Antenore, 1985).

61. Cf. Avicenna, *Liber canonis medicinae*, 1.1.

62. J. Agrimi, "La ricezione della *Fisiognomica* pseudoaristotelica nella facoltà delle arti," *Archives d'Histoire Doctrinale et Littéraire du Moyen Age* 64 (1997): 127–188.

63. See the constant references to animals in Peter of Abano's *Compilatio phisionomie*, a summary of other physiognomies.

Chapter 7

1. C. Lévi-Strauss, *The Savage Mind* (1972; repr., Oxford: Oxford University Press, 1996), p. 162.

2. C. Rudolph, *Artistic Change at St-Denis: Abbot Suger's Program and the Early-Twelfth Century Controversy over Art* (Princeton: Princeton University Press, 1990).

3. See, for example, F. Klingender, *Animals in Art and Thought to the End of the Middle Ages* (London: Routledge and Kegan Paul, 1971); J. R. Benton, *The Medieval Menagerie. Animals in the Art of the Middle Ages* (New York: Abbeville Press, 1992); B. Rowland, *Animals with Human Faces: A Guide to Animal Symbolism* (London: Allen and Unwin, 1974). More recent studies focus on particular aspects, such as bestiaries: see W. B. Clark, *A Medieval Book of Beasts. The Second-Family Bestiary: Commentary, Art, Text and Translation* (Woodbridge, UK: Boydell Press, 2006), with further literature.

4. J. R. C. Martyn, trans., *The Letters of Gregory the Great*, 3 vols. (Toronto: Pontifical Institute of Mediaeval Studies, 2004), 9.209, p. 674.

5. Ibid., 11.10, pp. 744–746, at p. 745.

6. Job 12:7–8.

7. M. Thiébaux, trans. and ed., *Dhuoda, Handbook for Her Warrior Son*. Liber Manualis (Cambridge, Cambridge University Press, 1998), pp. 112–115; J. Voisenet, *Bêtes et hommes dans le monde médiévale. Le bestiaire des clercs du Ve au XIIe siècle* (Turnhout, Belgium: Brepols, 2000), pp. 1–2.

8. The long-standing tradition of the lamb in Christian iconography, deriving from scriptural passages, is discussed in the Introduction, this volume.

9. For the *Physiologus*, see N. Henkel, *Studien zum Physiologus im Mittelalter* (Tübingen, Germany: Niemeyer, 1976), and the Introduction, this volume.

10. Augustine, *De doctrina Christiana*, c. XXV; Augustine, *On Christian Teaching*, trans. R. P. H. Green (Oxford: Oxford University Press, 1997), p. 85.

11. Voisenet, *Bêtes et hommes*, p. 58.

12. Cf. Introduction, this volume.

13. Cf. Introduction, this volume.

14. W. B. Clark, trans. and ed., *The Medieval Book of Birds. Hugh of Fouilloy's Aviarium* (Binghampton, NY: Medieval and Renaissance Texts and Studies, 1992), pp. 116–117.

15. Ibid., pp. 118–119.

16. Aberdeen, Aberdeen University Library, MS 24, http://www.abdn.ac.uk/bestiary/, trans. M. Gould and C. McLaren, fol. 25v–26r (accessed June 2, 2007).

17. R. Barber, *Bestiary* (Woodbridge, UK: Boydell Press, 1999), p. 96 (translation of Oxford, MS Bodley 764, mid-thirteenth century).

18. Trans. by R. Grant, *Early Christians and Animals* (New York: Routledge, 1999), p. 58.

19. Clark, *Book of Beasts*, p. 179 (sirens) and p. 158 (centaurs).

20. Klingender, *Animals*, p. 311.

21. M. Camille, *Image on the Edge: The Margins of Medieval Art* (London: Reaktion Books, 1992), pp. 68–70, interprets the "ram bishop" as a critique of clerical illiteracy.

22. Trans. by C. Rudolph, *The "Things of Greater Importance": Bernard of Clairvaux's* Apologia *and the Medieval Attitude toward Art* (Philadelphia: University of Pennsylvania Press, 1990), pp. 11–12.

23. Cf. Bernard of Clairvaux, *Apologia*, ca. 28, translated by C. Rudolf in *The "Things of Greater Importance": Bernard of Clairvaux's* Apologia *and the Medieval Attitude toward Art,* (Philadelphia: University of Pennsylvania Press, 1990), pp. 10–11.

24. T.E.A. Dale, "Monsters, Corporeal Deformities, and Phantasms in the Cloister of St-Michel-de-Cuxa," *The Art Bulletin* 83, no. 3 (September 2001): 402–436, with further literature.

25. Rudolph, *The "Things of Greater Importance,"* p. 58.

26. E. Panofsky, trans. and ed., *Abbot Suger on the Abbey Church of St-Denis and Its Art Treasures* (Princeton: Princeton University Press, 1496), pp. 48–49; cf. Rudolph, *Artistic Change*.

27. See Introduction, this volume.

28. The drawing of the elephant is included in his *Chronica majora*, Cambridge, Corpus Christi College, MS 16, fol. 4r. Cf., e.g., J. A. Givens, *Observation and Image-Making in Gothic Art* (Cambridge: Cambridge University Press, 2005), p. 39.

29. J. A. Giles, trans., *Matthew Paris's English History from the Year 1235 to 1273*, 3 vols. (1852–1854; repr., New York: AMS Press, 1968), vol. 3, p. 115.

30. Givens, *Observation*, chap. 2, pp. 37–81.

31. Villard de Honnecourt, Lion, Paris, BnF, MS Français 19093, fol. 24v.

32. D. Hassig, *Medieval Bestiaries: Text, Image, Ideology* (Cambridge: Cambridge University Press, 1995), p. 142. Cf. Givens, *Observation*, p. 78.

33. Paris, BnF, MS Français 2810.

34. Ibid., fol. 85r.

35. See Introduction, this volume.

36. Marco Polo, *The Travels*, trans. A. Ricci (London: Routledge, 1931), p. 330.

37. Cf. R. Wittkower, ed., "Marco Polo and the Pictorial Tradition of the Marvels of the East," in idem, *Allegory and the Migration of Symbols* (New York: Thames and Hudson, 1987), p. 113.

38. I. Ventura, "The *Curae ex animalibus* in the Medical Literature of the Middle Ages: The Example of the Illustrated Herbals," in *Bestiaires médiévaux. Nouvelles perspectives et les traditions textuelles*, ed. B. Van den Abeele (Louvain-la-Neuve, Belgium: Université Catholique de Louvain, 2005), pp. 213–248, at p. 225.

39. Schlatt, Eisenbibliothek, MS 20, fol. 22r. Cf. De Leemans and Klemm, chapter 6, this volume.

40. M. Camille, "Bestiary or Biology?" in *Aristotle's Animals in the Middle Ages and Renaissance*, ed. C. Steel, G. Guldentops, and P. Beullens (Leuven, Belgium: Leuven University Press, 1999), pp. 355–396, at p. 375.

41. See De Leemans and Klemm, chapter 6, this volume.

42. Paris, BnF, MS Français 160.

43. Ibid., fol. 6r.

44. J. Zahlten, *Creatio Mundi: Darstellungen der sechs Schöpfungstage und naturwissenschaftliches Weltbild im Mittelalter* (Stuttgart, Germany: Klett-Cotta, 1979).

45. Paris, BnF, MS Français 9.

46. J. A. Givens, *Observation and Image-Making in Gothic Art* (Cambridge: Cambridge University Press, 2005), pp. 134–168, esp. pp. 165–168.

47. For the uses of animals in heraldry see Page, chapter 1, this volume.

48. Camille, *Image*, pp. 36–47.

49. Cf., for example, M. Camille, *Mirror in Parchment. The Luttrell Psalter and the Making of Medieval England* (London: Reaktion Books, 1998).

BIBLIOGRAPHY

Abalo Buceta, J. M. "Literatura cinegética peninsular. La montería: contrastes y pecu-
    liaridades frente a otras tradiciones literarias europeas." In *Los libros de caza,* ed-
    ited by J. M. Fradejas Rueda. Tordesillas, Spain: Seminario de Filología Medieval,
    2005, pp. 9–28.
Aberdeen, Aberdeen University Library, MS 24, http://www.abdn.ac.uk/bestiary/.
Ælfric, *Lives of Three English Saints.* Edited by G. I. Needham. London: Methuen and
    Co., 1966.
Agrimi, J. "La ricezione della *Fisiognomica* pseudoaristotelica nella facoltà delle arti."
    Archives d'Histoire Doctrinale et Littéraire du Moyen Age 64 (1997): 127–88.
Aiken, P. "The Animal History of Albertus Magnus and Thomas of Cantimpré." *Specu-
    lum* 22, no. 2 (1947): 205–225.
Albertus Magnus. *Liber de principiis motus processivi.* Edited by B. Geyer. Münster,
    Germany: Aschendorff, 1955.
Albertus Magnus. *On Animals. A Medieval Summa Zoologica.* Translated by K. F. Kitch-
    ell Jr. and I. M. Resnick. 2 vols. Baltimore: Johns Hopkins University Press, 1999.
Alford, V. *The Hobby Horse and Other Animal Masks.* London: Merlin, 1978.
Al-kindi. *De radiis.* Edited by M. T. d'Alverny and F. Hudry. *Archives d'histoire doctri-
    nale et litteraire du moyen age* 41 (1974): 139–260.
Almond, R. *Medieval Hunting.* Stroud, UK: Sutton Publishing, 2003.
Alvarez de Miranda, A. *Ritos y juegos del toro.* Madrid: Taurus, 1962.
Aristoteles Latinus Database Release 2/2006. Turnhout, Belgium: Brepols, 2006.
Aristotle. *De animalibus: Michael Scot's Arabic–Latin Translation.* Pt. 3, bks. XV–XIX:
    Generation of Animals, edited by A. van Oppenraay. New York: Brill, 1992. Pt. 2,
    bks. XI–XIV, *Parts of Animals,* edited by A. van Oppenraay. Boston: Brill, 1998.
Aristotle. *De generatione animalium. Translatio Guillelmi de Moerbeka.* Edited by
    H. J. Drossaart Lulofs. Aristoteles Latinus XVII 2.v. Paris: Desclée de Brouwer, 1966.
    De historia animalium. Translatio Guillelmi de Morbeka. Prima pars: lib. I-V. Edited
    by P. Beullens and F. Bossier. Aristoteles Latinus XVII 2.i.i. Boston: Brill, 2000.
Aristotle. *History of Animals.* Bks. VII–X, edited and translated by D. M. Balme, prepared
    for publication by A. Gotthelf. Cambridge, MA: Harvard University Press, 1991.

Aristotle. *Parts of Animals,* with an English translation by A. L. Peck; *Movement of Animals, Progression of Animals,* with an English translation by E. S. Forster. Cambridge, MA: Harvard University Press, 1945.

Aristotle. *Problems.* Edited by W. S. Hett. 2 vols. Cambridge, MA: Harvard University Press, 1926.

Armitage, P. L. "A Preliminary Description of British Cattle from the Late 12th to the Early 16th Century." *The Ark* 7 (1980): 405–412.

Armitage, P. L. "Developments in British Cattle Husbandry from the Romano–British Period to Early Modern Times. *The Ark* 9 (1982): 50–54.

Arnold, J. "L'élevage du lapin au Moyen Age." *Ethnozootechnie* 59 (1997): 61–68.

Audoin-Rouzeau, F. "Les modifications du bétail et de sa consommation en Europe médiévale et moderne: le témoignage des ossements animaux archéologiques." In *L'homme, l'animal domestique et l'environnement du Moyen Age au XVIIIe siècle,* edited by R. Durand. Nantes, France: Ouest Éditions, 1993, pp. 109–126.

Audoin-Rouzeau, F. "Les ossements du cheptel medieval." *Ethnozootechnie* 59 (1997): 69–7.

Augustine. *De doctrina Christiana.* Translated and edited by R.P.H. Green. Oxford: Clarendon Press, 1995.

Avicenna Latinus. Liber de anima seu Sextus de naturalibus. Édition critique de la traduction latine médiévale par S. Van Riet. Introduction sur la doctrine psychologique d'Avicenne par G. Verbeke, 2 vols. Leuven, Belgium: Peeters, 1968–1972.

Avicenne Liber canonis medicine. Cum castigationibus Andree Bellunensis. 1527. Reprint of the edition of Venice: *in edibus Luce Antonii Junta,* Brussels, 1971.

Axton, R. *European Drama of the Early Middle Ages.* Pittsburgh: University of Pittsburgh Press, 1974.

Bacon, Roger. *Opera quedam hactenus inedita,* Vol. I, edited by J. S. Brewer. London, 1859.

Balis, A., K. De Jonge, G. Delmarcel, and A. Lefébure. *Les chasses de Maximilien.* Paris: Musée du Louvre, 1993.

Barber, R. *Bestiary.* Woodbridge, UK: Boydell Press, 1999.

Barber, R. *The Knight and Chivalry.* London: Longmans, 1970.

Barber, R., and J. Barker. *Tournaments: Jousts, Chivalry and Pageants in the Middle Ages.* New York: Weidenfeld and Nicolson, 1989.

Barney, S. A., W. J. Lewis, J. A. Beach, and O. Berghof, trans. *The Etymologies of Isidore of Seville.* Cambridge: Cambridge University Press, 2006.

Bartlett, R. *England under the Norman and Angevin Kings, 1075–1225.* Oxford: Clarendon Press, 2000.

Bath, M. *The Image of the Stag. Iconographic Themes in Western Art.* Baden-Baden, Germany: V. Koerner, 1992.

Bartosiewicz, L., ed. *Animals in the Urban Landscape in the Wake of the Middle Ages: A case study from Vác, Hungary.* B.A.R. 609. Oxford: B.A.R., 1995.

Bautier, R-H., and A.-M. Bautier. "Contribution a l'histoire de cheval au Moyen Âge: L'élevage du cheval." In *Bulletin philologique et historique du comité des travaux historiques et scientifiques, 1978.* Paris: Bibliothèque Nationale, 1980.

Baxter, R. *Bestiaries and Their Users in the Middle Ages,* Stroud, UK: Sutton Publishing, 1998.

Beda Venerabilis. *Libri Quatuor in principium Genesis usque ad nativitatem Isaac et eiectionem Ismahelis adnotationum,* edited by Ch. W. Jones. Turnhout, Belgium: Brepols, 1967.

Bell, D. N. *Wholly Animals: A Book of Beastly Tales*. Kalamazoo, MI: Cistercian Publications, 1992.

Bennet, H. S. *Life on the English Manor: A Study on Peasant Conditions, 1150–1400*. Cambridge: Cambridge University Press, 1937.

Bennett, M. "The Medieval Warhorse Reconsidered." In *Medieval Knighthood*, vol. 5, edited by S. Church and R. Harvey. Woodbridge, UK: Boydell, 1995.

Benson, R. L., and G. Constable, eds. *Renaissance and Renewal in the Twelfth Century*. Cambridge, MA: Harvard University Press, 1982.

Benton, J. R. *The Medieval Menagerie: Animals in the Art of the Middle Ages*. New York: Abbeville Press, 1992.

Berteloot A. and D. Hellfaier, *Jacob van Maerlants "Der naturen bloeme" und das Umfeld: Vorläufer, Redaktionen, Rezeption* (Münster, Germany: Waxmann, 2001).

Beullens, P. "A 13th-century Florilegium from Aristotle's Books on Animals: *Auctoritates extracte de libro Aristotilis de naturis animalium*." In *Aristotle's Animals in the Middle Ages and Renaissance*, edited by C. Steel, G. Guldentops, and P. Beullens. Leuven, Belgium: University Press, 1999, pp. 69–95.

Bianchi, L. "La felicità intellettuale come professione nella Parigi del Duecento." *Rivista di filosofia* 78 (1987): 181–199.

Biddick, K. "Pig Husbandry on the Peterborough Abbey Estate from the Twelfth to the Fourteenth Century a.d." In *Animals and Archaeology: Husbandry in Europe*, B.A.R. International Series 227, edited by C. Grigson and J. Clutton-Brock. Oxford: B.A.R., 1984, pp. 161–178.

Birkenmajer, A. "Le rôle joué par les médecins et les naturalistes dans la réception d'Aristote au XIIe et XIIIe siècles." In *Études d'histoire des sciences et de la philosophie du Moyen Age*, edited by A. Birkenmajer. Wrocław: Zakład narodowy im. Ossolinskich, 1970, pp. 73–87.

Biskho, C. J. "El Castellano hombre de llanura. La explotación ganadera en el área fronteriza de La Mancha y Extremadura en la Edad Media." In vol. I, *Homenaje a Jaime Vicens Vives*. Barcelona: Universidad de Barcelona, 1967, pp. 201–218.

Boase, T.S.R. *English Art, 1100–1216*. Oxford: Oxford University Press, 1953.

Bobis, L. "L'évolution de la place du chat dans l'espace social et l'imaginaire occidental, du Moyen Age au XVIIIe siecle." In *L'homme, l'animal domestique et l'environnement du Moyen Age au XVIIIe siècle*, edited by R. Durand. Nantes, France: Ouest Éditions, 1993, pp. 73–84.

Boccaccio, Giovanni. *Decameron*. Translated by J. Payne, revised by C. S. Singleton. 2 vols. Berkeley: University of California Press, 1982.

Boccassini, D. *Il volo della menta. Falconeria e Sofia nel mondo mediterraneo. Islam, Federico II, Dante*. Ravenna, Italy: Longo Editore, 2003.

Bokonyi, S. "The Development and History of Domestic Animals in Hungary: The Neolithic through the Middle Ages." *American Anthropologist* 73 (1971): 640–674.

Bolland, J., ed. *Acta sanctorum quotquot toto orbe coluntur*. 1643. Reprint, Turnhout, Belgium: Brepols, 1966–1971.

Bond, J. "Rabbits: The Case for Their Medieval Introduction to Britain." *Local History* 18 (1988): 53–57.

Borst, A. *Das Buch der Naturgeschichte. Plinius und seine Leser im Zeitalter des Pergaments*. Heidelberg: Winter, 1994.

Boughan, K. "Beyond Diet, Drugs, and Surgery: Italian Scholastic Medical Theorists on the Animal Soul, 1270–1400." Ph.D. diss., University of Iowa, 2006.

Boulnois, O. "Rapport de la table ronde sur le nouvel Aristote." In *L'enseignement des disciplines,* edited by O. Weijers and Louis Holtz. Turnhout, Belgium: Brepols, 1997, pp. 329–333.

Boureau, A. "L'animal scolastique." In *L'animal exemplaire au Moyen Âge* (Ve-XVe siècle), edited by J. Berlioz and M. A. Polo de Beaulieu. Rennes, France: Presses Universitaires de Rennes, 1999, pp. 99–109.

Bover, J. "La cetrería en las Islas Baleares: siglos XIII-XIV." In *Los libros de caza,* edited by J. M. Fradejas Rueda. pp. 9–20.

Braekman, W. L., ed. *Studies on Alchemy, Diet, Medecine [sic] and Prognostication in Middle English.* Brussels: Omirel, 1986.

Brams, J. *La riscoperta di Aristotele in occidente.* Milan: Jaca Books, 2003.

Bugnion, J. *Les chasses médiévales. Le brachet, le lévrier, l'épagneul, leur nomenclature, leur métier, leur typologie.* Paris: Edition Folio, 2005.

Bumke, J. *Courtly Culture: Literature and Society in the High Middle Ages.* Translated by T. Dunlap. Berkeley: University of California Press, 1991.

Burnett, C., trans. and ed. *Adelard of Bath, Conversations with His Nephew: On the Same and the Different, Questions on Natural Science, and On Birds.* Cambridge: Cambridge University Press, 1998.

Burnett, C. "Arabic Divinatory Texts and Celtic Folklore: A Comment on the Theory and Practice of Scapulimancy in Western Europe." *Cambridge Medieval Celtic Studies,* 6 (1983): 31–42.

Cadden, J. "Preliminary Observations on the Place of the Problemata in Medieval Learning." In *Aristotle's Problemata in Different Times and Tongues.* Leuven, Belgium: Leuven University Press, 2006, p. 1–19.

Caesarius of Heisterbach. *The Dialogue on Miracles.* Translated by H. von E. Scott and C. C. Swinton Bland. 2 vols. London: Routledge, 1929.

Camille, M. *Image on the Edge: The Margins of Medieval Art.* London: Reaktion Books, 1992.

Carmody, F. J., ed. *Physiologus Latinus. Éditions préliminaires versio B.* Paris: E. Droz, 1939.

Cavallar, O., S. Degenring, and J. Kirshner, eds. *A Grammar of Signs: Bartolo da Sassoferrato's Tract on Insignia and the Coat of Arms.* Berkeley: University of California Press, 1994.

Cawte, E. C. *Ritual Animal Disguise: A Historical and Geographical Study of Animal Disguise in the British Isles.* Cambridge: D.S. Brewer, 1978.

Chambers, E. K. *The Mediaeval Stage.* 2 vols. Oxford: Oxford University Press, 1903.

Chaucer, Geoffrey. *Troilus and Criseyde.* In *Riverside Chaucer,* edited by L. Benson. New York: Houghton Mifflin, 1987.

Chenu, M.-D. *Nature, Man and Society in the Twelfth Century: Essays on New Theological Perspectives in the Latin West.* Chicago: University of Chicago Press, 1968.

Chrétien de Troyes. *Arthurian Romances.* Translated by W. W. Kibler. Harmondsworth, UK: Penguin, 1991.

Clare, L. *La quintaine, la course de bague et le jeu des têtes: Étude historique et ethno-linguistique d'une famille de jeux équestres.* Paris: Centre National de la Recherche Scientifique, 1983.

Clark, J., ed. *The Medieval Horse and Its Equipment, c. 1150-c.1450.* 2nd ed. Woodbridge, UK: Boydell, 2004.

Clark, S. *Vanities of the Eye: Vision in Early Modern European Culture.* Oxford: Oxford University Press, 2007.

Clark, W. B. *A Medieval Book of Beasts. The Second-Family Bestiary: Commentary, Art, Text and Translation.* Woodbridge, UK: Boydell Press, 2006.

Clark, W. B., trans. and ed. *The Medieval Book of Birds. Hugh of Fouilloy's Aviarium.* Binghampton, NY: Medieval & Renaissance Texts and Studies, 1992.

Claxton, A. "The Sign of the Dog: An Examination of the Devonshire Hunting Tapestries." *Journal of Medieval History* 14 (1988): 127–179.

Clutton-Brock, J. *Domesticated Animals from Early Times.* London: Heinemann, 1981.

Cockayne, T. O. *Leechdoms, Wortcunning and Starcraft of Early England.* London: Longman, 1864–1866.

Cohen, E. "Animals in Mediaeval Perceptions: The Image of the Ubiquitous Other." In *Animals and Human Society Changing Perspectives,* edited by A. Manning and J. Serpell. London: Routledge, 1994, pp. 59–80.

Conrad, J. R. *The Horn and the Sword: The History of the Bull as a Symbol of Power and Fertility.* New York: Dutton, 1957.

Contamine, P. "Jalons pour une histoire du cheval dans l'économie rurale lorraine à la fin du Moyen Age." *Ethnozootechnie* 59 (1997): 51–59.

Cordero del Campillo, M. "Veterinary Medicine in the Medieval Period: The Christian Kingdoms in Spain." *Historia Medicinae Veterinariae* 22 (1997): 73–104.

Cummins, J. "*Aqueste lance divino:* San Juan's Falconry Images." In *What's Past is Prologue: A Collection of Essays in Honour of L. J. Woodward,* edited by S. Bacarisse and others. Edinburgh: Scottish Academy Press, 1984, pp. 28–32, 155–156.

Cummins, J. *The Hound and the Hawk. The Art of Medieval Hunting.* London: Phoenix Press, 2001.

Dalby, D. *Lexicon of the Mediaeval German Hunt.* Berlin: de Gruyter, 1965.

Dale, T.E.A. "Monsters, Corporeal Deformities, and Phantasms in the Cloister of St-Michel-de-Cuxa." *The Art Bulletin* 83, no. 3 (September 2001): 402–436.

Damascene, St. John. *De fide orthodoxa.* Edited by E. M. Buytaert. St. Bonaventure, N.Y.: Franciscan Institute, 1955.

Daston, L., and K. Park, eds. *Wonders and the Order of Nature, 1150–1750.* New York: Zone Books, 1998.

Davis, R.H.C. *The Medieval Warhorse: Origin, Development and Redevelopment.* London: Thames and Hudson, 1989.

Davis, S.J.M. *The Archaeology of Animals.* New Haven: Batsford, 1987.

D'Alverny, M-T. "Translations and Translators." In *Renaissance and Renewal in the Twelfth Century,* edited by R. Benson and G. Constable. Cambridge, MA: Harvard University Press, 1982, pp. 4421–4462.

De Asua, M. "Medicine and Philosophy in Peter of Spain's Commentary on *De animalibus.*" In *Aristotle's Animals the Middle Ages and the Renaissance,* edited by C. Steel, G. Guldentops, and P. Beullens. Leuven, Belgium: Leuven University Press, 1999, pp. 189–211.

De Asua, M. "Peter of Spain, Albert the Great and the *Quaestiones de animalibus.*" *Physis* 34 (1997): 1–30.

Dean, T., trans. and ed. *The Towns of Italy in the Later Middle Ages.* Manchester: Manchester University Press, 2000.

De Leemans, P. "Aristotle's *De progressu animalium* in the Middle Ages: Translation and Interpretation." In *Frontiers in the Middle Ages,* edited by O. Merisalo. Louvain-la-Neuve, Belgium: Fédération internationale des instituts d'études médiévales, 2006, pp. 525–541.

De Leemans, P. "The Discovery and Use of Aristotle's *De Motu Animalium* by Albert the Great." In *Geistesleben im 13. Jahrhundert,* Miscellanea Mediaevalia 27, edited by J. A. Aertsen and A. Speer. New York: de Gruyter, 2000, pp. 170–188.

De Leemans, P. "Medieval Latin Commentaries on Aristotle's *De Motu Animalium*: A Contribution to the *Corpus commentariorum medii aevi in Aristotelem Latinorum*." *Recherches de Théologie et Philosophie Médiévales* LXVII, no. 2 (2000): 272–360.

De Leemans, P. "Peter of Auvergne on Aristotle's *De motu animalium* and the ms. Oxford, Merton College, 275." *Archives d'Histoire Doctrinale et Littéraire du Moyen Age* 71 (2004): 129–202.

De Leemans, P. "La réception du *De progressu animalium* d'Aristote au Moyen Age." In *Textes et cultures: réception, modèles, interférences,* edited by P. Nobel. Vol. 1, *Réception de l'Antiquité.* Besançon, France: Presses universitaires de Franche-Comté, 2004, pp. 165–185.

De Leemans, P. "Internal Senses, Intellect, and Movement: Peter of Auvergne (?) on Aristotle's *De motu animalium*." In *Corpo e anima, sensi interni e intelletto dai secoli XIII-XIV ai post-cartesiani e spinoziani,* edited by G. Vescovini. Turnhout, Belgium: Brepols, 2006, pp. 139–160.

Deleito y Piñuela, J. *También se divierte el pueblo.* Madrid: Espasa-Calpe, 1944.

Delgado Ruiz, M. *De la muerte de un dios: La fiesta de los toros en el universo simbólico de la cultura popular.* Barcelona: Nexos, 1986.

Delort, R. *Les animaux ont une histoire.* Paris: Éditions du Seuil, 1984.

Delort, R. "Le Prince et la bête." In *Guerre, pouvoir et noblesse au Moyen Âge: Mélanges en l'honneur de Philippe Contamine,* edited by J. Paviot and J. Verger. Paris: Presses de l'Université de Paris-Sorbonne, 2000.

Dennys, R. *The Heraldic Imagination.* London: Barrie and Jenkins, 1975.

Digard, J.-P. "Perspectives anthropologiques sur la relation homme-animal domestique et sur son évolution." In *L'homme, l'animal domestique et l'environnement du Moyen Age au XVIIIe siècle,* edited by R. Durand. Nantes, France: Ouest Éditions, 1993.

Digby, G. W. *The Devonshire Hunting Tapestries.* London: Victoria and Albert Museum, 1971.

Dobiat, C. "Zur Herkunft der Falknerei aus archäologisch-historischer Sicht." *Alma Mater Philippina* (WS 1995–1996): 10–14.

Dronke, P. *Fabula: Explorations into the Uses of Myth in Medieval Platonism.* Leiden, The Netherlands: Brill, 1974.

Dronke, P., ed. *A History of Twelfth-Century Western Philosophy.* Cambridge: Cambridge University Press, 1988.

Duceppe-Lamarre, F. "Les réserves cynégétiques en France septentrionale, seconde moitié du XIIe siècle-fin XVe siècle." In *Forêt et chasse, Xe—XXe siècle,* edited by A. Orvol. Paris: L'Harmattan, 2006, pp. 29–42.

Duvernoy, J., ed. *Le Registre d'inquisition de Jacques Fournier (1318–1325).* 3 vols. Toulouse: Édouard Privat, 1965.

Dyer, C. *Everyday Life in Medieval England.* London: Hambledon, 2000.

Dyer, C. *Standards of Living in the Later Middle Ages.* Cambridge: Cambridge University Press, 1989.

Eco, U. *Kant and the Platypus. Essays on Language and Cognition.* London: Secker and Warburg, 1999, pp. 57–59.

Edgerton, S. Y. *Pictures and Punishment. Art and Criminal Prosecution during the Florentine Renaissance.* New York: Cornell University Press, 1985.

Edsman, C.-M. "The Story of the Bear Wife." *Ethnos* 1–2 (1956): 36–56.

Einarsson, B., ed. *Haraldskvaeði.* In *Agrip af Nóregskonunga Sogum, Fagrskinna-Noregs Konunga Tal,* vol. 29. Reykjavik: Islenzka Fornrit, 1985.

Ellis Davidson, H. R. "Shape-changing in the Old Norse Sagas." In *Animals in Folklore,* edited by J. R. Porter and W.M.S. Russell. Cambridge: D.S. Brewer, 1978, pp. 126–42.

Endrei, W., and L. Zolnay. *Fun and Games in Old Europe.* Budapest: Corvina, 1986.

Epstein, H. J. "The Origin and the Earliest History of Falconry." *Isis* 34 (1942–1943): 497–509.

Evans, E. P. *The Criminal Prosecution and Capital Punishment of Animals.* 1906. Reprint, Boston: Faber and Faber, 1987.

Favreau, R. "Fêtes et jeux en Poitou à la fin du Moyen Âge." In *Jeux, sports et divertissements au Moyen Âge et à l'Âge classique,* edited by J.-M. Mehl. Paris: Éditions du CTHS, 1993.

Filotas, B. *Pagan Survivals, Superstitions and Popular Cultures in Early Medieval Pastoral Literature.* Toronto: Pontifical Institute of Mediaeval Studies, 2005.

Fitzstephen, W. *Descriptio nobilissimae civitatis Londoniae.* Translated by H. E. Butler. In *Norman London,* with an essay by Sir F. Stenton. New York: Italica, 1990.

Forsyth, I. "The Theme of Cockfighting in Burgundian Romanesque Sculpture." *Speculum* 53 (1978): 252–82.

Fossier, R. "L'élevage médiéval. Bilan d'un problème." *Ethnozootechnie* 59 (1997): 9–20.

Fradejas Rueda, J. M. *Bibliotheca cinegetica hispanica: bibliografía crítica de los libros de cetrería y montería hispano-portugueses anteriores a 1799.* London: Grant & Cutler, 1991.

Fradejas Rueda, J. M. *El arte de Cetrería de Federico II.* Vaticano-Madrid: Testimonio, 2004.

Fradejas Rueda, J. M. *Literatura cetrera de la Edad media y el Renacimiento español.* London: Department of Hispanic Studies, Queen Mary and Westfield College, 1998.

Fradejas Rueda, J. M. *Suplemento 1.* London: Tamesis, 2003.

French, R., and A. Cunningham. *Before Science. The Invention of the Friars' Natural Philosophy.* Aldershot, UK: Scolar, 1996.

Friedman, M. "The Falcon and the Hunt: Symbolic Love Imagery in Medieval and Renaissance Art." In *Poetics of Love in the Middle Ages: Texts and Context,* edited by M. Lazar and N. Lacy. Fairfax, VA: George Mason University Press, 1989, pp. 157–175.

Froissart, Jean. *Chronicles.* Translated by G. Brereton. Harmondsworth: Penguin, 1978.

Fumagalli, V. "Gli Animali e l'Agricoltura." In *L'uomo di fronte al mondo animale nell'Alto Medioevo, Settimane di Studio del Centro Italiano di studi sull'Alto Medioevo XXXI* I (1985): 579–609.

Gaier, C. "Quand l'arbalète était une nouveauté. Réflexions sur son rôle militaire du Xe au XIIIe siècle." *Le Moyen Age* 101 (1995): 137–144.

García Martín, P., coord. *Cañadas, cordeles y veredas.* Valladolid, Spain: Junta de Castilla y Leon, 2000.

Garnier, F. "Les significations symboliques du faucon dans l'illustration des Bibles moralisées de la première moitié du 13e siècle." In *La chasse au vol au fil des temps.* Gien, France: Editions du Musée International de la Chasse, 1994, pp. 135–142.

Gasser, C. "Attività venatoria e documentazione scritta nel Medioevo. L'esempio dell'uccellagione." In *Los libros de caza,* edited by J. M. Fradejas Rueda. Tordesillas, Spain: Seminario de Filología Medieval, 2005, pp. 69–82.

Gasser, C. "Imago venationis. Jagd und Fischerei im Spätmittelalter zwischen Anspruch und Wirklichkeit." In *Schloss Runkelstein. Die Bilderburg*. Bolzano, Italy: Athesia, 2000, pp. 411–430.

Gasser, C., and H. Stampfer. *La caccia nell'arte del Tirolo*. Bolzano, Italy: Athesia, 1995.

Geertz, C. "Deep Play: Notes on a Balinese Cockfight." *Daedalus* 101 (1972): 1–37.

George, W., and B. Yapp. *The Naming of the Beasts: Natural History in the Medieval Bestiary*. London: Duckworth, 1991.

Gerald of Wales. *Topographia Hibernica*. Translated by J. O'Meara. London: Penguin, 1982.

Germain, R. "Jeux et divertissements dans le centre de la France à la fin du Moyen Âge." In *Jeux, sports et divertissements au Moyen Âge et à l'Âge classique*, edited by J.-M. Mehl. Paris: Éditions du CTHS, 1993, pp. 45–58.

Gervase of Tilbury. *Otia Imperialia* (1210–14), II, 12. Translated and edited by S. E. Banks and J. W. Binns. Oxford: University Press, 2002.

Giles, J. A., trans. *Matthew Paris's English History from the Year 1235 to 1273*. 3 vols. 1852–1854. Reprint, New York: AMS Press, 1968.

Gillmeister, H. "Medieval Sport: Modern Methods of Research—Recent Results and Perspectives." *The International Journal of the History of Sport* 5 (1988): 53–68.

Gillmor, C. "Practical Chivalry: The Training of Horses for Tournaments and Warfare." *Studies in Medieval and Renaissance History* 13 (o.s. 23, 1992): 5–29.

Givens, J. A. *Observation and Image-Making in Gothic Art*. Cambridge: Cambridge University Press, 2005.

Goldberg, J.P.J. "Pigs and Prostitutes: Streetwalking in Comparative Perspective." In *Young Medieval Women*, edited by K. Lewis, N. J. Menuge, and K. M. Phillips. Stroud, UK: Sutton Publishing, 1999, pp. 172–193.

Goldin, Frederick, trans. *Chanson de Roland (The Song of Roland)*. New York: W.W. Norton, 1978.

Goldstein, T. "Gérard du Breuil et la zoologie aristotélicienne au XIIIe siècle." *Positions des thèses de l'École des Chartes* (1969): 61–68.

Gómez-Tabanera, J. M., ed. "Origenes y determinantes de las fiestas taurinas in España." In *El Folklore Español*, edited by J. M. Gómez-Tabanera. Madrid: Instituto Español de Anthropologia Aplicada, 1968, pp. 269–95.

Gottfried von Strassburg. *Tristan*. Translated by A. T. Hatto. 1960. Reprint, London: Penguin, 1967.

Les Grandes Chroniques de France. Paris: Librairie ancienne Honoré Champion, 1937.

Grant, A. "Animal Resources." In *The Countryside of Medieval England*, edited by G. Astill and A. Grant. Oxford: Basil Blackwell, 1988, pp. 149–187.

Grant, J., ed. *La Passiun de Seint Edmund*, Anglo-Norman Text Society 36 (London, 1978).

Grant, R. *Early Christians and Animals*. New York: Routledge, 1999.

Gray, J. *Straw Dogs: Thoughts on Humans and Other Animals*. London: Granta Books, 2002.

Green, R. F. *Poets and Princepleasers: Literature and the English Court in the Late Middle Ages*. Toronto: University of Toronto Press, 1980.

Guldentops, G. "Albert the Great's Zoological Anthopocentrism." *Micrologus* 8 (2000): 217–236.

Habig, M. A. *St Francis of Assisi: Writings and Early Biographies*. Chicago: Franciscan Herald Press, 1983.

Hackwood, F. W. *Old English Sports*. London: T. Fisher Unwin, 1907.

Hahn, D. *The Tower Menagerie: The Amazing 600-Year History of the Royal Collection of Wild and Ferocious Beasts Kept at the Tower of London*. New York: Penguin Group, 2004.

Hallam, H. E. *Rural England, 1066–1348*. Glasgow, UK: Fontana, 1981.

Hamesse, J. *Les Auctoritates Aristotelis. Un florilège médiéval*. Louvain-la-Neuve, Belgium: Publications Universitaires; Paris: Béatrice-Nauwelaerts, 1974.

Hamesse, J. "Johannes de Fonte, compilateur des 'Parvi flores.' Le témoignage de plusieurs manuscrits conservés à la Bibliothèque Vaticane." *Archivum Franciscanum Historicum* 88 (1995): 515–531.

Hamburger, J. F. *The Rothschild Canticles: Art and Mysticism in Flanders and the Rhineland circa 1300*. New Haven: Yale University Press, 1990.

Hanawalt, B. *Growing Up in Medieval London: The Experience of Childhood in History*. Oxford: Oxford University Press, 1993.

Hanawalt, B. *The Ties That Bound: Peasant Families in Medieval England*. Oxford: Oxford University Press, 1986.

Hansen, J. *Quellen und Untersuchungen zur Geschichte des Hexenwahns und der Hexenverfolgung im Mittelalter*. Bonn: Georgi, 1901.

Harris, R. "The White Stag in Chrétien's *Erec et Enide*." *French Studies* 10 (1956): 55–61.

Hartmann von Aue. *Gregorius*. In *Arthurian Romances, Tales and Lyric Poetry: The Complete Works of Hartmann von Aue*, translated by F. Tobin, K. Vivian, and R. H. Lawson. University Park: Pennsylvania State University Press, 2001.

Hasse, D. N. *Avicenna's De Anima in the Latin West. The Formation of a Peripatetic Philosophy of the Soul 1160–1300*. London: University of London. Warburg Institute, 2000.

Hassig, D. *Medieval Bestiaries: Text, Image, Ideology*. Cambridge, Cambridge University Press, 1995.

Henkel, N. *Studien zum Physiologus im Mittelalter*. Tübingen, Germany: Niemeyer, 1976.

Henisch, B. A. *Fast and Feast. Food in Medieval Society*. University Park: Pennsylvania State University Press, 1976.

Henricks, T. S. "Sport and Social Hierarchy in Medieval England." *Journal of Sport History* 9 (1982): 20–37.

Heywood, W. *Palio and Ponte: An Account of the Sports of Central Italy from the Age of Dante to the XXth Century*. 1904. Reprint, New York: Hacker Art Books, 1969.

Hoffmann, G. "Falkenjagd und Falkenhandel in den nordischen Ländern während des Mittelalters." *Zeitschrift für deutsches Altertum* 88 (1957): 115–149.

Holmes, T. U. *Daily Living in the Twelfth Century. Based on the Observations of Alexander Neckam in London and Paris*. Madison: University of Wisconsin Press, 1952.

Hoßfeld, P. *Albertus Magnus als Naturphilosoph und Naturwissenschaftler*. Bonn: Albertus-Magnus-Institut, 1983.

Hudson, H., ed. *Sir Tryamour*, in *Four Middle English Romances*. Kalamazoo, MI: Medieval Institute, 1996.

Humbert of Romans. *Treatise on the Formation of Preachers*. Translated by S. Tugwell. In *Early Dominicans: Selected Writings*. New York: Paulist Press, 1982.

Hünemörder, C. "Thomas von Aquin und die Tiere." In *Thomas von Aquin. Werk und Wirkung im Licht neuerer Forschungen*, edited by A. Zimmermann and C. Kopp. New York: de Gruyter, 1988, pp. 192–210.

Hünemörder, C. "Die Zoologie des Albertus Magnus." In *Albertus Magnus. Doctor Universalis, 2180/1980,* edited by G. Meyer and A. Zimmermann. Mainz, Germany: Matthias-Grünewald-Verlag, 1980, pp. 235–248.

Hyland, A. *The Horse in the Middle Ages.* Stroud, UK: Sutton Publishing, 1999.

Hyland, A. *The Medieval Warhorse from Byzantium to the Crusades.* Phoenix Mill, UK: Alan Sutton, 1994.

Ingold, T. *What Is an Animal?* New York: Routledge, 1994.

Jacquart, D. "Aristotelian Thought in Salerno." In *A History of Twelfth-Century Western Philosophy,* edited by P. Dronke. Cambridge: Cambridge University Press, 1988, pp. 407–428.

James, M. R. *The Bestiary.* Oxford: Roxburghe Club, 1928.

James, M. R., ed. "Twelve Medieval Ghost Stories." *English Historical Review* 37 (1922): 413–422.

Jamroziak, E. "Rievaulx Abbey as a Wool Producer in the Late Thirteenth Century: Cistercians, Sheep and Debts." *Northern History* XL, no. 2 (2003): 197–218.

Janson, H. W. *Apes and Ape Lore in the Middle Ages and the Renaissance.* London: Warburg Institute, 1952.

Jean de Jandun. *Questiones super libros de anima.* Venice, 1480 (on http://gallica.bnf.fr).

Jenkins, D. "Hawk and Hound: Hunting in the Laws of Court." In *The Welsh King and his Court,* edited by T. C. Edwards and others. Cardiff: University of Wales Press, 2000, pp. 255–280.

Jennings, B. *Yorkshire Monasteries: Cloister, Land and People.* Otley, UK: Smith Settle, 1999.

Jordan, M. "The Construction of a Philosophical Medicine: Exegesis and Argument in Salernitan Teaching on the Soul." *Osiris,* second series, 6 (1990): 42–61.

Jordan, W. C. *The Great Famine. Northern Europe in the Early Fourteenth Century.* Princeton: Princeton University Press, 1996.

Jusserand, J. J. *English Wayfaring Life in the Middle Ages.* Translated by L. Toulmin Smith. 1889. Reprint, London: Methuen, 1950.

Jusserand, J. J. *Les sports et jeux d'exercice dans l'ancienne France.* Paris: Plon-Nourrit, 1901.

Kaimakis, D. *Der Physiologus nach der ersten Redaktion.* Meisenheim am Glan, Germany: Hain, 1974.

Keen, M. *Chivalry.* New Haven: Yale University Press, 1984.

Kieckhefer, R. *Forbidden Rites: A Necromancer's Manual of the Fifteenth Century.* University Park: Pennsylvania State University Press, 1997.

Kiser, L. J. "Animals in Sacred Space: St. Francis and the Crib at Greccio." In *Speaking Images: Essays in Honor of V. A. Kolve,* edited by R. F. Yeager and C. C. Morse. Asheville, NC: Pegasus, 2001, pp. 56–73.

Kisling, V. N. ed. *Zoo and Aquarium History: Ancient Animal Collections to Zoological Gardens.* Boca Raton, FL: CRC, 2001.

Klein, J. *The Mesta: A Study in Spanish Economic History, 1273–1836.* Cambridge, MA: Harvard University Press, 1920.

Klemm, M. "Medicine and Moral Virtue in the *Expositio Problematum Aristotelis.*" *Early Science and Medicine* 11 (2006): 302–335.

Klingender, F. *Animals in Art and Thought to the End of the Middle Ages.* London: Routledge & Kegan Paul, 1971.

Kluge, F. *Etymologisches Wörterbuch der deutschen Sprache.*, 7th ed. Strassburg, France: Trubner, 1910.

Köhler, T. W. *Grundlagen des philosophisch-anthropologischen Diskurses im dreizehnten Jahrhundert. Die Erkenntnisbemühung um den Menschen im zeitgenössischen Verständnis.* Boston: Brill, 2000.

Kristeller, P. O. "The School of Salerno: Its Development and Its Contribution to the History of Learning." *Bulletin of the History of Medicine* 17 (1945): 138–194.

Kristeller, P. O. "Bartholomaeus, Musandinus, and Maurus of Salerno and Other Early Commentators of the *Articella* with a Tentative List of Texts and Manuscripts." *Italia medioevale et umanistica* 19 (1976): 57–87.

Laguna Sanz, E. *Historia del Merino.* Madrid: Ministerio de Agricultura, 1986.

Lambros, S. P., ed. *Excerptorum Constantini de natura animalium libri duo. Aristophanis historiae animalium epitome.* Berlin: Reimer, 1885.

Langdon, J. *Horses, Oxen and Technological Innovation: The Use of Draught Animals in English Farming from 1066–1500.* Cambridge: Cambridge University Press, 1986.

L'art d'archerie. Sur les traces du premier livre d'archerie. 2nd ed. St-Egrève: Emotion Primitive, 2002.

Leach, A. F. *The Schools of Medieval England.* London: Methuen, 1915.

Lecoy de la Marche, A., ed. *Tractatus de diversis materiis praedicabilibus.* In *Anecdotes historiques, légendes et apologues.* Paris: Librairie Renouard, 1877.

Le Goff, J. "Ecclesiastical Culture and Folklore in the Middle Ages: Saint Marcellus of Paris and the Dragon." In idem, *Time, Work and Culture in the Middle Ages.* Chicago: University of Chicago Press, 1980, pp. 159–188.

Le Goff, J., and E. Le Roy Ladurie. "Mélusine maternelle et défricheuse." *Annales. Economies, Sociétés, Civilisations* 26 (1971): 587–622.

Lévi-Strauss, C. *The Savage Mind.* 1972. Reprint, Oxford: Oxford University Press, 1996.

Levitan, B. "Medieval Animal Husbandry in South West England." In *Studies in the Palaeoeconomy and Environment of South West England,* edited by N. D. Balaam and others. BAR British Series, 181. Oxford: B.A.R., 1987, pp. 51–80.

Lindner, K. "Die Anfänge der deutschen Jagdliteratur. Ihre Entwicklung vom 14. Jahrhundert bis zur Zeit der Reformation." *Zeitschrift für Jagdwissenschaft* X (1964): 41–51.

Lindner, K. *Queen Mary's Psalter.* Berlin: Paul Parey, 1966.

Linnard, W. "The Nine Huntings: A Re-examination of *Y Naw Helwriaeth.*" *The Bulletin of the Board of Celtic Studies* 31 (1984): 119–132.

Lipton, S. "Jews, Heretics, and the Sign of the Cat in the *Bible moralisée.*" *Word and Image* 8 (1992): 362–77.

Lloyd, T. H. "Husbandry Practices and Disease in Medieval Sheep Flocks." *Veterinary History* 10 (1977–1978): 3–14.

Loisel, G. *Histoire des menageries de l'antiquité a nos jours.* 3 vols. Paris: Octave Doin et Fils, 1912.

Luibheid, C., and P. Rorem, *Pseudo-Dionysius, The Complete Works.* New York: Paulist Press 1987.

Mahony, E. "Sense, Intellect, and Imagination in Albert, Thomas, and Siger." In *The Cambridge History of Later Medieval Philosophy. From the rediscovery of Aristotle to the Disintegration of Scholasticism 1100–1600,* edited by N. Kretzmann, A. Kenny, and J. Pinborg. Cambridge: Cambridge University Press, 1982, pp. 602–622.

Malacarne, G. *Le cacce del principe. L'ars venandi nella terra dei Gonzaga.* Modena, Italy: Il Bullino, 1998.

Malacarne, G. *I Signori del cielo. La falconeria a Mantova al tempo dei Gonzaga.* Mantova, Italy: Artiglio Editore, 2003.

Marie de France. *The Lais of Marie de France.* Translated by G. S. Burgess and K. Busby. Harmondsworth, UK: Penguin, 1986.

Marrone, S. "Medieval Philosophy in Context." *The Cambridge Companion to Medieval Philosophy,* edited by A. S. McGrade. Cambridge: Cambridge University Press, 2003, pp. 10–43.

Martin, J. D. "Sva lykr her hverju hestaðingi: Sports and Games in Icelandic Saga Literature." *Scandinavian Studies* 75 (2003): 25–44.

Martinez Gazquez, J. "El 'Liber de animalibus' de Pedro Gallego, adoptación del "Liber animalium aristotelics," in *Roma magistra mundi,* ed. J. Hamesse (Lauvain-la-Neuve: FIDEM, 1998), pp. 563–74. His edition of the text (Florence: SISMEL Edizioni del Galluzo, 2000) contains too many errors to be used as a work of reference.

Martyn, J.R.C., trans. *The Letters of Gregory the Great.* 3 vols. Toronto: Pontifical Institute of Mediaeval Studies, 2004.

McCulloch, F. *Medieval Latin and French Bestiaries.* Chapel Hill: University of North Carolina Press, 1960, revised 1962.

McKitterick, D., ed. *The Trinity Apocalypse.* London: The British Library, 2005.

McLean, T. *The English at Play in the Middle Ages.* Windsor Forest, UK: Kensal, 1983.

McNeill, J. T., and H. M. Gamer. *The Medieval Handbooks of Penance.* New York: Columbia University Press, 1990.

Mehl, J.-M. *Les jeux au royaume de France du XIIIᵉ au début du XVIᵉ siècle.* Paris: Fayard, 1990.

Mellinkoff, R. *Averting Demons: The Protective Power of Medieval Visual Motifs and Themes.* Los Angeles: Ruth Mellinkoff Publications, 2004.

Mellinkoff, R. "Riding Backwards: Theme of Humiliation and Symbol of Evil." *Viator* 4 (1973): 154–66.

Meyer, P., ed. *L'Histoire de Guillaume le Maréchal, comte de Striguil et de Pembroke.* 3 vols. Paris: Société de l'histoire de France, 1891–1901.

Migne, J. P., ed. *Honorii Augustodunensis Opera omnia.* Patrologiae Latinae tomus 172. Reprint Turnhout, Belgium: Brepols, 1970.

Mills, M., ed. *The Anturs of Arther.* London: Dent, 1992.

Mills, M., ed. *Sir Percyvell of Gales.* London: Dent, 1992.

Mitchell, T. *Blood Sport: A Social History of Spanish Bullfighting.* Philadelphia: University of Pennsylvania Press, 1991.

Mitchell, T. *Violence and Piety in Spanish Folklore.* Philadelphia: University of Pennsylvania Press, 1988.

Montanari, M. "Gli animali e l'Alimentazione umana." In *L'uomo di fronte al mondo animale nell'Alto Medioevo,* Settimane di Studio del Centro Italiano di studi sull'Alto Medioevo XXXI. Spoleto, Italy: La Sede del Centro, 1985, vol. I, pp. 619–663.

Moore, J. H. "The Ox in the Middle Ages." *Agricultural History* 35, no. 2 (1961): 90–93.

Morenzoni, F. "La capture et le commerce des faucons dans les Alpes occidentales au XIVe siècle." In *Milieux naturels, espaces sociaux. Etudes offertes à Robert Delort,* edited by E. Mornet and F. Morenzoni. Paris: Publications de la Sorbonne, 1997, pp. 287–298.

Moseley, C.W.R.D., trans. *The Travels of Sir John Mandeville.* London: Penguin, 1983.

Muchembled, R. *Popular Culture and Elite Culture in France, 1400–1750.* 1985. Reprint, Baton Rouge: Louisiana State University Press, 2004.

Müller, H. H. "Falconry in Central Europe in the Middle Ages." In *Exploitation des animaux sauvages à travers le temps.* Juan-les-Pins, France: Editions APDCA, 1993, pp. 431–437.

Myers, A. R. *London in the Age of Chaucer.* Norman: University of Oklahoma Press, 1972.

Neckam, A. *De naturis rerum,* and *De laudibus divinae sapientiae.* Edited by T. Wright. London: Longman Green, 1863.

Neumeyer, M. "Le bestiaire héraldique. Un miroir de la chevalerie." In *Il mondo animale.* Florence: Sismel, 2000, vol. 1, pp. 145–164.

Nicoll, A. *Masks, Mimes and Miracles: Studies in the Popular Theatre.* New York: Cooper Square, 1931.

Niedermann, C. *Das Jagdwesen am Hofe Herzog Phillipps des Guten von Burgund.* Brussels: Archives et Bibliothèques de Belgique, 1995.

Nischik, T.-M. *Das volkssprachliche Naturbuch im späten Mittelalter. Sachkunde und Dinginterpretation bei Jacob van Maerlant und Konrad von Megenberg* (Tübingen, Germany: Niemeyer, 1986).

Nussbaum, M. C. *Aristotle's De Motu Animalium.* Princeton: Princeton University Press, 1985.

O'Connor, R., trans. *Icelandic Histories and Romances.* Stroud, UK: Tempus 2002.

O'Connor, T. P. "The Archaeozoological Interpretation of Morphometric Variability in British Sheep Limb Bones." PhD diss., University of London, 1982.

O'Neill, Y.V. "Another Lock at the "Auatoria Para'," Viator (1970), pp. 115-24.

Offermans, D. *Der Physiologus nach den Handschriften G und M.* Meisenheim am Glan, Germany: Hain, 1966.

Oggins, R. S. *The Kings and the Hawks. Falconry in Medieval England.* New Haven: Yale University Press, 2004.

Onions, C. T. *Oxford Dictionary of English Etymology.* Oxford: Clarendon Press, 1966.

Orme, N. *Medieval Children.* New Haven: Yale University Press, 2001.

Oschinsky, D. *"Walter of Henley" and other Treatises on Estate Management.* London: Clarendon Press, 1971.

Painter, S. *William Marshal.* Baltimore: Johns Hopkins University Press, 1933.

Pálsson, H., trans. *Hrafnkel's Saga and Other Icelandic Stories.* Harmondsworth, UK: Penguin, 1971.

Panofsky, E., trans. and ed. *Abbot Suger on the Abbey Church of St-Denis and Its Art Treasures.* Princeton: Princeton University Press, 1946.

Park, K. "The Organic Soul." In *The Cambridge History of Renaissance Philosophy,* edited by C. B. Schmidt and Q. Skinner. Cambridge: Cambridge University Press, 1988, pp. 464–484.

Pastoureau, M. "La chasse au sanglier: histoire d'une dévalorisation (IVe-XIVe siècle)." In *La chasse au Moyen Age. Société, traités, symboles,* edited by A. Paravicini Bagliani and B. Van den Abeele. Florence: Sismel, 2000, pp. 7–24.

Pérez Martínez, L., and M. Pascual Pont. *Jaime III Rey de Mallorca. Leyes Palatinas.* Palma de Mallorca, Spain: Olañeta, 1991.

Peter of Abano. *Compilatio phisionomie.* Padua, 1474 (on http://gallica.bnf.fr).

Peter of Abano. *Expositio problematum.* Venice, 1482 (on http://gallica.bnf.fr).

Peter of Auvergne. *Questions on Aristotle's De caelo. A Critical Edition with an Interpretative Essay by G. Galle.* Leuven, Belgium: University Press, 2003.

Peters, H. "Falke, Falkenjagd, Falkner und Falkenbuch." In *Reallexikon zur Deutschen Kunstgeschichte*, vol. VI. Munich: A. Druckenmüller, 1971, col. 1261–1366.

Petit, G., and J. Théodoridès. *Histoire de la zoologie des origines à Linné*. Paris: Hermann, 1962.

Pingree, D., ed. *Picatrix Latinus*. London: The Warburg Institute, 1986.

Pitman, J. H., trans. *The Anglo-Saxon Physiologus*. New Haven: Yale University Press, 1921.

Plato Latinus. *Timaeus a Calcidio translatus commentarioque instructus*. Edited by J. H. Waszink (Plato Latinus IV). London: Warburg—Brill, 1962.

Pliny. *Natural History*, trans. and ed. H. Rackham. Cambridge, MA: Harvard University Press, 1983.

Pluskowski, A. *Wolves and the Wilderness in the Middle Ages*. Woodbridge, UK: Boydell Press, 2006.

Pohl-Resl, B. *Rechnen mit der Ewigkeit. Das Wiener Bürgerspital im späten Mittelalter*. Munich: Oldenbourg, 1996.

Polo, Marco. *The Travels*. Translated by R. Latham. London: Penguin, 1958.

Powers, E. *Medieval English Nunneries c. 1275–1535* (Cambridge: Cambridge University Press, 1922), pp. 305–309, 412–413.

Prévot, B. *La Science du cheval au mogen âge. Le* Traité d'hippiatric de Jordauus Rufus (Paris: Klincksieck, 1991).

Rackham, J. "Physical Remains of Medieval Horses." In *The Medieval Horse and Its Equipment, c. 1150–c. 1450*, edited by J. Clark. London: HMSQ, 1995, pp. 19–32.

Randall, L. *Images in the Margins of Gothic Manuscripts*, Berkeley: University of California Press, 1966.

Reed, R. *The Nature and Making of Parchment*. Leeds, UK: Elmete Press, 1975.

Reeves, C. *Pleasures and Pastimes in Medieval England*. Phoenix Mill, UK: Sutton, 1997.

Reina, M. E. "Un Abbozzo di polemica sulla psicologia animale: Gregorio da Rimini contro Adamo Wodeham." In *L'homme et son univers au moyen âge*, edited by C. Wenin. Louvain-la-Neuve, Belgium: Éditions de l'Institut supérieur de philosophie, 1986, pp. 598–609.

Resl, B. *Understanding Animals, 1150–1350*. Basingstoke, UK: Palgrave Macmillan, forthcoming.

Richter, W., and R. Richter-Bergmeier, eds. Petrus de Crescentiis, *Ruralia commoda. Das Wissen des vollkommenen Landwirts um 1300*. Heidelberg: C. Winter, 1995–1998.

Riondato, E., and Olivieri, L., eds. *Pietro d'Abano, Conciliator. Ristampa fotomeccanica dell'edizione Venetiis apud Iuntas 1565*. Padua, Italy: Editrice Antenore, 1985.

Riu y Riu, M. "Agricultura y ganadería en el Fuero de Cuenca." *Estudios en memoria del Professor D. Salvador de Moxó*, vol. II (1982): 369–386.

Rodrigues, A.-M. S.A. "Le taureau dans les fêtes aristocratiques et populaires du Moyen Âge." In *Jeux, sports et divertissements au Moyen Âge et à l'Âge classique*, edited by J.-M. Mehl. Paris: Éditions du CTHS, 1993, pp. 181–192.

Rösener, W., ed. *Jagd und höfische Kultur im Mittelalter*. Göttingen, Germany: Vandenhoeck & Ruprecht, 1997.

Rooney, A. *Hunting in Middle English Literature*. Rochester: Boydell Press, 1993.

Rowland, B. *Animals with Human Faces: A Guide to Animal Symbolism*. London: Allen & Unwin, 1974.

Rudolph, C. *Artistic Change at St-Denis: Abbot Suger's program and the early-twelfth century controversy over art*. Princeton: Princeton University Press, 1990.

Rudolph, C. *The "Things of Greater Importance."* Philadelphia: University of Pennsylvania Press, 1990.

Ryder, M. L. "The History of Sheep Breeds in Britain." *Agricultural History Review* XII (1964): 1–12, 65–82.

Ryder, M. L. "Livestock Remains from Four Medieval Sites in Yorkshire." *Agricultural History Review* IX (1961): 105–110.

Sabine, E. "City Cleaning in Medieval London." *Speculum* XII (1937): 24–25.

Salisbury, J. E. *The Beast Within: Animals in the Middle Ages*. New York: Routledge, 1994.

Saly, T. "Tristan chasseur." In *La chasse au Moyen Age. Société, traités, symboles*, edited by A. Paravicini Bagliani and B. Van den Abeele. Florence: Sismel, 2000, pp. 436–441.

Sánchez-Belda, A., and M. C. Sánchez Trujillano *Razas ovinas españolas*. Madrid: Ministerio de Agricultura, 1989.

Sannino, A. "Ermete mago e alchimista nelle biblioteche di Guglielmo d'Alvernia e Ruggero Bacone." *Studi Medievali* 40 (2000): 151–209.

Santi, F. "Cani e gatti, grandi battaglie. Origini storiche di un conflitto ancora aperto." *Micrologus* 8 (2000): 31–40.

Sbordone, F., ed. *Physiologus*. Rome, 1936.

Schmitt, J.-C. *The Holy Greyhound*. Cambridge: University of Cambridge Press, 1983.

Schroeder, H. J. *Disciplinary Decrees of the General Councils: Text, Translation and Commentary*. St. Louis, MO: B. Herder, 1937.

Scott-MacNab, D. *A Sporting Lexicon of the Fifteenth Century*. The J.B. Treatise, Oxford: The Society for the Study of Medieval Languages and Literature, 2003.

Serjeantson, D. "Animal Remains and the Tanning Trade." In *Diet and Crafts in Towns: The Evidence of Animal Remains from the Roman to the Post-Medieval Periods*, edited by D. Serjeantson and T. Waldron. BAR British Series 199, Oxford, BAR, 1989, pp. 129–146.

Seymour, M. C., and others, eds. *John Trevisa's Translation of Bartholomaus Anglicus "De proprietatibus rerum."* New York: Clarendon Press, 1988.

Shenton, C. "Edward III and the Symbol of the Leopard." In *Heraldry, Pageantry and Social Display in Medieval England*, edited by P. Coss and M. Keen. Woodbridge, UK: Boydell, 2002.

Siebert, G. "Falkner und Beizjagd in den Miniaturen der Grossen Heidelberger Liederhandschrift." *Deutscher Falkenorden Jahrbuch* (1968): 89–95.

Smalley, B. "Thomas Waleys O.P." *Archivum Fratrum Praedicatorum* 24 (1954): 50–107.

Smets, A. "*Dés faucons*: les quatre traductions en moyen français du *De falconibus* d'Albert le Grand. Analyse lexicale d'un dossier inédit." PhD diss., K.U. Leuven, 2003.

Smets, A. "L'image ambiguë du chien à travers la littérature didactique latine et française (XIIe-XIVe siècles)." *Reinardus* 14 (2001): 243–253.

Smets, A. "Les traductions françaises médiévales des traités de fauconnerie latins: vue d'ensemble." In *Le bestiaire, le lapidaire, la flore*, edited by G. Di Stefano and R.M. Bidler. Montréal: CERES, 2004–2005.

Smets, A., ed. Le "Liber accipitrum" de Grimaldus: un traité d'autourserie du haut Moyen Âge. Nogent-le-Roi: J. Laget—LAME, 1999.

Smets, A., and B. Van den Abeele. "Manuscrits et traités de chasse français du Moyen Âge. Recensement et perspectives de recherche." Romania 116 (1998): 316–367.

Smithers, G. V., ed. Kyng Alisaunder. EETS, Oxford: Oxford University Press, 1952.

Solski, L. "Zoological Gardens of Central-Eastern Europe and Russia." In Zoo and Aquarium History: Ancient Animal Collections to Zoological Gardens, edited by V. N. Kisling. Boca Raton, FL: CRC, 2001.

Sorabji, R. Animal Minds and Human Morals. Ithaca, NY: Cornell University Press, 1993.

Southern, R. W. "The Schools of Paris and the School of Chartres." In Renaissance and Renewal in the Twelfth Century, edited by R. Benson and G. Constable. Cambridge, MA: Harvard University Press, 1982, pp. 113–137.

Southworth, J. The English Medieval Minstrel. Woodbridge, UK: Boydell Press, 1989.

Sperber, D. "Why are Perfect Animals, Hybrids and Monsters Food for Symbolic Thought?" Method and Theory in the Study of Religion 8, 2 (1996): 143–169.

Stecher, R. M., and L. Gross. "Ankylosing Lesions of the Spine." Journal of Veterinary Medical Association 138 (1961): 248–265.

Steckelberg, U. Hadamar von Laber 'Jagd'. Überlieferung, Textstrukturen und allegorische Sinnbindungsverfahren. Tübingen, Germany: Niemeyer, 1998.

Steel, C., G. Guldentops, and P. Beullens, eds. Aristotle's Animals in the Middle Ages and the Renaissance. Leuven, Belgium: Leuven University Press, 1999.

Strehlow, H. "Zoological Gardens of Western Europe." In Zoo and Aquarium History: Ancient Animal Collections to Zoological Gardens, edited by V. N. Kisling. Boca Raton, FL: CRC, 2001.

Strubel, A. "Le débat entre fauconniers et veneurs: un témoignage sur l'imaginaire de la chasse à la fin du moyen âge." Travaux de littérature 10 (1997): 49–64.

Strutt, J. The Sports and Pastimes of the People of England. 1801. Reprint, Bath: Firecrest, 1969.

Stuart, F., ed. Averrois Cordubensis Commentarium Magnum in Aristotelis De anima libros. Cambridge, MA: Medieval Academy of America, 1953.

Stutvoet-Joanknecht, C. M. Der byen boeck. De Middelnederlandse vertalingen van Bonum universale de apibus van Thomas van Cantimpré en hun achtergrond (Amsterdam: VU, 1990).

Summers, M. trans., Malleus maleficarum (1928; repr. New York: Dover publications, 1971), pt. 1, quest. 10 and pt. II, quest. 1, chap. 8, pp. 61–65 and 122–24.

di Svevia, Federico II. De arte venandi cum avibus. Edited by A. L. Trombetti Budriesi. Rome: Editori Laterza, 2000.

Swaen, A. E. H. De valkerij in de Nederlanden. Zutphen: W.J. Thieme & Cie, 1936.

Stürner, W. Friedrich II., Teil 2. Der Kaiser, 1220–1250. Darmstadt, Germany: Wissenschaftliche Buchgesellschaft, 2000.

Szabo, T. "Die Kritik der Jagd. Von der Antike zum Mittelalter." In Jagd und höfische Kultur im Mittelalter. Göttingen, Germany: Vandenhoeck & Ruprecht, 1997, pp. 167–230.

Thiébaux, M., trans. and ed. Dhuoda, Handbook for Her Warrior Son. Liber Manualis, Cambridge: Cambridge University Press, 1998, pp. 112–115.

Thiébaux, M. The Stag of Love: The Chase in Medieval Literature. Ithaca, NY: Cornell University Press, 1974.

Thomas Aquinas. A Commentary on Aristotle's De anima. Translated by Robert Pasnau. New York: Yale University Press, 1999.

Thomas Aquinas. *Summa Theologiae*. Vol. I, *Christian Theology* (Ia.1). Translated by T. Gilby. New York, 1964.

Thomas of Cantimpré. *Liber de natura rerum*. Edited by H. Boese. New York: de Gruyter, 1973.

Thomas, K. *Man and the Natural World: Changing Attitudes in England, 1500–1800*. Oxford: Oxford University Press, 1983.

Thorndike, L. *The History of Magic and Experimental Science*, vol. 4. New York: Columbia University Press, 1933.

Thorpe, L. "Tristewell et les autres chiens de l'enfer." In *J. Misrahi Memorial Volume. Studies in Medieval Literature*, edited by H. R. Hunte, H. Niedzielski, and W. L. Hendrickson. New York: Columbia University Press, 1977, pp. 115–135.

Thrupp, J. "On the Domestication of Certain Animals in England between 7th and the 11th Centuries." *Transactions of the Ethnological Society of London* 4 (1866): 164–172.

Tilander, G. *Les Livres du Roy Modus et de la Royne Ratio*. Paris: SATF, 1932, I, pp. 307–309.

Tomlins, T. E., and others, eds. *Statutes of the Realm*. 9 vols. 1810–1822. Reprint, London: Dawson, 1963.

Trevisa, John. *On the Properties of Things: John Trevisa's Translation of Bartholomaeus Anglicus. De Proprietatibus Rerum*. Edited by M. C. Seymour. 3 vols. Oxford: Oxford University Press, 1975.

Trombetti Budriesi, A. L. Federico II di Svevia, *De arte venandi cum avibus* (Rome: Editori Laterza, 2000); C. A. Wood and F. M. Fyfe, trans., *The Art of Falconry, Being the "De arte venandi cum avibus" of Frederick II of Hohenstaufen* (Stanford, CA: University Press, 1943).

Turville-Petre, E. O. G. *Myth and Religion of the North: The Religion of Ancient Scandinavia*. London: Weidenfeld and Nicolson, 1964.

Ulrich von Liechtenstein. *The Service of Ladies (Frauendienst)*. Translated by J. W. Thomas. Woodbridge, UK: Boydell Press, 2004.

Van den Abeele, B. "Falken auf Goldgrund. Illuminierte Handschriften lateinischer Jagdtraktate des Mittelalters." *Librarium* 47 (2004): 2–19.

For details on birds and techniques, cf. B. Van den Abeele, *La fauconnerie au Moyen Âge. Connaissance, affaitage et médecine des oiseaux de chasse d'après les traités latins* (Paris: Klincksieck, 1994).

Van den Abeele, B. *La fauconnerie dans les lettres françaises du XIIe au XIVe siècle*. Leuven, Belgium: Leuven University Press, 1990.

Van den Abeele, B. "Le 'De animalibus' d'Aristote dans le monde latin: modalités de sa réception médiévale." *Frühmittelalterliche Studien* 33 (1999): 287–318.

Van den Abeele, B. "Le faucon sur la main. Un parcours iconographique médiéval." In *La chasse au Moyen Age. Société, traités, symboles*, edited by A. Paravicini Bagliani and B. Van den Abeele. Florence: Sismel, 2000, pp. 87–109 and pls. 1–12.

Van den Abeele, B. *La littérature cynégétique*. Turnhout, Belgium: Brepols, 1996.

Van den Abeele, B. "Trente et un nouveaux manuscrits de l'Aviarium: regards sur la diffusion de l'oeuvre d'Hugues de Fouilloy." *Scriptorium* 57 (2003): 253–271.

Van den Abeele, B. "Une version moralisée du De animalibus d'Aristote." In *Aristotle's Animals in the Middle Ages and Renaissance*, edited by C. Steel, G. Guldentops, and P. Beullens. Leuven, Belgium: University Press, 1999, pp. 338–354.

Van den Abeele, B., ed. *Bestiaires médiévaux. Nouvelles perspectives sur les manuscrits et les traditions textuelles*. Louvain-la-Neuve, Belgium: Université Catholique de Louvain, 2005.

Van den Abeele, B., and J. Loncke. "Les traités médiévaux sur le soin des chiens: une littérature technique méconnue." In *Inquirens subtilia diversa. Dietrich Lohrmann zum 65. Geburtstag,* edited by H. Kranz and L. Falkenstein. Aachen, Germany: Shaker, 2002, pp. 281–296.

Van Oppenraay, A. "The Reception of Aristotle's History of Animals in the Marginalia of Some Latin Manuscripts of Michael Scot's Arabic–Latin Translation." *Early Science and Medicine* 8, no. 4 (2003): 387–403.

Van Oostrom, F. *Maerlants wereld* (Amsterdam: Prometheus, 1996).

Varese, R., ed. *Atlante di Schifanoia.* Modena, Italy: Francesco Cosimo Panini, 1989.

Vaultier, R. *Le Folklore pendant la guerre de Cent Ans d'après Les Lettres de Rémission du Trésor des Chartres.* Paris: Librairie Guénégaud, 1965.

Veale, E. M. *The English Fur Trade in the Later Middle Ages.* 1966. Reprint, Oxford: Oxford University Press, 2003.

Venantius Fortunatus. "Vita s. Hilarii." In *Monumenta Germaniae Historica, Scriptores rerum Merovingicarum* 4, 2, edited by B. Krusch. Hannover, Germany: MGH, 1902.

Ventura, I. "The *Curae ex animalibus* in the Medical Literature of the Middle Ages: The Example of the Illustrated Herbals." In *Bestiaires médiévaux. Nouvelles perspectives et les traditions textuelles,* edited by B. Van den Abeele. Louvain-la-Neuve, Belgium: Université Catholique de Louvain, 2005, pp. 213–248.

Voisenet, J. *Bêtes et hommes dans le monde médiévale. Le bestiaire des clercs du Ve au XIIe siècle.* Turnhout, Belgium: Brepols, 2000.

Voisenet, J. "L'espace domestique chez les auteurs du Moyen Ages, d'Isidore de Séville a Brunetto Latini." In *L'homme, l'animal domestique et l'environnement du Moyen Age au XVIIIe siècle,* edited by R. Durand. Nantes, France: Ouest Éditions, 1993.

Walker, C. G. "An Edition with Introduction and Commentary of John Blount's English Translation of Nicholas Upton's *De Studio Militari*." PhD diss., University of Oxford, 1998.

Walker-Meikle, K. "Late Medieval Pet-Keeping: Gender, Status and Emotions." PhD diss., London, forthcoming.

Walz, D. "Falkenjagd—Falkensymbolik." In *Codex Manesse, Katalog zur Ausstellung,* edited by E. Mittler and W. Werner. Heidelberg: Braus, 1988, pp. 350–371.

Wattenbach, W., ed. "Continuatio Claustroneoburgensis III." In *Monumenta Germaniae Historica, Scriptores* 9. Hanover, Germany: MGH, 1851, pp. 613–624.

Wattenbach, W., ed. "Continuatio Novimontensis." *Monumenta Germaniae Historica, Scriptores* 9. Hanover, Germany: MGH, 1851, pp. 669–677.

Wattenbach, W., ed. "Continuatio Sancrucensis II." *Monumenta Germaniae Historica, Scriptores* 9. Hanover, Germany: MGH, 1851, pp. 637–646.

Wattenbach, W., ed. "Historia Annorum 1264–1279." *Monumenta Germaniae Historica, Scriptores* 9. Hanover, Germany: MGH, 1851, pp. 649–654.

Weick, R. *Der Habicht in der deutschen Dichtung des 12. bis 16. Jahrhunderts.* Göppingen, Germany: Kümmerle Verlag, 1993.

Weijers, O., and L. Holtz, eds. *p des disciplines à la Faculté des arts (Paris et Oxford, XIIIe-XVe siècles).* Turnhout, Belgium: Brepols, 1997.

Weill-Parot, N. *Les "images astrologiques" au Moyen Âge et à la Renaissance.* Paris: Honoré Champion, 2002.

Wenzel, S., ed. *Fasciculus Morum: A Fourteenth-Century Preacher's Handbook.* University Park: Pennsylvania State University Press, 1989.

Wetherbee, W. "Philosophy, Cosmology, and the Twelfth-Century Renaissance." In *A History of Twelfth-Century Western Philosophy*, edited by P. Dronke. Cambridge: Cambridge University Press, 1988, pp 21–53.

White, K. "Two Studies Related to St. Thomas Aquinas' Commentary on Aristotle's *De sensu et sensato*, Together with an Edition of Peter of Auvergne's *Quaestiones super Parva Naturalia*." Ph.D. diss., University of Ottawa, 1986.

White, L., Jr. *Medieval Technology and Social Change*. Oxford: Clarendon, 1962.

Wickham, C. "Pastoralism and Underdevelopment in the Early Middle Ages." In *L'Uomo di fronte al mondo animale nell'Alto Medioevo*, Settimane di Studio del Centro Italiano di Studi sull'Alto Medioevo XXXI. Spoleto, Italy: La Sede del Centro, 1985, pp. 401–451.

Wickham, G. *The Medieval Theatre*. 3rd ed. Cambridge: Cambridge University Press, 1974.

William of Auvergne, *Opera omnia*, 2 vols. (1674; repr. Frankfurt, 1963).

William of Conches. *Dragmaticon philosophiae*, edited by I. Ronca. Turnhout, Belgium: Brepols, 1997.

William Durandus. *Rationale divinorum officiorum*. Edited by A. Davril and T. M. Thibodeau. Turnhout, Belgium: Brepols, 1995.

Williams, E. *Hunting the Deer: Some Uses of a Motif-Complex in Middle English Romance and Saint's Life*. In *Romance in Medieval England*, edited by M. Mills and others. Cambridge: D.S. Brewer, 1991, pp. 187–206.

Willis, R., ed. *Signifying Animals*. London: Routledge, 1994.

Wilmart, A. "La légende de Ste. Édith en prose et vers par le moine Goscelin." *Analecta Bollandiana* 56 (1938): 5–101.

Wiseman, J. *The Pig. A British History*. London: Duckworth, 2000.

Wittkower, R. *Allegory and the Migration of Symbols*. New York: Thomas and Hudson, 1987.

Wittkower, R. "Marvels of the East: A Study in the History of Monsters." *Journal of the Warburg and Courtauld Institutes* 5 (1942): 159–197.

Wood, C. A., and F. M. Fyfe, trans. *The Art of Falconry, Being the "De arte venandi cum avibus" of Frederick II of Hohenstaufen*. Stanford, CA: University Press, 1943.

Wolfram von Eschenbach. *Parzifal*. Translated by Helen M. Mustard and Charles E. Passage. New York: Vintage, 1961.

Wolter-von dem Knesebeck, H. "Aspekte der höfischen Jagd und ihrer Kritik in Bildzeugnissen des Hochmittelalters." In *Jagd und höfische Kultur im Mittelalter*, edited by W. Rösener. Göttingen, Germany: Vandenhoeck & Ruprecht, 1997, pp. 493–572.

Yapp, B. "The Illustrations of Birds in the Vatican Manuscript of 'De arte venandi cum avibus' of Frederick II." *Annals of Science* 40 (1983): 597–534.

Zeuner, F. E. *A History of Domesticated Animals*. London: Hutchinson, 1963.

Ziolkowsky, J. *Talking Animals: Medieval Latin Beast Poetry, 750–1150*. Philadelphia: University of Philadelphia Press, 1993.

NOTES ON CONTRIBUTORS

Pieter Beullens is researcher at the De Wulf-Mansion Centre for Ancient and Medieval Philosophy. He is editor of *Aristotle's Animals in the Middle Ages* (1999) and of *Aristotelis De historia animalium. Translatio Guillelmi de Morbeka* (2000).

Pieter De Leemans is postdoctoral researcher at the De Wulf-Mansion Centre for Ancient and Medieval Philosophy of the K.U.Leuven (Belgium) and secretary of the Aristoteles Latinus project. He has published several studies about medieval Greek-Latin translations of Aristotle (especially of his biological works) and their reception in the Middle Ages and the Renaissance.

Lisa J. Kiser is professor of English at The Ohio State University. She is the author of *Telling Classical Tales: Chaucer and the Legend of Good Women* (1983), *Truth and Textuality in Chaucer's Poetry* (1991), and many articles on medieval environmental history, the history of animal and/or human relationships, and other aspects of the premodern natural world.

Matthew Klemm is assistant professor of history at the University of Nebraska at Kearney. His research is about natural philosophy and learned medicine in the late Middle Ages and early Renaissance. He has published on the relationship between physiology and psychology in the Italian philosopher and physician, Pietro d'Abano.

Sophie Page is lecturer in late medieval European history at University College London. Her research focuses on medieval magic, religion, cosmology, and attitudes to the natural world. Her recent publications include "Image-Magic Texts and a Platonic Cosmology at St Augustine's, Canterbury, in the late middle ages," in C. Burnett and W. F. Ryan, eds., *Magic and the Classical Tradition* (2006) and *Magic in Medieval Manuscripts* (2004).

Esther Pascua is lecturer in the Department of Medieval History of the University of St. Andrews (Scotland). Her research focuses on the environmental history of the Middle Ages. Her publications include "Las otras comunidades: pastores y ganaderos en la Castilla medieval," in Ana Rodriguez, ed., *El lugar del campesino. En torno a la obra de Reyna Pastor* (2007), "Communautés de propriétaires et resources naturelles a Saragosse lors du passage du Moyen Age a l'époque moderne," in Pierre-Yves Laffont, ed., *Transhumance et estivage en Occident des origines aux enjeux actuels* (2006), and "Around and About Water: Christians and Muslims in the Ebro Valley," in Peter Linehan and Simon Barton, eds., *Cross, Crescent and Conversion: Studies on Medieval Spain and Christendom in Memory of Richard Fletcher* (2008).

Brigitte Resl is professor of Medieval history at the University of Liverpool. She is author of *Rechnen mit der Ewigkeit* (1996). Her current research focuses on the cultural history of animals in the Middle Ages. Recent publications include *Understanding Animals, 1150–1350* (2008).

An Smets is research fellow in the research unit French, Italian, and Comparative Linguistics at the K.U.Leuven (Belgium). Her research areas include the origin and creation of a scientific vocabulary in vernacular languages starting from the (Middle French) translations of scientific texts in medieval Latin, medieval (French) hunting literature and the image of animals in medieval literature. She is author of *Le "Liber accipitrum" de Grimaldus: un traité d'autourserie du haut Moyen Âge* (1999) and *'Des faucons': le De falconibus d'Albert le Grand en moyen français* (forthcoming).

Baudouin van den Abeele is researcher at the Belgian FNRS and works in the history department of the Université catholique de Louvain. His research focuses on medieval falconry, bestiaries, animal symbolism, and encyclopedias as well as Renaissance zoology. His publications include *La fauconnerie au Moyen Age: connaissance, affaitage et médecine des oiseaux de chasse d'après les traités latins* (1994), *Bestiaires médiévaux* (2005), *Bartholomaeus Anglicus, De proprietatibus rerum. Texte latin et réception vernaculaire* (2005).

INDEX